The Street Philosopher and the Holy Fool

The Street Philosopher and the Holy Fool

A Syrian Journey

Marius Kociejowski

First published in 2004 by Sutton Publishing Limited

This paperback edition first published in 2006

Reprinted in 2011 by
The History Press
The Mill, Brimscombe Port,
Stroud, Gloucestershire, GL5 2QG
www.thehistorypress.co.uk

British Library Cataloguing in Publication Data
A catalogue record for this book is available from the British Library.

ISBN 978 0 7509 3807 5

Typeset in 10/12.5pt Sabon.
Typesetting and origination by
Sutton Publishing Limited.
Printed and bound in England.

Contents

for Christopher Middleton

Truly it is good to speak, and to hear is better and to converse is best, and to add what is fitting to the fortunes of one's friends, rejoicing with them in some things, sorrowing with them in others, and to have the same return from them; and in addition to these there are ten thousand things in being near to one another.

Libanius, *Orat*. xi, 214

Part One

ONE

A Full Moon Over Antioch

Know ye the land where the cypress and myrtle
  Are emblems of deeds that are done in their clime?
Where the rage of the vulture, the love of the turtle,
  Now melt into sorrow, now madden to crime?

Lord Byron, *The Bride of Abydos. A Turkish Tale*

As we passed through the Syrian Gates my thoughts were not where I'd trained them to be, on Strabo or Alexander, but on a turtle I had encountered a few days earlier on the road from Urgüp to Mustafapasha. I had been walking the five miles that separate those two places with a young American woman, Grace, who was all that her name implies, a ghost of the Old South in her voice. Although oddly out of place, she had come to Cappadocia in search of the late Byzantine. We were walking through one of the world's stranger landscapes, the tufa formations like dream cities in the distance, when we came upon a turtle standing at one side of the road, debating whether or not to cross over to the other side. I had a grim vision of asphalt spattered with turtle, so I picked up the creature, intending to move it a few feet over onto the grassy verge. At that moment a red car sped around the corner, from the direction of Mustafapasha, and screeched to a stop. The driver jumped out, opened the boot of his car, came up to me, muttered a single word in Turkish, plucked the turtle out of my hands, dropped it into the boot – *clunk* – and, as if this were his sole mission in life, jumped back into his car, made a U-turn and drove back from whence he came. All this happened so quickly that any protest I might have made was only just beginning to take shape.

'Well, I reckon there goes somebody's supper,' said Grace.

Was this mockery in her voice? The fact is, by drawing attention to the turtle's existence I had become the agent of its destruction.

A couple of days later, I met Grace again, on a guided tour of Cappadocia. Our guide, Mustafa, whose enthusiasm for his subject was genuine, was pointing out some of the more extraordinary rock formations near Göreme, inviting us to draw visual comparisons.

'You see Napoleon over there,' he said, the joke dying on his lips, probably for the thousandth time.

'And there you'll see one resembling a—'

'Turtle!' Grace and I simultaneously exclaimed.

What we saw, perched upon one of the pillars of stone, like some terrible ghost summoned to remind us of old crimes, did indeed resemble the hapless chelonian of a couple of days before. (I have to confess that although, by and large, I've shed the skin of a North American childhood I am still prone to call a tortoise a turtle.) Mustafa smiled uneasily at the tears of laughter in our eyes.

'Do Turks eat turtles?' I asked him.

A look of disgust formed around his mouth.

'No, the French do.'

I told him the story of my turtle.

'Maybe he was rescuing it from *you*,' he answered.

My spirits lifted to an imagined newspaper banner:

MAN SAVES TURTLE

Our bus climbed slowly through the twisting pass of the Amanus Mountains, the Syrian Gates, where Alexander the Great came, fresh from victory, in 333 BC, over Darius on the plain of Issos. The Crusaders came this way too. Along the roadside were small trees which the *hari kaya*, the winter mistral that blows through these parts, whipped into grotesque shapes. The fertile plain of Amuk was in the distance and beyond that, Antakya, the modern Turkish name for Antioch.

Antioch, ah, the very sound that word made.

I had read about 'the fair crown of the Orient' (*Orientis apicem pulcrum*) whose streets were positioned at such an angle that they would catch the breeze blowing off the Orontes. Antioch was, after Byzantium, the most magnificent city in the eastern Roman Empire but, as though such beauty were not sustainable, it was built over two zones of seismic disturbance. The ancients said that when Jupiter in his rage struck the dragon, Typhon, at the foot of Mount Amanus, Typhon, fleeing the god's thunderbolts, burrowed deep into the ground, his subterranean panic resulting in earthquakes. It was here, in the middle of the first century, beneath the gaze of the goddess Tyche, that Christianity got its name. Antioch has also been described as 'the eye of the Eastern church'. What fascinated me above all, though, were the third-century figures of Libanius, the last great pagan orator, author of the *Antiochikos*, the celebrated encomium of his town, and his pupil, John Chrysostom, 'John of the Golden Mouth', arguably the greatest Christian orator of his time. If the legend is true, and it sounds too attractive not to believe, when Libanius was on his deathbed his disciples begged that the school he founded be put in the hands of his most brilliant student, and he answered, 'It ought to have been John had not the Christians stolen him from us.' Libanius's melancholic disposition could be put down to his having been struck on the head when young by a bolt of lightning. We know he suffered from migraine. Christianity, which in his own writings he disdains to mention by name, must have struck him like a second bolt. A habitual bather, Libanius recoiled from the unwashed monks in their dark sackcloth, these fools spouting pieties. If they wished to free themselves of earthly passions, he reasoned, why undo the very education that provided them with the means to do so? Was not classical Greek literature mankind's most precious possession, its study the most effective means of receiving moral training? And was not a rhetorical education the main ingredient of civilisation? My sympathies were with this old heathen whose singed head ached all the more to see the ancient Hellenistic world with its civilised values possessed by 'the Galilean madness'.

As for Chrysostom, he truly was one of 'Christ's athletes'. Like so many ascetics of the day he ate but little, went into the desert to engage in contemplation and wore threadbare clothes. What distinguished him from the Great Unwashed, however, was his magnificent eloquence. When he preached the cathedral filled and it is said his sermons were frequently interrupted with applause. The common people who spoke only Syriac would gather around a deacon who translated from the Greek while Chrysostom spoke. Moreover, Chrysostom knew the hearts of the people he preached to, and with his acute sensitivity to matters of the human soul and his deep knowledge of the Scriptures he would render even the most difficult concepts in terms to which his listeners could immediately relate. If the world were about to break in two, with Antioch perched on its fault line, it would do so to the clamour of great voices. Antioch was already becoming for me a poetic landscape, every bit as potent as Yeats's Byzantium, a theatre of the imagination where pagan and Christian are locked in perpetual struggle. Historically, Syria is almost unthinkable without Antioch. If Damascus were Syria's historical centre, Antioch would still be my mythical one.

A young man in a turtleneck sweater, who – how shall I say this? – resembled a turtle, kept glancing over at me. He was reading a newspaper, the front and middle pages of which appeared to be devoted to some woman with a slightly mannish face or perhaps a man with a rather womanish one.

'Zeki Müren is dead,' he said with a curious grin on his face.

The previous night Zeki, one of Turkey's most popular singers, collapsed and died of heart failure, only minutes after being presented, on live television, with the gift of his (or her) first ever microphone.

'At precisely one minute to nine!'

My neighbour seemed to attach much significance to the time of death.

'You see, it could have happened at one minute *past* nine which means people would have said he died at about ten o'clock, rather than nine. A minute in Turkey can be the same as an hour.'

'Are you telling me Zeki was a transvestite?'

'Sorry?'

I pointed to a photograph of Zeki looking most fetching in a one-piece woman's bathing costume. Quite clearly, the waves had gone nowhere near her (or his) pompadour.

'It would appear,' I said, not wishing to ruffle Ottoman sensibilities, 'that she was in fact a *he*.'

The young man pondered this for a moment.

'Yes, maybe!'

There had been a fresh attack on the Kurds in the east of the country, news of which occupied only a square inch of space, whereas the death of Zeki, one of Turkey's national treasures, filled most of the paper.

'Zeki Müren was born in 1931, in Bursa.' My neighbour began to translate for me one of the many articles. 'His grandfather was a muezzin at the mosque there, and it was from him that Zeki learned to sing. The girls used to crowd around him, and, at the age of six he fell in love with Ayten, a girl with green eyes.'

I struggled with this early instance of heterosexual love.

'. . . At sixteen, Zeki made his first record—'

'What can you tell me about turtles?'

The young man, his shaven head protruding from the dark shell of his clothes, seemed not in the least unsettled by my sudden change of direction. I told him about the troublesome business on the road to Mustafapasha.

'Well, it was quite obviously *his* turtle.'

After mulling over the issue, however, he returned with a fresh explanation.

'I read not so long ago, in the newspaper, of an American who believes he has discovered a cure for cancer, which is drinking the blood of turtle.'

TURTLE SAVES MAN

According to Pliny the Elder the flesh of the turtle is an antidote 'highly salutary for repelling the malpractice of magic and for neutralising poisons' (*Nat. Hist.* xxxii, 14) and as such appears in his catalogue of remedies sixty-six times. My heart sank, and before I could prevent my neighbour from reaching the obvious conclusion, he explained, 'You see, this man who took your turtle might have read the same article.'

As we approached 'the fair crown of the Orient' I saw in the distance women in bright colours picking cotton. They had been trucked in, magenta scarves whipping about their faces, from the nearby towns and villages. They were the lucky ones, my companion explained to me. Every morning these women would gather in the marketplace, hoping to be among the few chosen from the many poor willing to break their backs for a pittance.

When I reached modern Antakya my heart sank in the time it takes for a stone to reach the bottom of the Orontes. Although I knew to expect little, I was appalled nevertheless. Antakya was not the sleepy backwater I had imagined – it was ugly, congested, and seemingly without a centre. The ghosts of Chrysostom and Libanius seemed to dissolve in the traffic fumes. I stood on a 'Roman' bridge somewhere in the body of which presumably was the original stone. A traveller standing on this same bridge, in 1847, wrote of the wonderful and fearful sight the swollen river made 'as it tears by, roaring and foaming towards the sea'. And he wrote of being able to see from there distant blue mountains, pastures and green hillocks, poplars and evergreens, handsome buildings on one side and crumbling old ruins, minarets and mosques, on the other. It was difficult now to imagine Mounts Staurus, Orocassius and Silpius as cradle to the third city of the Roman Empire, and that upon their slopes lived monks and hermits, many of them holy fools, who had turned their backs on a civilisation given to seeking pleasure, whether it be at the theatre, at the horse races or in easy sexual encounters at Daphne. 'The loss of Antioch is as if the sun dropped into a hole and left its rays behind it,' wrote Freya Stark, 'for its influence is still visible in spite of all.' The town has changed still more since Gertrude Bell and Freya Stark first recorded their impressions. The Orontes, which the Turks call the Asi Nehri, is now a slow, green effluence, its concrete banks covered with advertisements. I stared down at a slowly moving plastic bottle.

A white object flashed upon the water.

A young man with an oversized head and piercing eyes was walking with a close friend through the gardens alongside the Orontes. They were both wearing the coarse, sleeveless robes – lebiton *– which bespoke their withdrawal from the world and its vanities. Their solemn, abstracted movements suggested a monkish attitude. They spoke, heads bowed, in hushed tones. They were on their way to visit a martyr's shrine when they noticed the floating object which at first they took to be a piece of linen. When they, both of them eager bibliophiles, saw it was an unbound book they took turns in trying to fish it out, joking all the while, wondering who would secure the prize. The friend teased the book to shore.*

'I will have shares in this,' the other laughed.

'But first let us see,' said the winner, 'what in the world it is.'

The soggy pages were covered with magical formulae.

'You realise whose book this was?'

The other nodded. They guessed immediately who the previous owner was, a man who earlier had been carried all about the city in bonds and then executed. This man thinking to escape the authorities threw the incriminating object into the Orontes – all in vain, for further evidence (as if further evidence were needed) was brought against him. What both young men knew was that if caught with the manuscript they would suffer the same fate. Their failure to take immediate action reflected a certain grim fascination. The young man with the big head and spidery frame was John Chrysostom; the friend may have been Evagrios, or perhaps Theodore or even Maximus, any one of whom would qualify for the role, for like Chrysostom they too had turned their backs on the excesses of the material world.

Such was the mood in Antioch at that time, when, according to Ammianus, men crept about 'as if in Cimmerian darkness'. It was the late autumn of AD *371; the emperor Flavius Valens was newly arrived in Antioch. The whole city was in a tremble. A bigoted, deeply superstitious Christian, a man not without foes, Valens had heard rumours of divination by which means it could be ascertained when he would die, under what circumstances, and, more vitally, who his successor would be. Ouija boards had been used to produce oracles, which responded in Greek hexameters. Also theurgy involving magical techniques for religious enlightenment was widely practised. Libanius writes of* alektromanteia, *a form of divination which involved scratching the letters of the alphabet on the ground and laying a grain of wheat on top of each one; fowl would be set loose, and, according to the sequence in which they picked the grain, the enquirer would be provided with answers to his questions. Valens had to contend with an entire culture of magic, both pagan and Christian. Valens 'carrying death at the tip of his tongue, blew everything down with an untimely hurricane, hastening to overturn utterly the richest houses.' His soldiers combed the city for evidence, particularly books of sorcery and magic. Whole libraries were put to the torch, and even those books which could be read in perfect innocence or which the authorities passed over the Antiochenes themselves burned. An innocuous passage read by ignorant eyes could amount to a death sentence. Anyone caught dabbling in the black arts or even possessing books on the subject was tried and, in most instances, summarily executed. Ironically, the judges would ask 'conspirators' whether they had predicted their own fate.*

'Everywhere,' Ammianus writes, 'the scene was like a slaughtering of cattle.' A man had been executed for consulting the horoscope of another Valens who was in fact his own brother; another, Bassianus, who sought by divination to determine the sex of his unborn child, had all his property confiscated. Some unfortunates who made the mistake of passing a tomb at night were suspected of seeking to communicate with the dead and, because raising the ghosts of the dead was a capital offence, shortly after followed them to the grave. A farmer who used amulets and magical charms for summoning good weather and crops was driven into exile. A philosopher called Coeranius wrote to his wife, telling her to 'crown the door of the house', a common expression of the time meaning that something of greater importance than usual was to be done; he was executed after savage torture. An old woman was put to death for treating a fever with charms, a technique that she had applied with success to the daughter of the very man who passed sentence on her. A youth was beheaded because he had been spotted in the baths touching the marble and then his breast, while reciting the seven vowels of the Greek alphabet. The vowels with their mystical connection to the seven planets were often used in magical formulae; the youth in question was suffering from a bellyache. Many had been condemned to death before they themselves knew they were under suspicion.

A celebrated case in Scythopolis revealed 'an endless cable of crimes'. A tripod of laurel wood was displayed in a courtroom as evidence of a séance. A circular metal plate with the twenty-four letters of the Greek alphabet engraved on its rim was placed beneath it, and suspended by a thread from the apex of the tripod was a ring which, when set in motion, would spell out in hexameter verses responses to the questions asked of it. The séance was conducted in a house purified with Arabic perfumes. The emperor would die on the plains of Mimas, it said. When the participants of the séance asked who would succeed him the pendulum swung to four letters: theta, epsilon, omikron *and* delta. *Although there were many names beginning with 'THEO' suspicion fell upon one Theodorus, an imperial secretary of high birth and erudition, who was a popular figure among the people. If the participants in the séance had finished spelling the name, Theodorus might have escaped; ironically, the four letters would have applied equally well to Theodosius who in fact succeeded Valens. Theodorus was so despairing of justice that he attended the trial wearing black robes. One of the witnesses, Hilarius, said that Theodorus was completely ignorant of what had taken place. When examined by the judge, Theodorus, after lying prostrate praying for pardon, dryly remarked that there was no need for an attempt on the throne since fate would bring about the outcome in any case. All the witnesses were strangled, save for one, a young philosopher, Simonides, who stood motionless amid the flames.*

All this must have been passing through the minds of Chrysostom and his friend while they stared at the mysterious signs and formulae. A soldier approached, and for the next few minutes paced back and forth between them and the river. Years later, in one of his homilies, Chrysostom would speak of themselves as being 'congealed with fear'. They could neither toss the book away nor tear it to pieces without attracting notice. 'God gave us means', although what these were Chrysostom does not say; perhaps the pages were stuffed in an intimate place. Finally, when the soldier was at a safe distance, they cast the book aside and quickly made their departure. Chrysostom, relating this youthful adventure, one of a number of such cases, pointed to God's intervention when 'we have fallen into dangers and calamities' as being good cause for people to glorify Him.

Antioch was not always the most congenial of places.

That evening, beneath an almost full moon, I walked through what little survives of the old town, the narrow streets with the appearance of stone walls, their continuity broken only by shuttered wooden balconies and closed entrances. A century ago, women in the houses would have peered down through the slats, hidden from public gaze. The area was almost attractive. I heard drums and singing in the distance, and, following the sound, soon found myself peering in at the open entrance of a house.

The music stopped, I was waved inside.

A space was made for me, and within minutes I was offered apples, pomegranates and coffee. The women recommenced beating their drums and singing with an even greater rhythmic fervour. It was a wedding party, although the actual ceremony would be taking place the next day, at the registry office. When the couple danced together just the once, probably the only time in their lives they would ever do so, there was no meeting of the eyes. The people gathered here appeared happier for the couple than the couple were for themselves. The clapping of hands and the beating of drums would chase away devilish uncertainties. Such glumness, however, was only part of the ritual; it would be poor manners for the happy couple to appear overjoyed at the prospect of leaving home. An older Arab woman with a stern face got up to dance. She snaked her hands through the air, closed her eyes and smiled. The drums beat louder and faster. She shook her ample breasts wildly while the other women encouraged her with their ziraleet.

'And light your shrines and chaunt your ziraleets,' writes Thomas Moore in 'The Veiled Prophet of Khorassan' from his *Lalla Rookh*. The ziraleet is that sound which Alexander Russell, in his *A Natural History of Aleppo* (1794), describes as 'the common manner of a company of women expressing joy, or any sudden exultation. The words expressed are Lillé, Lillé, Lillé, repeated as often as the person can do at one breath, and, being rapidly uttered in a very shrill tone, they are heard at a great distance.' Russell continues with a comparison to passages from ancient Greek literature, pointing to when, for example, upon Xenophon's retreat, the Greek women attending the army shout in this manner; and also when Penelope, after the first transports of grief on the discovery of her son's departure, prepares a sacrifice to Minerva, and having finished her supplication makes a similar sound:

> She ceas'd: shrill ecstasies of joy declare,
> The fav'ring goddess present to the pray'r:
> The suitors heard, and deem'd the mirthful voice
> A signal of her hymeneal choice.
>
> *Odyssey,* iv, 1013–6 (Pope trans.)

A friend of the bridegroom, Ibrāhīm, spoke English. He had lived for a couple of years in Ealing and expressed a deep affection for England. Or was it only for Ealing Broadway? I had little sense of his having been elsewhere. Ibrāhīm, his eyes mournful behind thick spectacles, looked as though he had spent an eternity filing papers in a dusty office, where neither youth nor old age would ever trouble him. If there was anything he could show me in Antakya he would be free to do so the following morning, he told me. I expressed a desire to see the old Ottoman houses.

'Ah, easily done,' he said, 'I know many old houses.'

'Would we be able to go inside them?'

'Yes, yes, I know people.'

The next morning Ibrāhīm seemed only dimly aware of our conversation of the night before.

'Old houses? Huh! Yes, ah, houses.'

'Only if it's not too much trouble.'

'What trouble?' he snapped. '*Where's* trouble?'

Ibrāhīm was all nerves. We entered one courtyard only to find the broken outlines of what once must have been quite a handsome residence. Anything of aesthetic value had been destroyed. Sheets of corrugated iron patched holes in the walls. A waterless fountain stank of garbage.

'This is an old house,' he explained.

'Do you know its date?'

'Yes, old!'

Ibrāhīm seemed not to understand what I was looking for. I surmised that perhaps he was feeling awkward about knocking at strangers' doors but at the same time did not want to disappoint me. I wondered how I might, without offending him, release him from his earlier promise.

'The mosque of Ḥabīb al-Nadjdjār.'

We sped by without stopping to look inside.

'Who was he?'

'A Muslim saint who lived alone in a cave up on the mountain. When they cut off his head it rolled all the way down the mountainside, and where it stopped they built the mosque.'

'Who killed him and why?'

Ibrāhīm seemed not to hear me and, as though he had entered upon some mad trajectory of his own, rushed me through a dismal area of dilapidated houses. I stopped to look behind me. The mosque was perhaps a mile or more from the foot of the mountain. I wondered how it might be possible for a severed head to roll that distance. After a few minutes we found ourselves at a door upon which Ibrāhīm knocked hard several times. There was a crazed look in his eyes. A man in pyjamas answered, and, shrugging his shoulders at our architectural mission, summoned us inside.

'If these people knew who I was,' said Ibrāhīm, 'we would be asked to leave.'

We were invited to sit in a row of chairs in the courtyard where in the middle stood a tree, a single pomegranate hanging from one of its branches. A woman sliced onions, only rarely looking up from her task while a group of children with sores on their faces silently watched me. A chained dog whimpered beneath an unsupported stone staircase. The man in pyjamas, perhaps following the movement of my eyes, walked over to the tree, and, as though against my willing him not to, picked the only pomegranate that was hanging there and put it in front of me, together with a knife. The dog whined. Our host, his wife and their children watched as I cut into what might have been the last fruit in the universe. A red drop ran down over its green surface. The fruit was not yet ripe, and its bitter seeds wrung the moisture from my mouth. A midday sun filled the courtyard.

Ibrāhīm invited me to inspect the rooms upstairs. Would the steps with nothing beneath them finally collapse? I felt like part of an invading force. The master of the house followed us as though he, too, might make a few discoveries.

The rooms upstairs were in a considerably worse state than the area below. Ibrāhīm scowled with disgust as we inspected one where the walls had begun to bubble.

'Ibrāhīm, should we be here?'

I was hugely embarrassed, but he wasn't listening to me.

'I used to play in this room,' he hissed.

'What? You've been here before!'

Any answer he gave now was not to me but to some other question coiled like a snake deep within himself. Ibrāhīm submitted himself to its poisonous lashes.

'This was my grandmother's house. My second childhood home! See what these people have allowed it to become.'

Our host smiled uncomprehendingly.

'When my grandmother died they squatted this place. This happens all the time, especially with these old houses, and because the squatters cannot afford to make repairs to them the houses are falling apart.'

'And this is the first time you've returned?'

'Yes!'

I wondered at what point the idea occurred to him to make this dark pilgrimage. Clearly I had provided him with an excuse to come here.

'What's worse, if one of these people has an accident we can be held legally responsible. If one of these fools goes through the floor and breaks his neck we can be sued. It's the crazy law here. What can we do? My family fought to have them removed, but the legal costs were too great for us to be able to pursue the case.'

We stopped at the entrance to one of the bedrooms. I could see through a breach where floor and wall had separated a boy parking his bicycle. The floorboards felt spongy, as though about to give.

'Her bedroom!' Although I could comprehend Ibrāhīm's sorrow I felt sympathy too for the family who lived here. 'She was from Aleppo and was legendary for her beauty.'

Ibrāhīm noticed me searching, perhaps a little too closely, for traces of that same beauty in him.

'My mother was beautiful too, she *still* is, but not me.'

All this was said without a smile. Ibrāhīm's eyes were beady with murderous rage for those who now occupied his family's house.

'Where do you live now?'

'We moved in the seventies like everybody else, into the new apartment blocks north of the river, and when we left people from the villages moved into our old place.' There was a fresh note of pity in his voice. 'They really are poor, these people.'

We left the house, Ibrāhīm clearly much shaken by the experience. I bowed out of going to the wedding, saying that I did not wish to intrude. In truth, I was relieved to make my escape.

The next morning I walked along the Kurtuluş Caddesi, which follows the course of the famous street that Herod and Tiberius built. Almost two miles in length, this ancient thoroughfare with its many shops, its second-storey galleries and covered colonnades was one of Antioch's glories. There, one might sip cooled wine in the shade, watch camels and asses being led through the porticoes 'as though they were brides', jugglers and acrobats, pipers and dancers, barefoot monks and bearded philosophers, girls carrying amphorae on their shoulders, schoolboys chaperoned by slaves, women in brightly coloured carriages drawn by mules. A noisy road now, with miserable shops on either side, there is nothing for the mind to settle upon, unless it be the garage advertising AMERICAN PARTS or the small shop where all the bottles of water were thickly covered with dust. I followed this dismal stretch to where a path turned off up to the Grotto of St Peter, or, as the Turks call it, Sen Piyer Kilisesi.

A special Mass was being said, in Italian, for a group of pilgrims.

It may have been at this cave, on the west side of Mount Staurus (Mount of the Cross), that, according to Acts 11:26, the followers of a new religion were called Christians for the first time. A damp space thirteen metres long and nine metres wide constitutes what local tradition says is the first church in existence. If true, scholars and theologians are silent on the matter. The Crusaders were perhaps a little too enthusiastic to find holy places. When, under Bohemond, they conquered Antioch on 3 June 1098 and slaughtered all the Turks so that the streets were filled with corpses and then pillaged the houses of Muslims and, yes, even Christians, they might well have felt the need for spiritual solace. The remains of mosaic on the floor of the cave and the barely visible frescoes on the right side of the altar appear to date from between the fifth and seventh centuries, thereby suggesting that when they came this already was a site of importance. The Crusaders extended the cave by a couple of metres, adding two arches; the oriental façade was erected in 1883 and is soon to be replaced. With what, concrete?

Did St Peter actually preach here? All we know for certain is that he was in Antioch between AD 47 and 54 and that, with Paul and Barnabas, he founded one of the world's first Christian communities, most importantly, the first congregation to include Jews *and* Gentiles. On 29 June each year, the anniversary of St Peter's martyrdom, the small Christian population of Antakya congregates for a special service. There is a legend that fishermen used to come to bathe and be cleansed of their sins in a small sculpted building not far from here, but of this there is no archaeological evidence. The priest celebrating Mass, Padre Domenico, invited me to visit him the next day at his church in Antakya.

Only a hundred yards or so from the Grotto is a stone bust carved out of limestone, which the Antiochenes called the Charonian. The white stone is visible to most of the town. The Byzantine historian, John Malalas, writing in the sixth century, notes that during the reign of Antiochus IV Epiphanes (175–163 BC) the town was struck by plague. A soothsayer by the name of Leios told Antiochus to construct an image of Charon, the boatman who carried souls into the underworld. A smaller draped figure standing to the right of this may represent the Syrian goddess of Hierapolis, a figure connected to the underworld. The unfinished state of the carvings suggests that when the plague stopped, the sculptors, seeing little need to continue, downed their tools. The presence, at such close quarters, of pagan and Christian antiquities revived in me certain old dichotomies.

That evening the moon was full.

I went to a restaurant where, to my dismay, a television set dominated the dining space. When the news came on, almost all of its thirty minutes were devoted to further developments on Zeki's death. The waiters stood about in silence. There was ample footage of Zeki's last public appearance only minutes before he died. The camera kept zooming in on Zeki's right hand. Was there something going on here, which nobody had noticed before? Were these, the commentator asked, the early signs of Zeki's demise? The camera invited the audience to look again. Yes, there did appear to be a slight tremble. The woman presenting Zeki with the gift of his old microphone had a plunging neckline. I, too, might have trembled. I wanted a glass of Cappadocian wine. The waiters continued to stand in silence. I signalled as though into a terrible void or as a ghost might to a passing cab. If earth and moon were about to collide, no matter, Zeki would still be the big news, perhaps bigger than he ever was in life, for many days to come.

Padre Domenico, a Capuchin priest from Modena, Italy, has lived in Turkey for twenty-five years, the last eight of which have been spent in Antakya. When I asked him if he was ever homesick for Italy he nodded at the bags of Lavazza coffee. After making espresso for me, he proudly took me on a tour of the church and the surrounding premises. Some years before, he took over one of the crumbling Ottoman houses, and, employing the services of a local architect, Selahattin Altınöz, produced a model of what, given the right resources, can be done with these dilapidated buildings. The Catholic church stands only a few yards away from a synagogue, backs on to a mosque, and is quite close to the Orthodox church. A tourist brochure describes this as an 'ecumenical triangle'. Was there some irony in the phrase?

Padre Domenico is a popular figure. Throughout our conversation people kept coming and going and there was, in the manner in which they greeted him, both much affection and respect. Although there are few Catholic families in Antakya, probably not more than a dozen, the congregation includes a large number of Orthodox Christian worshippers who follow the Syriac rite and whose bishops and patriarchs are still titled 'of Antioch', although they are now based in Damascus. The following week a group of Protestants from America were coming to borrow the premises.

'Perhaps they'll think better of Rome.'

'I hope so,' he smiled.

A man not to be pushed to profundity he answered my questions with only the most perfunctory sentences, 'Yes, I like Antakya', and again, when asked if he could supply any anecdotes about the place, 'I'm afraid not much happens here.' I noticed Padre Domenico moved nervously from chair to chair, as though not wishing to be trapped by any one of them.

Chrysostom?

'Ah yes, Chrysostom,' he murmured, as though dimly recalling an old schoolmate.

'What of the first Capuchin priest who came here?'

'Basilio Galli! I remember!'

The Latin rite was brought back, on the authorisation of Pius IX, to Antioch in 1846, after an absence of several centuries. Padre Basilio was the good messenger. Some months later, I stumbled upon a small portrait of him in F.A. Neale's memoir, *Eight Years in Syria, Palestine, and Asia Minor, from 1842 to*

1850. Neale, who was attached to the consular service in Syria, resided at Antioch for eight months in 1847, and together with Basilio ('Père Bazelio') and an unnamed Italian doctor formed the European society of Antioch. The society of three soon became two. The doctor would never go to Mass on Sunday and consequently, Neale relates, this 'irreclaimably lost sheep' found himself exiled from Basilio's affections. An elderly but indefatigable figure, Basilio won the respect of the whole town; he established a school and a chapel, although the congregation never amounted to more than a dozen people.

Basilio's great passion was antiquities.

> With his staff in one hand, and a morsel of bread in the other, he toiled up mountains and down ravines in search of mouldering ruins and rusty antiques, appeasing his appetite from his scanty wallet, and quenching his thirst from one of the many streams that so plentifully abound round Antioch.

Nothing delighted Basilio more than the discovery of an old coin or a stone with some inscription, which was only barely visible. Whenever they met on neutral ground the doctor from Rome would quarrel with Basilio, saying that it was humbug to suppose anything had survived the many earthquakes. Basilio held his ground, no matter how shaky it was. The arguments would rapidly escalate 'with as much gesticulation and noise, as ever two Roman senators could have used in debating the most weighty affairs of the State', and such was the heat between the two Latins the townspeople feared there would be violence. One may suppose their quarrels constituted a deeper friendship. What Neale did not know, when his book was published in 1852, was that some months earlier, on 12 May 1851, Basilio's throat had been cut by unknown figures.

'Muslims killed him?'

'Yes, I believe so,' said Padre Domenico.

'Why?'

'Jealousy maybe.'

'What about the relationship between Muslims and Christians now?'

'Good.'

'Will it remain so?'

'Yes, why not?'

As of late, the Turks have not been noted for their religious tolerance, but several people I spoke to in Antakya suggested that the local situation was otherwise. Muslims and Christians got on well, I was told, things were different here. Padre Domenico showed me an old photograph of a Roman stone bridge spanning a turbulent Orontes.

'They destroyed this bridge in order to make way for a new one.'

'The people here have no sense of their own history?'

'Yes, it's most upsetting to observe.'

The doubting ghost of the Italian doctor must have got into me.

'Do you believe the Grotto's where St Peter preached?'

'There can be no positive "yes" or "no" to that question, but I feel that it probably is.'

Padre Domenico supported my earlier notion, that the presence of mosaics from an age predating that of the Crusades, even if it proves little, points to there already having been a strong tradition of worship in that spot. As we spoke, he leaned closer to me.

'This simple cave is very important to me,' he continued. 'Unlike the Vatican, which reflects the strength of man, this place is informed by the power of the Holy Spirit.'

The morning newspaper was filled with further revelations about Zeki. Whether scandals or miracles, these the Turkish language concealed from me. A television blasted pop videos over the breakfast tables. There could be no escaping junk culture, yet the moon above Antakya is the same as that which hung above Antioch. One may still glean from the surrounding stone something of permanence. I was just about to get onto a bus for Aleppo when Ibrāhīm arrived, saddened that I could not accept an invitation to his mother's house. We spoke unconvincingly of future dates. The demon that seemed to have possessed him a couple of days before had gone.

The Romans in this part of the world are said to have used turtles as walking candleholders. I enter into a debate with myself as to whether this was cruel, *immensely* cruel that is. Would the turtle have felt through its thick shell the dripping wax, and, if so, would it have accelerated? At what speed would a turtle have to move in order to extinguish the flame? Was the fate of a walking candle not preferable to that of turtle consommé? Of what do turtles dream?

TWO

To Aleppo Gone

Her husband's to Aleppo gone, master of the *Tiger*.

Macbeth, I. iii

A butcher came up to me near the Bāb Anṭākī (Antioch Gate), one of the main entrances to the main souq of Aleppo, and pressed his hand sticky with blood into mine. A couple of goat's heads lay on the ground by his feet. A quick death had frozen their professorial smiles. With his other hand the man, who might have been mad, friendly or hostile, grabbed my wrist, grinning foolishly all the while. I pulled myself free, and, with the goat's blood congealing between my fingers, I sped through the covered streets, looking for somewhere to wash.

'Hello, mister, welcome!'

A merchant pushed artificial silk scarves at me.

'Français?'

The voices seemed to come from all directions at once.

'English? Hello, Manchester United!'

I pressed myself against the wall, attempting to squeeze past a couple of small vehicles belching fumes, their drivers leaning on their horns at some boys perched on braying mules that kept going round in circles. The boys with their soprano voices slapped the arses of the mules. The poor creatures became even more confused, their eyes glassy with unintelligence. A small crowd of people who were the secondary cause of the obstruction gathered to watch the primary cause, an argument between two men who were eyeing each other with murderous rage. There was much shouting and waving of arms between them and several shoves but no determining punches. Almost five minutes of all show and no action passed before the men skulked off in opposite directions, the crowd dispersed, the boys stopped slapping the mules, the mules quit braying, the drivers let up beeping their horns and I was free to move.

'Deutsch?'

'Come inside just one minute. No need to buy anything. Just look. You like to drink some tea with me?'

The merchant's offer of brew and conversation is almost always perfectly genuine. The Syrian merchant will say there is more to life than making money and although he will demonstrate the truth of this one suspects that he is, in comparison to his Turkish counterpart whose prime objective is making a quick sale, the more skilful of the two salesmen. I accepted his offer for reasons other than conversation.

'May I wash my hands here?'

According to legend, the prophet Abraham, on his journey south to the land of Canaan, stopped and milked his cows on the mound where the citadel of Aleppo now stands. Alexander Russell, in his *The Natural History of Aleppo* (1794), which, despite its occasional lapses into prejudice, remains the finest book on Aleppo in the English language, refers to a manuscript in his possession, entitled *Tareeh Haleb* (The History of Aleppo). According to its author the Patriarch used daily to distribute milk to the poor of a neighbouring village, who at certain hours, in expectation of his bounty, assembled at the bottom of the hill, and by frequently repeating '*Ibrāhīm haleb*' ('Abraham has milked') gave occasion to the name Haleb being conferred on the town. Haleb is still the Arabic name for the town. As for the epithet *Shahbā'* that is frequently given to the city, Russell's manuscript contains a further variation on the Abraham legend. In the Patriarch's herd there was a singular cow, remarkable for its variegated colour and distinctive moo. *Shahbā'* denotes streaks of grey and white. When she was milked, the populace waiting below, upon hearing her moo, would remark to one another, '*Ibrāhīm haleb al-Shahbā'!*' (Abraham has milked the pied cow!) On the other hand, the town's epithet may be derived from the colour of the soil and buildings. If we find the legend of Abraham doubtful, it was not so in 1167 when Nūr al-Dīn built a mosque on the mound in the Patriarch's honour, preserving there the stone upon which he is supposed to have sat. According to Hittite records there was a settlement here between 2000 and 1400 BC. There have been settlements here going back to the eighth millennium and it seems likely that the hill was fortified long before Abraham's time and may not therefore have allowed for such a pastoral scene. That the story should survive at all, however, suggests a core of truth at its centre.

The Aleppo souq, the finest in the Middle East, is a marvel of covered passages. A foreigner should go invisibly there, so as not to precipitate too much change. Although there is a tourist trade, unlike the Grand Bazaar in Istanbul, which is almost wholly given over to that purpose, the Aleppo souq for the most part still serves the needs of the local populace. Authenticity, which usually means the cosmetic has been more smoothly applied than elsewhere, is uncalculated here. The concerns are what they always were, the buying and selling of gold continues as an insurance against hard times, the barrels of dried henna which when boiled up into a paste still decorate the palms of Bedouin women, the dried flowers which when brewed provide a cure for stomach troubles, the rope – why, with the nomadic life on the wane, so much rope? Although some areas of the souq are no longer given over to just one trade, meat is still to be found in one place, sheep carcasses hanging from the doorways, and elsewhere one finds specific areas for nuts, vegetables, cotton, textiles, tent trappings, sheepskins, confectionery, perfumes, leather, gold and silver jewellery, copper, brass and metal utensils, the spice market with its smells of nutmeg, coriander, cumin, saffron, cinnamon, pepper, cardamom and cloves and aloes. A foreigner will not go unnoticed, of course. Young boys rush through the streets keeping track of each person who goes there and will try to entice his prey back to the shop of an older brother, father or uncle.

This massive labyrinth, largely unchanged since the sixteenth century and in parts dating back to the thirteenth, covers seven kilometres. The vaulted stone ceilings, dusty shafts of light penetrating the gloom every so often, keep the area cool in summer and dry during the winter rains. It is a world of many contrasts – subterranean in feel yet above ground, timeless yet operating always in the present tense, orderly and chaotic. Aleppo, almost midway between where desert ends and sea begins, is also where East meets West and where, for centuries, European mercantile interests were also Oriental ones. If Shakespeare thought he could sail to Aleppo then either the doomed *Tiger* was dragged overland by a thousand camels or the coastline has greatly altered. Aleppo is seventy miles away from the sea and is further separated from Antakya by a mountain range. Or perhaps he did not blunder at all and was only speaking in the figurative sense. Alexandretta, on the Hatay coast, used to be considered Aleppo's port in the same way Seleucia was regarded Antioch's. Aleppo was certainly known in Shakespeare's day – the English Levant Company had a factory here and the town was a vital stage in the overland route for commerce with the East. Along the paths in the souq one can see what were once the magnificent courtyards of the khans or caravanserais where foreign merchants took up residence.

There is much here to make the heart sink, however, and in fact any journey to the Orient is in part a struggle to unscramble surfaces. The ugly and the beautiful dwell not side by side, but rather they occupy the same plane. A sweet rose contends with stinking garbage. So much magnificence runs to waste and indeed many of the old khans now serve as storage spaces. I noticed a particularly lovely minaret with three fluorescent tubes attached near the top, an illustration of just how much has gone wrong with the Arabic culture, in particular the distortion of its beautiful line. The Arabs themselves have imported the straight line. They must be held accountable.

Everywhere one looks there are electrical cables, makeshift repairs, advertising posters and fluorescent tubes. Who first brought in the fluorescent tube? Where's the punishment to fit the crime? One finds everywhere, even in the most beautiful mosques, the violence this harsh light has done. This imported identity is completely out of keeping with the gracefulness of Arabic architecture. The pollution in Aleppo is some of the worst I have ever experienced. The situation is, if anything, even worse in the souq where, with nowhere for the fumes to escape, one experiences a continual burning in the throat and eyes. The civil authorities seem unable, at present, to protect what they have. This is a problem that greatly exercises Aḥmad Mallāḥ, a tour guide whose knowledge of the souq and its hidden treasures is perhaps unrivalled. Aḥmad who picks up his clientele at the corner of the Souq al-Atarin and the street running south towards the Māristān Arghūn is informed by something more important than the need of an income – a genuine love of the place.

'Although the responsibility for the preservation of the souq falls ultimately to the wealthier people,' he complains, 'who among them will open their purses?'

Although less drastic than in Antakya the scenario is much the same, with the wealthy having abandoned the traditional houses for the modern quarters while the poor migrants who cannot afford the upkeep of the old houses came in droves. The population of Aleppo, over a million, has more than doubled since the 1960s.

'You must understand many of these people have come from the poorest villages. This to them is a kind of paradise. If I say to them, "You are destroying paradise", they'll think I am insane.'

Aḥmad stood, appropriately enough, in one of the courtyards of the Māristān Arghūn al-Kamilī, a hospital for the insane, constructed in 1354 by a wealthy Mamlūk governor who gave the place his name. The year before, on my first visit to Aleppo, a boy of angelic beauty kept trying to bring me here. *Why will you not come with me to see the madhouse?* There was a terrible disturbance in his eyes and, a couple of days later, when he whispered to me that he did not believe in God the gravity of what he was telling me shook his slight frame. *You will not tell anyone, please, my life would be made impossible.* The boy never smiled once, and I wondered how at the age of fourteen or fifteen despair had so completely possessed him. After a while I took pains to avoid him, but he would always find me. *Will you come with me now to the madhouse?*

Aḥmad pointed out the architectural wonders of the place.

'I must speak quickly because you see there are many less knowledgeable guides about and what they do is listen to me, gathering any information which they can use.'

A man stood nearby, a possible spy in the house of madness.

'Natural light and gentle sounds, the sound of fountains, were used in the treatment of the insane. Flowers were planted along the walls and around the pools so the mad could smell their perfume.'

At one end of the courtyard was an *īwān* where hired musicians played soft music and passages from the Qur'ān were read aloud. According to one medieval writer, Ibn Abī Uṣabi'a, the first doctors were the inventors of the reed pipe, who healed with their playing. Most Islamic medical writers recommended music as a cure for melancholia. The notion that music expressed the harmony of the heavenly spheres and directly influenced the soul was inherited from the Greeks. The Arabs were careful to distinguish between the various forms of madness – 'madness is of many kinds' – between the imbecile (*aḥmaq*), the possessed (*majnūn*), and 'the fool for God's sake' (*majdhūb*) to name but three. The late Michael W. Dols, in his monumental study, *Majnū n: The Madman in Medieval Society*, asking the meaning of madness in Islamic society, answers his own question:

> Conversely, what was sanity? In the medieval scheme of things, the human being was the microcosm of the universe, sharing with the plants and animals the qualities of growth

> and sensation but also sharing with the angels and heavenly beings the qualities of reason and the desire for beatitude. Reason was pivotal – it was the link between the visible and the invisible, the body and the soul, and the individual and society. Reason was the prerequisite for a Muslim's full participation in his community. Yet, paradoxically, the madman was accommodated by society, so that he was not a pariah, an outcast, or a scapegoat.

Aḥmad spoke of the importance of natural light but deeper inside the hospital, where in the twelve cells surrounding an octagonal courtyard the most dangerously insane were kept in chains, there was only darkness. Here, the worst cases were kept in chains and regularly beaten. It seemed extraordinary that one should find beneath one roof both enlightenment and sheer brutality. I asked Aḥmad what the present attitude to madness was.

'We try to cure them.'

'Yes, but how?'

Aḥmad seemed to want to evade my question, speaking instead of the need for spiritual balance, although he did say that life here was not without its attendant cruelties and also how easily one could be made to feel alone. The past may have been for him a safer country. Alexander Russell, who was a physician and would have paid close attention not only to the disorders of the body but to those of the mind, presumably was thinking of this place when he wrote:

> The power of invisible spirits over the human frame, a notion of such ancient date in the East, is still universally received; and, in various diseases, recourse is had to exorcism, as often as to medicine. Insane persons are not however all treated alike. The furious madman is kept in chains, and consigned to the care of doctors, or exorcists; mere drivellers are kept within doors, or, become the sport of idle boys in the street; whilst those who are but slightly disordered in mind, and who are guilty of no

> alarming excesses, are always used with the most compassionate tenderness; and if, happening to take a religious turn, they are capable of prayer, or can occasionally repeat some sentences of the Koran, they are then considered as persons divinely inspired, and sometimes admitted, in tattered garments, with their limbs naked, to sit down familiarly with people of the first rank, and even allowed to kiss their cheek. The inspired shaykhs are sometimes also consulted as physicians, and return advice truly oracular. It is diverting to observe men, in other respects of strong plain sense, make serious exertions to unravel the incoherent wanderings of a madman.

When we left the hospital, as if on cue a man ran down the street babbling nonsense, his eyes staring, a thin line of froth about his mouth, his body stiffly upright as though strapped to an invisible board, 'his arms flat against his sides like two capital I's', as the brothers Goncourt wrote in a rather different context.

'We say of such people,' Aḥmad whispered, 'the light's on in the house, but nobody's home.'

That evening Aḥmad and I went to a Sufi meeting at the Mosque al-ʿĀdiliyya. The practice of *dhikr* (remembrance) is derived from those Qur'ānic verses that enjoin the faithful to remember God often and its techniques involve the rhythmic repetition of a phrase in which one of the hundred names of God appears. The collective *dhikr* is carefully regulated with close attention paid to breath control and physical movement by which means the five senses as well as the psyche and imagination are brought into close proximity to God. The session we attended began with a recitation of Qur'ānic verses which lasted almost an hour, after which the men often with their young sons beside them stood holding hands in several circles, the organisers deciding who should go near the front in order to be closer to the centre of power and who should stay at the rear. They began jumping up and down in their places, continuing to do so until the movements were involuntary. As they jumped and made a *hu, hu, hu* sound an *ʿālim* ran between the lines of people, encouraging anyone who was slackening in pace. At the centre, from which all the power seemed to emanate, a shaykh danced in slow circles. After some minutes, the crowd was a single beating pulse. After perhaps half an hour of this a signal was made and the jumping stopped, and as the bodies relaxed the sound was like that of a panting animal. Russell describes a similar scene:

> The shaykh, placed in the centre of a circle, consisting perhaps of twenty persons, begins the service by chanting a prayer, while all the rest remain in an attitude of devout attention. He then repeats the words *Ullah hu! Ullah hu!* accompanying them with a slow movement of the body backward and forward, the whole circle at the same time following his example. After a short while, moving the body more quickly, they drop the word *Ullah!* and continue incessantly to repeat the word *hu!* This ceremony lasts almost an hour, the shaykh all the while barking like the others, and from time to time turning slowly, so as to front the circle successively. His countenance appears strangely agitated, and he at length sits down as if quite exhausted by the exercise.

The French traveller, Herbelot, from whom Byron derived much of his knowledge of the East, writes of a remarkable figure, Bābā Bazarlu, who shut himself up in a cell so he might spend his days in contemplation. The wall of his cell being his only page he inscribed on it, in characters so large as to occupy the whole surface, the single word *Hu*, 'He who is', one of the hundred names of Allāh, which is often placed at the beginning of Islamic texts.

As we were leaving the mosque a man, his eyes watery with laughter, blocked our way.

'AlllllllllllaaaaaaaaaaAhhh!'

Quite often I would hear Allāh's name stretched like this with a closing down hard on the *ah*, as if it were at once a spiritual and vocal exercise.

'ʿAbdul is a Saʿdīya Sufi,' Aḥmad told me, 'a fool by his own admission. ʿAbdul, will you speak to our visitor here.'

The sentences only barely connected to each other yet, as rendered in Aḥmad's translation, were complete in themselves, like different coloured stones strung on a single thread.

'This is a gift I have from Allāh. *Ha ha ha!* Allāh is free in choosing those people who serve Him. Yes, I make people laugh. *Ha, ha!* Allāh says, "I am the one who makes people smile and I am the one who makes others weep." When we mix laughter with weeping they become equal. Can you describe honey for me, if I never tasted it? Sufis taste the beauty of Allāh. *Ha, ha, ha!* The beauty of Allāh is equal to His mightiness. They mix the two descriptions of Allāh. They are not like this, angry or frowning. I am not normal. *Ha, ha!* We are supported by Allāh, the one who started the universe. Without Him all is perishable. We don't hate or despise the atheist, but we hate his atheism. We love him for Allāh's sake. Our hearts are compassionate for him, for Allāh's sake. You are a manifestation of Allāh. Absolutely. *Ha, ha, ha!* When I sit with you I am talking to Allāh. *Ha!* I will not ignore you if you are an atheist or a Christian because you, too, were created by Allāh. Who made your hair, your eyes? *Ha, ha, ha!* We should be polite with the creatures of Allāh.'

When I returned to my hotel, the *Najem Akhdar* (Green Star), I met Amal, the son of the proprietor, who seemed to be in love with some Western image of himself, complete with jogging outfit and baseball cap. I mentioned in passing that I was working on a book about Syria.

'Ah, then perhaps you know my good friend in London—'

I had almost dreaded him saying the name.

'—Robert Tewdwr Moss. He always stays here. We quite often travel together. I am expecting him soon.'

'I'm afraid, Amal, I've got bad news.'

Shortly before I left England somebody handed me an obituary notice, containing the photograph of a strikingly handsome man 'arch, precise and hysterical' with a wild bohemian look in his eyes. A tabby sat on the step beside him. Robert Tewdwr Moss. It was the first time I had encountered his name. A lobbyist for the Cat Protection League, a passion for the Middle East, 'an ear for the bizarre' – the credentials were impressive. Tewdwr Moss had been putting the finishing touches to a book of travels in Syria, *Cleopatra's Wedding Present*, when he was mysteriously murdered, suffocated, in his Paddington flat. The computer containing his book in its final form was stolen. The murder, if one read between the lines, appeared to stem from the circumstances of a life boldly lived. A flamboyant figure, Tewdwr Moss 'like some ghost of the *fin de siècle* past,' the obituarist Philip Hoare wrote, 'moved through literary, journalistic and café society, clad in velvet and brocade, surreptitiously passing on a morsel of gossip here, imparting some arcane piece of knowledge there'. He was thirty-five years old when he died. Pursued by men, glamorous women and mad countesses, there seemed to be a kind of blighted perfection in his life. An hour later, Amal was precisely where I'd left him, his eyes fixed on some point in the floor.

'Why kill a man so gentle?'

The narrow streets of the Jdeide quarter, the traditionally Christian area, are north of the walled city. The architecture with its overhanging balconies, latticework and shutters is in some respects a Mamlūk version of Tudor. As seen from the outside walls one cannot guess at the beauty inside. Most of the houses are built around a courtyard with a fountain at the centre, an *īwān* at one end and with highly decorative walls which incorporate elements of rococo and Mamlūk. One of the most exquisite of the old houses is the Beit Ajiqbash, built in 1757 for a wealthy Christian family, and which now houses the Museum of Popular Traditions.

A year before, in the courtyard of this house, I met Yasser for the first time. Although he was born in Syria he considers himself a Palestinian first. With each sentence he began he would point a finger as though conducting the flow of his thoughts. A lover of English literature, Yasser began to recite, 'Yet once more, O ye Laurels, and once more/Ye Myrtles brown, with Ivy never-sear . . .'. The words tripped so mechanically from his lips I wondered if they were not learned by rote. 'Who would not sing for *Lycidas*? he well knew/Himself to sing, and build the lofty rhyme.' I remarked on his Arabic cadences, how they seemed to turn an English into an Arabic poet. Yasser seemed rather upset by what I had intended as a compliment.

'I learned this from a tape of an English actor reading the poem.'

I suggested that he flatten his reading of the lines a little. Yasser looked uneasy, as though some part of his education were being undone. The poem in its celebration of the tender friendship between two males began to strike me as very Arabic indeed. Yasser asked me about D.H. Lawrence. Because he was reluctant at first to express his own views on the subject I told him that for me the key to Lawrence's character was in his paintings. If, in comparison to his writings, the paintings were poor, they were still a remarkable pointer to how he perceived himself, as occupying a messianic role.

'As good as Lawrence can be,' I continued, 'while reading him I always get the sense of the author breathing down my neck, telling me what to think.'

Yasser geared himself up to ask what for him was obviously an awkward question.

'Can you tell me,' he whispered, 'do English people actually speak in Lawrence's pornographic language?'

I tried to explain that since Lawrence's day we have developed a rather tougher linguistic palate. Suddenly, beneath a Syrian sun, I was for the first time in years discussing, and criticising, an author whom I had treated once with reverence.

'So perhaps,' Yasser said, 'Lawrence represents the demise of spiritual values in Western culture.'

'I think he would have said he was upholding them.'

'Yes perhaps, but I fear the decay has already begun. The Arabs have taken only the worst from Western culture, which is why for Muslims the greatest revolution this century, equivalent only to the French Revolution in your sphere, has been the rise of the Āyatollāh Khomeinī and with him the restoration of spiritual values.'

'At what cost though?'

'When you consider what's at stake, very little.'

I recalled the public execution of the Shah's white horses. So many thousands of people died, yet the image that stayed with me was of those horses.

'Sometimes excesses are necessary,' he concluded.

Later that evening we drank coffee in the park, a Ferris wheel behind us, which although empty of people kept revolving like some presentiment of the utterly futile. We moved inevitably towards the Palestinian question.

'Arafat has undone everything we have sought to achieve,' Yasser said, 'and by doing so he has become the Zionists' policeman.'

'How then, do you perceive the future?'

'We cannot begin to discuss the future until we have properly considered the past.'

In the Middle East the past stretches further back than in most places. For the next hour or so Yasser took me back to the Middle Ages when, as he explained to me, the position of the Jew in Europe was as a movable part in a rigid feudal system.

'The Jew was essential to making that system work. It was only through him that usury was possible. When the feudal system collapsed there was no longer any need for him, hence the beginnings of "the Jewish problem".'

I followed him down many complicated routes into the present.

'What do you think of our military operations?'

'You choose your words with considerable care,' I said. 'I would not describe as a military operation anything that results in the deaths of innocent people.'

'Listen,' Yasser whispered, 'I do not hate Jews. I have no wish to kill Jews, but perhaps you should explain to me *who* these innocent people were, who levelled my family's village to the ground, wiping from the maps even its name and who afterwards built their own settlement there.'

Although I expressed my sympathy for the Palestinian cause, I argued there was now a younger generation of Israelis many of whom wanted to make a lasting peace.

'Perhaps,' I suggested, 'the moment is ripe for compromise.'

'Your father is Polish?'

'Yes.'

'A supporter of the Communist regime?'

'No.'

'Does he hate the Russian people?'

'No.'

'Ah then, tell me! At what point did your father believe the time had come to compromise on the Soviet domination of Poland? We may despise the Zionist regime, but not the Jewish people.'

'So how would you feel about the creation of an independent Palestinian state?'

'Yes, that would be fine by me!'

'And if so, an Israel that you would recognise?'

'Yes, because once such a step has been taken Israel would disappear of its own accord. It would cease to be of substance not only to itself but to its American paymasters too.'

'You're dreaming. The Israelis will never consider such a possibility, so what then will your position be?'

'The answer is very simple. They must go back to from where they came, or else accept Palestinian nationality and live in peace.'

'You know that is not going to happen.'

'Why not? The Crusaders went away after a couple of hundred years.'

When I met him again a year later, despite the recent moves towards Palestinian self-determination, Yasser had hardened in his attitude. He was working now for al-Fatah, counselling those who had begun to waver in their resistance to the Zionist cause.

'You should be afraid to speak to me.'

'Why so?'

'Because I am a terrorist.'

I wondered what his counselling was like. The progress Arafat had made was, according to him, of little consequence, for in accepting a few bits of land and some empty promises he had betrayed the Palestinian struggle. Jordan was to blame. As was just about everybody else, the English too. The tunnel in Jerusalem that the Israelis had just reopened, despite the offence it would cause to Muslims by running close to the mosque, had been constructed in 1890 by an English engineer who had thereby served the Zionist cause. The digging into the past went deeper still. Yasser explained how Israeli archaeologists had falsely deciphered the Ebla stones, finding in them evidence of Jewish autonomy in the region. We were speaking here of inscriptions four thousand years old. There was little that could not be traced to the great Zionist plot, and although there were grains of truth in much of what he told me the smallest suspicions ballooned into conspiracy theories. Our conversation, like the Ferris wheel of a year before, had moved again in a familiar circle, though perhaps more rapidly this time, and when once again the question of 'military operations' came up I told him that these had resulted a few months earlier in the deaths of several Jewish children.

'They should not have been there,' he answered.

This was the same man who a year before sang Milton's verses.

'You will come over to our side,' he continued.

'I shall be with those who want peace.'

As I watched Yasser walk away, probably feeling certain of his victory over me, I saw in that shadow blending into the greater darkness the true horror of the dispossessed, the murderous abstraction of which only the ideologically pure are capable. We did not speak again. When later, in Damascus, I spoke of this my listener replied, 'When a duck sinks in the pond, the Zionists are to blame.'

When, a year later, I returned to Aleppo with my wife, an elderly man selling socks from the open window of a small wooden kiosk summoned me.

'Excuse me,' he asked, 'what do you do?'

Nouri ʿAjamī sat in his wooden enclosure like a marionette with one string broken, for his movements were like those in a film jumping several frames at a time. His sad, longish face was deathly pale against the dark piles of socks behind and to either side of him.

'I am a poet,' I replied.

If I were more direct about describing myself so than I would be at home, it was with the prior knowledge that being a poet in Syria meant being able to skip the banter and to get down to matters of importance.

'In that case,' Nouri ʿAjamī said, 'would you mind listening to this.'

He recited from memory a poem, not a particularly good one, but in a voice so mellifluous that any defects in the poem were briefly concealed.

In silence we do stay
Embowered with deep grief,
We cast our last glance
On him who passed away.

What can he have to offer
As a gift of departure
Besides our ailing sore
But a wreath of flower?

We can give him nothing more
Then the tears which are saline

Those can only do spangle
His unblemished coffin.

'Tell me,' he asked, 'is that a poem?'
'Yes, I believe it is.'
He savoured this information for a moment.
'Would you mind if I recited another one?'

Love songs cannot be sung by me

As he recited the poem Nouri ʿAjamī seemed to escape the narrow confines of his world.

. . . Then have a heart full of desire
The desire that tortured me.

'Is that, too, a poem?'

'Yes,' I said, although in truth it was much clumsier in construction than the last one. Nouri ʿAjamī pulled from beneath a pile of socks a notebook containing upwards of a hundred poems, all of them his, and all written in English. I read through a number of them and with his permission copied out the first poem into my notebook. They were obviously so much more than a mere poetaster's exercises: they were of a world he had made for himself. Their very existence ought to make a thousand better poets feel humble.

'You write in Arabic, too?'

'No, I can't. I have tried to. I can write only in English.'

'Do you read English poetry?'

'At school I learned some by heart, otherwise, no, I do not read poetry, Arabic or English. One day, when I was about fifty, I had to write a poem. I had never done so before. The words, when they came, were in English. It was the only way they would come. I cannot write poems any other way. I care for neither fame nor money. I want simply to pass the time and to be able to write my poems.'

I asked him if he would tell me anything of his life.

'My father escaped the Urfa massacres of 1924, in Turkey. I am an Urfalee Christian. We lived for some time in a tent, in a camp on the outskirts of Aleppo. We did not know the Arabic language, of course, and had little food. Those were difficult times. My father had been a stonecutter, but in Aleppo he became a goldsmith, a famous jeweller in the souq. I became a jeweller too.'

I did not ask him how he came to be selling socks.

'Do you write anything else?'

'I am producing an Aramaic/Arabic dictionary. Also, I am collecting Aramaic words that are commonly spoken in the city. So far I have found about 350.'

Nouri ʿAjamī peered down through his thick glasses.

'What do you call the pink,' he said to my wife, 'at the end of your breast?' Without even so much as a hint of lasciviousness in his voice, for here was a man wholly devoted to scholarship, he added, 'Tit, yes?'

My wife swallowed a smile.

'In Aramaic, *tido*.'

THREE

The Street Philosopher & the Holy Fool

When I die, amid my bones will be found the gold your friendship gave me.

Arabic proverb

The Syrian novelist Rafik Schami writes that the citizens of an ancient city inherit the accumulated eccentricities of its past inhabitants and that this alone should account for why there are so many strange people in Damascus. Damascus is reputably the oldest of all cities – or at least the oldest continually inhabited one. I am not sure that this does not also explain a suffocating conformity, a rigid pattern whose every layer is a little harder and more brittle than the previous one. 'We lack democracy not only in our politics but in our lives,' a carpet seller told me. 'You may think my words are free and often I go against the opinions of many fellow Syrians, yes, but in the end you must remember mine is an Oriental mind and however much I might complain I will resign myself to this fate.' Still, given the number of fascinating people I would meet in Damascus, there can be little arguing with the novelist's words.

This was my return journey here.

I will pass over my first visit in silence. While the several misadventures I had to endure were of great interest to me, the world, if it were to be apprised of them, would say I fell among clichés. What made me return were matters of a gentler and less hackneyed nature. I had it in me to write a particular book. The fact that I failed to do so causes me no displeasure. Such plans as I had made were to be soon replaced by others, and almost immediately I began to ignore the map I brought with me, which I had so carefully plotted with red crosses.

A yellow cab blistered all over with rust took me to the Ṣāliḥiyya district, on the slope of Mount Qāsiyūn, where I hoped to find Sulaymān again. Ṣāliḥiyya, now a suburb of Damascus but once upon a time a separate village, has been long associated with holy figures. There are many saints' tombs and residences of holy men. The most important tomb of all, on the main thoroughfare, Madares Assad al-Dīn, is that of the saint and mystic, Ibn al-ʿArabī, 'the great master', arguably the most influential of all Sufi teachers. If one were to seek a figure of comparable stature in Christianity it would probably have to be St Thomas Aquinas. Such is his importance that it is better to produce a thumbnail sketch than to even attempt a larger picture, for truly his works are close to unfathomable. If, for his Sufi followers, he represents the height of mystical theory, for the orthodox Muslim he continues to present problems; there is and will always be much debate as to whether he was a monist or a pantheist. It is probably a measure of his greatness that neither label sticks to him, for his system, if that is a term he himself would allow, is based on the notion of the unity of being. Ibn al-ʿArabī regarded the teaching of poetry above all the sciences, saying it is 'the archive of the Arabs' – his own verses are both mystical and erotic. He was born in Spain in 1165 and died in Damascus in 1240. Today pilgrims from all over the world visit his tomb, sit before it in silence, hoping to draw from it spiritual strength for themselves. If I stress his importance the reason is because Ibn al-ʿArabī is a major spiritual element in the lives of my two main protagonists; it is in his writings that the idea of the 'holy fool', as a conduit for God's word, reaches its highest expression and it is there, too, that one finds much of appeal to the 'street philosopher', although human logic, in this most demandingly intelligent of figures, is not of prime importance.

A couple of minutes away from the mosque where Ibn al 'Arabī's tomb is, in the busy street market, Sulaymān, perched behind his open suitcase of tattered volumes and old magazines, pointed me out to his companion. There was no show of surprise. A second could not have passed between my appearance and his recognising me. I heard him say the word *shāʿir*. The other looked up, all alert, like a dog at the mention of a bone.

'An English poet,' he cried, 'I have yet to meet one of those!'

Sulaymān, meanwhile, remained a picture of perfect calm, dressed as I remembered him from a year before, like some figure out of the *Arabian Nights* – in a pointed turban, collarless shirt and balloon trousers. Anywhere in the world he would have stopped people with his gaunt face, amazingly high cheekbones and piercing eyes. Sulaymān was half Bedouin, the family on his father's side having originally come from Saudi Arabia. His mother, whom I caught a glimpse of once, as she vanished from the hallway of his family's house, was Damascene. What first drew me to Sulaymān was his magical ability to communicate beyond the confines of spoken language. It didn't matter if he spoke not a word of English nor I Arabic, for he was a master of nuance. Also, he used his hands with the most graceful movements I had ever witnessed in a human being, such that even in his conversations with other Arabs the words themselves seemed but mere subsidiaries to the elaborate gestures that he would sometimes freeze for as long as ten or twenty seconds at a time. I had on that first occasion spent a whole hour with him, mostly in silence. All the while he wrote between the printed lines of a huge book he balanced on his knees, apparently copying out the text and here he was, a year later, still doing so. The strangeness of that first meeting would later revisit me in dreams and indeed were it not for Sulaymān and the longing for *otherness* that he inspired in me I might not have returned to Syria.

Abed, his companion, glowered at me with a slightly crazed smile. A young man with beautiful green eyes, he had a strong yet strikingly gentle face, modishly unshaven, a slight turning down at the mouth suggestive of much pain. Although handsome there was also something physically clumsy, almost oafish about him. A woman will frequently despise her best features, desiring normality where she is most fetchingly unique, and if there was something of this in Abed this is not to say he was not physically masculine, only that his awkwardness was somehow feminine. These may be later impressions spread over early ones, true, but Abed made as immediate an impact on me as, say, a first reading of Dostoevsky's youthful characters, God-haunted and inwardly driven by their own scourge; later, he became for me rather more of an Oblomov figure. When I asked him how he was, Abed spoke of life's vicissi*si*tudes, throwing in an extra syllable.

'A word I picked up from Oscar Wilde!'

I would have asked him from which work it came, but already he was telling me how he always strove for the most sophisticated word, and how, in order to reach into the soul of another people, one must always seek out their language's cutting edge. Also, he told me how much he liked the English sense of humour, without which the English would not be what they are. 'One must never smile when making a joke' – an English manual on acting had taught him this. 'One must listen carefully to other people.' A peculiar, elevated tone such as one finds in translations of Arabic tales, although a bit artificial on the page, gave his speech its peculiar charge. It was infiltrated by bits of English and American slang he picked up here and there. 'Cheesy, huh?' was one of his favourite expressions, by which means he would frequently send up his own poetic excesses.

'You come at a new dawn in my life.'

I watched for his sun to rise.

'Aren't you going to congratulate me? Will you not say to me, "Abed, this is good, I have arrived at precisely the right moment." I give you news of a great triumph and all I get in return is your silence.'

'What, then, shall we celebrate?'

'The girl I want to marry finds me acceptable.'

'Acceptable? Can you not hope for more?'

'She is sixteen – you may say *only* sixteen – but full in body and in mind.'

Abed made a sweeping gesture that managed somehow to convey both her physical and mental attributes.

'Her name is Ghufrān, which in our language means "forgiveness". So you see, *forgiveness* will be my bride! I was in torment for eight years, but now that my family has found me a girl whom I like – a girl whom I will *love* – my anguish will be removed. Yesterday, a mediator brought me the good news and now I'm waiting to see whether her father will accept me.'

'Are we not being a little premature, then?'

'No, no!' Abed waved away the shadow my words made. 'You mustn't say anything negative. You will contaminate my hopes.'

'If her father approves, will you stop biting your nails?'

Abed's fingernails were chewed down almost completely to the flesh, so severely I could see he was at pains to hide them and immediately I regretted my question.

'Yes, and perhaps I will stop smoking too. Arnold Schwarzenegger used to smoke two cigars a day. Then he got married and now smokes only one.'

'Which means he's found only half the happiness he was looking for,' I replied. 'The balance is in his remaining cigar.'

'Ah, this is a poetical response!'

I assured him it was a mathematical one.

'You must forgive me asking you this, but what can a girl of sixteen who has never left home possibly know of life?'

'You have the usual Western prejudice against arranged marriages, even when so few of your own survive. Here, a girl of sixteen is ready for marriage. Anyway, there is a period during which time if one finds the other unacceptable the engagement can be broken without too much damage to either side. There may be two, even three such engagements before anything is decided. A man in his twenties will usually marry a girl of sixteen, a man in his thirties a woman in her twenties—'

'And if the woman is beyond being marriageable?'

'Then the man must be very old indeed.'

Abed smoked furiously, always lighting a new cigarette

with the glowing stub of his previous one. Sulaymān did not smoke at all. He seemed to be able to divine most of our conversation, adding comments in his strangely high-pitched voice, winding up each sentence with an impish smile. Abed would immediately translate, and Sulaymān, mind-reader that he was, would correct him from time to time. I remarked Sulaymān had lost no time in recognising me.

'That is because he is a Sufi and because of their great mental discipline Sufis are blessed with incredible memory.'

All the while, Sulaymān was writing in his book, barely looking down at the page.

'Ibn al-ʿArabī's *al-Futūḥāt al-Makkīya*, *The Mecca Revelations*,' Abed explained, 'the four great Sufi books. Ibn al-ʿArabī is the Kaʿba of saints, the one towards whom the hearts of all other saints are directed, and these books, his greatest achievement, are so complex that even religious scholars have trouble deciphering them. A single misunderstanding can lead one into heresy. Sulaymān is copying out the text so as to remember it better.'

'To what order does Sulaymān belong?'

'The Naqshbandī. The strange clothes he wears are not for the tourists but are of his particular sect. His guru is Shaykh Nāzim.'

Sulaymān showed me on the inside of the top of his suitcase a poster of Sufi eminences. A white-bearded figure he pointed to was Shaykh Nāzim. Sulaymān repeated his name fondly several times.

Shaykh Muḥammad Nāzim ʿAdil al-Ḥaqqani is the spiritual world leader of the Naqṣhbandī Sufi movement. A native of Cyprus, although he lives in London part of the year, he has sought to revive Islam in the face of much opposition from the secular Turkish government and for his efforts he has been jailed many times. At one point the state brought one hundred and fourteen cases against him. A moderate, he steers a middle course which his followers describe as true Islam, that runs between the severity of the fundamentalists on one hand and the permissiveness of other groups on the other. His lineage goes back, on his father's side, to Jalāl al-Qādir al-Jīlāni, founder of the Qadirīyya order, and, on his mother's side, to Jalāl al-Dīn Rumī, poet and founder of the Mevlevi order.

'Sulaymān's quest is for knowledge, the knowledge that comes from God and not from the reading of books, which is given by Him only to special people, sometimes with the help of St George.'

'Khiḍr,' interjected Sulaymān.

Khiḍr is one of the most mysterious figures in Islam and, if not exactly interchangeable with the Christian St George and with the Jewish Elijah, may be said to share their characteristics to the extent that he puts on their spiritual clothes and even, on occasion, bears one or the other's name; as a figure of fecundity and renewal he may predate all three religions. There are hints of him even in the Gilgamesh epic and he is said to have accompanied Alexander the Great on his travels. Khiḍr is for Muslims what St George is for us, the patron saint of travellers; he is supposed to have drunk of the waters of immortality and is frequently invoked in the healing of the mentally deranged. One important detail which no Sufi will allow one to forget is that Khiḍr, as opposed to the martyred St George, is still very much alive – madmen and mystics speak of their meetings with him in much the same way Christians will speak of meeting Jesus. Many Sufis receive their initiation from him, through visions, and are thus directly connected to the highest source of mystical inspiration. 'The Green One', which is how his name translates, invites countless other analogies. I would suggest the figure who emerges from all three religious traditions is not an imagined saint, as Calvin described St George, but a saint of the imagination. I dare say Abed and Sulaymān would protest at these words. Although I have little doubt our St George is based on a historical figure there is no actual road that will lead to his bones. There is and will always be flesh on Khiḍr's bones.

Although he is never named in the Qur'ān it is Khiḍr who, in the *sūra* called The Cave, accompanies the prophet Moses on his journeys. Khiḍr tells Moses he will remain in his company but also warns him that his actions will seem so strange that finally the other will not be able to bear his company. Firstly, they board a ship in the hull of which Khiḍr proceeds to make a hole. Moses is shocked by what he believes will result in a wanton loss of life. Secondly, they come across a youth and, without any word of explanation, Khiḍr kills him. Again Moses protests. 'Did I not tell thee,' Khiḍr answers, 'that thou couldst not bear with me?' Finally, they go to a town and ask for food from the inhabitants who turn them away. They come across a dilapidated wall that Khiḍr restores. Moses asks why they should repair a wall belonging to people who refused them sustenance. Once again, he is rebuked. 'This is the parting between thee and me,' says Khiḍr, but before taking his leave he explains his actions, saying everything he did was not of his own choosing but an order from God. The ship that Khiḍr damaged was being pursued by a pirate king who would have taken it by force. The boy had good and decent parents whom, if given the chance, he would have driven out of their faith; God replaced the boy with another more pious. The wall belonged to orphan boys whose father was a righteous man. Later, the orphans would find beneath the wall a treasure the father had hidden for them and which God wanted them to have. I must confess there is much concerning the morality of this *sūra* that continues to baffle me.

I asked Abed if he were a Sufi as well.

'There are ninety-nine definitions of Allāh, and it may be in one's destiny to get spiritual support through one of those names and also the knowledge concerning that name. Allāh the Beautiful. No, I am an aesthete, although I consider myself a philosopher too.'

'Would you not describe this as a kind of fatalism?'

'If one is an aesthete, aestheticism is already in the blood. This is not fatalism. There are two kinds of fatalism. One is a gift from God – talent, for example. The other is that which comes through sustained effort. If my path is through aestheticism, philosophical enquiry, Sulaymān's path is in his tireless efforts to reach the truth through hunger, silence – the five pillars of Sufism.'

'In the quest for beauty can one not fall on the side of heresy?' I asked. 'Is it not possible to love the things of this earth more than Him who put them there?'

'Yes, if you worship human beauty which is not eternal, whereas God is beyond getting old. So what's left, one must ask, when beauty fades? This is a delicate point. When God wants to give you a great thing He will give you the respect of his creatures and, whatever your creed, you will appreciate His qualities. The Prophet Muḥammad, peace be upon his name, is a present for all people. In Sufism, people attribute their talent to God. Both knowledge and mercy are essential, as one without the other is useless and because knowledge on its own can be destructive. You need only think of atomic power, its uses and abuses. When God wants something to happen He will temporarily remove the sanity of the people and when that thing He wishes to happen happens He returns to them their sanity. This is beyond human logic and power, and although seemingly an illusion is truth also. I will give you an example – if God wants you to marry a certain girl and her father is very materialistic and you are poor He will temporarily wipe away the father's way of thinking so that he will agree to the marriage.'

'And how, Abed, does that pertain to you?'

Abed smiled from the bottom of his verbal transparencies.

'Sir Marius, I will address you from now on by this name.'

Sulaymān, on the other hand, unable to manage the 'i-u-s' sound, always called me Marcie.

The following day I returned to Ṣāliḥiyya.

'Sir Marius, stop where you are!'

Abed signalled to me like a railwayman flagging down an engine.

'At this distance you look thirty-five. Now, step back five paces. Yes, good, now you look thirty. This, you see, is our Arabic art of flattery.'

Sulaymān immediately went for tea and when he returned his suitcase was closed up to become a table for our glasses. The bookshop was closing early that day. Abed and Sulaymān would tell me the story of their lives.

Abed's father was a retired textile merchant who wanted more than anything for his two sons to escape the endless competition of the souq. A religious lawyer was the future he envisioned for Abed while for his other son he hoped he would become a teacher. As it turned out, the latter followed in his father's footsteps and worked in textiles, while Abed, much to his family's despair, did very little at all – or so it seemed to them, for Abed considered himself a tireless worker in 'adventures of the mind'. Abed's doubting father gave him a monthly pocket allowance, just enough, that is, for tea and cigarettes. Physically drained by the previous evening's discourse, Abed would rise only in time for midday prayers and his first cigarette. Afterwards, he would visit his closest friend Sulaymān and together they would sit in the market talking and when the market closed they would go to the park or down into old Damascus for tea at the Nofara Café where they talked late into the evening. Sulaymān sold the odd, greatly out of date, magazine on electronics or a magazine on Egyptian film stars or the Arabic equivalent of a cheap Harlequin romance. Abed would go through all of them extracting whatever information might prove of use in his philosophical enquiries. Odd bits of information, such as Arnold Schwarzenegger's liking for cigars, would sooner or later be employed in Abed's conversation.

'How long have you known Sulaymān?'

'Five years of earthly time, a thousand years in the secondary world.'

Abed told me he owed more to Sulaymān than to anyone else in his life, saying he had been rescued by him on numerous occasions. Meanwhile, his family considered Sulaymān a bad influence. 'Why do you waste your time on that fool?' they cried. 'What good will he ever do you? And what are these crazy visions of his?' Abed would not be dissuaded, however.

There is a proverb, Abed told me, which best described the nature of their friendship.

'When I die, amid my bones will be found the gold your friendship gave me. This is not too cheesy, huh? Once, when writing a school essay I wrote this line, passing it off as my own. I forget where it comes from, but it describes perfectly my feelings for Sulaymān. At a critical point in my life, he became my lifeline, taught me how to appreciate life and enjoy it, so by meeting him my appreciation and enjoyment of existence multiplied a thousand times. I had always been on the outside. It is never my decision to be so, rather I was pushed there. I am probably cerebral by nature – getting a piece of information is more important to me than getting a thousand dollars. Again, this was never my choice. Since childhood, years before I met Sulaymān, since I was eight or nine, I was aware of my difference. I was mocked by others of my own age because my head was physically large. Sometimes, I would fall to the ground because of the size of my brain. So, in 1990 my body and my brain found a balance, but the scars were still there in my psyche. All those childhood experiences had stuck to me. Often, I joke to Sulaymān that we both studied at the University of Pain. I was born with this talent for philosophical enquiry but such a talent needs to be adopted, embraced by someone. At the age of twenty, instead of meeting someone who likes to intermingle with society – in other words, a "mainstreamer" – I met Sulaymān instead. He alone understood this strange talent I have for being on the outside. Why him? Because, if one may defend someone this way, he is the lord of outsiders. So he embraced and contained me, and with his guidance my talent grew and flourished. And for his part Sulaymān trusts me, knows that because I understand things in a correct way I can help him sometimes. Also, he knows of my Western tendencies, my desire to be open to the whole world. We are bound together by our love of tourists.'

I asked Abed if this were not another example of Arab flattery.

'A tourist comes for the sake of comfort and change, but if his response to what he finds here is a deep one then this transcends any financial estimation. Likewise, a tourist has power in himself to give.'

'Yes, but surely tourism can be a destructive force?'

'About five years ago I began talking to tourists, finding in this an inexplicable ecstasy. This made me stick out like a sore thumb in our deeply homogenous society. I still don't know if I was right or wrong in doing so, but it seemed that by making my conscience ache I'd find comfort because, you see, I like to be truthful with myself. So when I spoke to tourists I felt a sense of comfort because they accepted me. As a result I drifted away from our society. The West pulled me to its side. All this is a prelude to telling you why I immediately liked Sulaymān. I had been criticised for having a Westernised personality. I had become aloof with my own people and even teasing them gave me solace because I had at last found acceptance by others. I met Sulaymān and found in him a similar love of tourists. In our society, as in yours, a priest or religious person is respected, and usually priests are puritanical in nature. So when Sulaymān, who is a deeply religious, puritanical person argued that Westerners, too, are worthy of being loved my conscience ceased to ache. Also, he explained to me why the Arab people deserved to be criticised. Now, for a holy person to criticise Muslims while praising Europeans stunned me. Prophet Muḥammad, peace be upon him, taught us not to lie but to be truthful and helpful to other people regardless of their creed. So why do so few Arabs follow him? Why have Arabs forsaken Islam though their identity, on paper, is Muslim? For a Muslim to commit a lie is equal to heresy, but now Arabs have become professional liars – lying has become sacred to them, never mind their other faults like greed, superficiality and so forth. Shaykh Nāzim says the Arabs are dead, the Europeans are asleep. You can wake up a sleeping person, but not a dead one. That is why he left for Europe thirty years ago and why he has converted as many Europeans to Islam as he has. The great paradox, one that stunned me, is that for all his love of the West, Sulaymān is the most devout of Muslims. It adds to his credibility as a Sufi that he recognises the beauties of the Western individual. So he is not drifting in Islam. I am attracted to rather than repelled by Sulaymān's devotion. My appreciation for life and aesthetics was enhanced and, most importantly, new horizons were added to my sphere. If the bad things of my worldliness or of my being mundane were incoherent with my personality they were removed and replaced by things that cohered with my aestheticism. The years of my friendship with Sulaymān have been the period of my mellowing. But in answer to your question about tourism being a destructive force, if one celebrates the meeting between tourist and one of us God Himself will be pleased.'

'And if some tourists move only upon the surface of things?'

'Yes, but each moves in his own sphere. The prophet Abraham did not like to eat alone, so he invited a passer-by, saying he should eat with him. During the meal Abraham asked his guest what religion he belonged to. "I have no religion," came the answer. "Then you are no longer allowed to eat with me," Abraham replied. Upon hearing this, God scolded him. "I created this seventy-year-old man, this infidel, and throughout those seventy years I have fed him, pampered him like a child, and now you, Abraham, because you want him to join you for one meal, demand that he belong to your faith? Unless you beg him for forgiveness, I will remove your name from the list of prophets." Abraham begged forgiveness of his guest, and upon hearing this the infidel repented. The Prophet Muḥammad says, "No religion by coercion!"'

'And Sulaymān, what about him?'

Abed laughed, 'Sulaymān is already annihilated, just waiting to be shoved into the grave. As I said before, he too is an outsider. Many of his fellow Sufis find him too abnormal, too exotic, too eccentric. Sulaymān says it is out of his control, so rather than quarrel with them he tries to remain on friendly terms.'

'Would you say Sulaymān is a holy fool?'

'Any answer to this requires some knowledge of his life. The question really is whether he is sane or insane. Whether or not you believe in Sufism it is a reality, not an illusion, and revelations do take place. Certain Sufis are fated to have powerful revelations from God. Who is God? The creator of billions of galaxies, each one containing billions of stars. In the Qur'ān God defines Himself by saying He is not like anything. So how can you imagine what God is like, if He is unlike anything you can imagine. Ibn al-ʿArabī says in defining the relation between a Sufi and God nobody, not even Sufis, can reach Him. We are only bits of dust in the universe. Who are we to be able to reach God, the creator of everything? Some Sufis are destined to be intelligent and reasonable. They have wit and spirit – they can talk to people, and through their common sense invite them into Islam. Others, during the process of becoming a Sufi, experience revelations, some of which are overwhelmingly strong. One, for example, might see St George, the most beautiful of creatures, more so than any woman – meeting such a figure would be like looking into the sun and if you do not have the capacity you will waste yourself. Some Sufis see St George or Khiḍr as a physical presence or else in dreams or waking dreams, and lose or at least partially lose their minds. The best, like Shaykh Nāzim, are fostered by a meeting with him. Sulaymān told me, after seeing St George two years ago, that by comparison to him all the things of this world had become trashy, even the mind that we suppose to be so precious. This is Sulaymān's case, not a generalisation. The mind has become secondary for him. So he is moved not by his mind but by what he likes – spiritually, not logically – and in this his likings are sometimes wrong, sometimes right. We may say Sulaymān's state is good, but not perfect. With Shaykh Nāzim and his peers there is completeness because spirit and mind work together. There may be a defect in Sulaymān but, if so, this defect is his destiny. It might be corrected, perhaps not. This is why most people will not accept him altogether and why some even think he is an impostor. Why so? Because followers of St George follow what they like, spiritually that is. They are not normal people.

'A few years ago, Sulaymān was a normal young man, with the same interests and desires of any Damascene his age. He liked cars, girls. He was even married for a while. Sulaymān was too pure for his first wife. A woman needs some impurities in a man so that she can think him normal. What a man must do is goose her. You say this in English, *goose*? Although the woman pretends not to, actually she appreciates this. It is not the act she appreciates but the fact of his being impure. You see, Sir Marius, women are children of the devil.'

'What happened to his marriage?'

'She could not understand anything. She knew enough to pray five times a day, otherwise she gossiped all the time. Sulaymān knew enough to show only his normal side to her, but as time went on he grew cold toward her. She was annoyed by his apparent laziness, although they got by, as do most families. She tried to control him but try as she did she always failed. Acceptance is the greatest form of love. She was already divorced once, had a screw loose.'

'And there have been no other women?'

'One night Sulaymān met a whore. She was standing outside a nightclub, with her painted face. Sulaymān looked at her and what he saw was a victim, an outcast. What happened then is he spoke to her because he knew he would benefit her more than he could normal people, because her need was so much greater than theirs. Sulaymān felt not physical but spiritual ecstasy just by looking at her, by knowing she could benefit from his warmth and compassion. Compare him now to the rest of society, especially those *imams* who would never even look at such a creature. This is yet another example of Sulaymān doing as he likes, and because there is no conformity in him "sane" and "insane" become baggy words, again because with him there is no definition of what *is* or *is not*. Sulaymān is neither saint nor impostor, and to suggest he is either would be to fall into the trap of rigidity. I have heard it said many times that Christianity is the religion of love. Somebody asked Shaykh Nāzim once, "If this is so, what then is Islam?" "Islam is the religion of compassion," he replied. "So what, then, is the meaning of compassion?" "Your wife might love you, but in the absence of compassion she might out of jealousy poison your food so you'll become ill and wholly dependent on her. Love on its own can be perilous, which is why love and compassion should always be together."

'When he was twenty-two Sulaymān had a major crisis in his life and, struck by some mysterious power, became speechless. He felt, among other things, a tremendous pressure on the nape of his neck. This experience annihilated his affinities for life. The five ways of Sufism are hunger, silence, seclusion, sleeplessness and prayer. Sulaymān excelled in all of these. After several months, he was freed of all desire. He spent two years in the graveyard. It was two years before he was able to adapt again to the company of other people.'

The description Abed gave was similar to that of many famous Sufis whose careers began with a religious crisis. The eleventh-century Persian mystical poet, Abū Saʿīd ibn Abī 'l-Khayr, described his days as a novice, the fasting, the physical discomforts he endured, the mysticism which in the eyes of the world was madness: 'In my seeing I was blind, in my hearing deaf, in my speaking dumb. For a whole year I conversed with no one. People called me a lunatic, and I allowed them to give me that name, relying on the Tradition that a man's faith is not made perfect until he is supposed to be mad.' In the biographies of Ibn al-Jawzī and Ṣafī al-Dīn there are many accounts of holy fools who lived in cemeteries. The figures they interrogated were usually hermits, living on a diet of nuts and herbs; they tended to be melancholic and anxious. One famous *imam*, ʿAlī al-Kurdī, quit Damascus in order to live in a cemetery and stayed there until he died. I asked Sulaymān about the time he spent in the graveyard.

'I spent two years there. It was a rejection, a ripping away of the outer world. I developed a strong relationship with the dead and even now I always feel comfortable when walking past a graveyard. I would watch the coffins being lowered and felt as though I were actually descending with the dead because, although my eyes were open and theirs closed, I too was cut off, finished with the world. I could feel whether a certain dead man was comfortable or not. My father lost all hope in me, but my uncle who had seen similar cases among the Bedouin reassured him, saying I would soon return. Our world is different from the world of the dead, this being a world of religious, personal and communal conflicts, where every one wants to be in control, whereas the dead are finished with these things. If, when alive, somebody harmed people he will have a bad afterlife. During this time I never spoke to people and was always hungry. I would stand near food, but could never ask for any and gradually I reached the stage when I ate only one date a day. Nevertheless, people would give me money and when I was in this state would you believe I had the same income as I do now. I never begged, however. A Sufi, says al-Rifāʿī, does not beg and does not refuse. Nor should he save. It is better not to think about saving, although you can save without thinking. Put money in your hands, but not in your hearts. At the end of this period I took an oath with St George, who came from a world of light, a very beautiful man. When I saw him I said, "You are Khiḍr. My soul identified you." St George replied with a smile. After two years of this I gradually came back to the world, back to normal life. I was able to smile again after two years of not being able to do so. I spoke to people. All the physical pain was gone. I was healed. Can one be a fool for God, you ask me. A fool is so only in the eyes of other people, and sees things the others can't. If there is to be an earthquake, a fool will be the first to cry out long before others realise what is happening. When beside a fool we are like ignorant people sitting beside an astronomer. There are different kinds of fools, holy fools and idiots. When you see a holy fool you see the signs of God's power in his face. There are other types of fools. One who is disturbed overwhelmingly is, in Sufism, called "the wild beast".

A beast walks on its feet, and but for the sake of his physical presence is not *here*. People have compassion for him, give him money, feed him. This fool is one who has gone to the other world and has not returned, whereas the other kind of fool God returns to this world in order that he might benefit other people. Although he may be distracted you can at least talk with him and benefit from his knowledge.'

'Can holy fools divine hidden knowledge?'

'About four years ago,' Abed said, 'an American invited Sulaymān and me to his hotel room. We were talking, when Sulaymān suddenly announced that people were eavesdropping on our conversation. To my certain knowledge there was nobody else in the room. I thought Sulaymān was mad. I went towards the window in front of which there was a heavy curtain. I pulled it aside. Three people were standing on the balcony outside. I asked Sulaymān how he knew they were there. "I saw their spiritual silhouettes," he answered. Sulaymān had many visions, or, if you prefer, revelations, as many as twice a week sometimes, and early on he had one in which he saw himself reading *The Mecca Revelations*. Although Sulaymān was only semi-literate and at first could understand nothing he kept reading them, despite warnings from other people not to. They feared he would go mad or else would become a heretic by mistake. Gradually, however, he understood and reached a stage whereby he was able to help people far more literate than himself with textual difficulties. Also, he is able to heal people. When he places his hand over a mad person's eyes the patient sleeps and meets prophets in heaven, receives support from the spiritual world. With ordinary adults, Sulaymān puts his hand on their eyes and instructs them to say the word of God, not verbally but in their hearts only. After five minutes of concentration, with Sulaymān concentrating, too, the person will see colours, each colour representing a different spiritual value. "I see red," says one. "Good," Sulaymān replies, "but you must keep concentrating." Sometimes, they see only yellow. A few people see green, the colour of St George, and the highest value.

The colour a person sees depends on his spiritual capacity. Children are probably the only ones who completely understand Sulaymān. It is not so much a matter of understanding but of innocence, and he in turn feels comfortable with them. They are like white sheets of paper upon which you may write whatever you wish. Sulaymān has administered spiritual healing to many children, mostly between the ages of eight and fourteen. A child is easier to treat than an adult because he is immaculate, whereas with an adult you cannot make him *go* to the spiritual world. Some of the children Sulaymān treats speak of meetings in the other world with prophets. "I was in the Kaʿba in Mecca," one said, "and I saw Jesus and Muḥammad there. I talked with them." The children will answer Sulaymān's questions in ways far too sophisticated for their limited knowledge. A child of eight does not lie about such matters. In one instance, Sulaymān was challenged by the uncle of one of these children. The child was put to sleep and when asked by Sulaymān to speak of his uncle mentioned problems this uncle had had throughout his life, things this child could not possibly have known. Sulaymān has even treated people with cancer, but only on condition that they make right their wrongs, for those who misuse another's knowledge will be punished mercilessly. Your intention must always be pure.'

One of the odder aspects about my stay in Damascus was how I would oscillate between pleasure and despondency, as if the one were dependent upon the other. One day, as I followed my usual route, cutting through to Martyr's Square, where I took morning tea before going into the old city, I passed a dead cat. It lay against the perimeter of a construction site where I never saw any work being done. There were quite a few of these buildings, hideous concrete shells, which never seemed to develop beyond that phase. The cat lay in a frozen arc, its teeth bared against the heavens, as if ready to strike at whoever or whatever killed it. As the days passed I would have to walk in ever wider curves to avoid the smell. Admittedly, I could have taken a different route altogether but in some strange way I had become attached to this poor creature's fate. The cat lay where thousands of other people had to pass, and *still* nobody came to remove it. The city did not apparently have the means to be able to deal with an animal's corpse. What was it about this place that so simple a thing could not be done? Sometimes, I would feel myself on the treadmill of the interminable. And there were days I would have to fight against a terrible weight inside me, a dead cat's weight, constantly pulling me down. I entered a peculiar rhythm whereby one day I would feel elation and involve myself in much activity and on the next find myself barely able to move.

'Sir Marius, you must pray for me.'

Abed was nervously pacing back and forth.

'There are fresh obstacles.'

'What do you mean?'

'Her father sees me for a tramp. What am I to do?'

'Secure the woman first, but in order to do this you are going to have to impress her father. You are going to have to choose a direction in your life.'

'Such as?'

'You must provide for her.'

'What should I do?' Abed pointed to a blank stretch of wall. 'Should I put up some shelves there?'

'And what will you put on them?'

'Oriental crafts.'

'Abed, I am not sure if selling crafts is in your destiny.'

'Yes, you see! A philosopher should not have to put up shelves. Am I to become a mainstreamer? She already accepts me as I am. This girl is everything to me. If this engagement fails, I will be plunged into such sorrow I won't know what to do. I am lost, I have no will.'

'Precisely, Abed, if I were in her father's shoes I would be worried too. You must make even a pretence at strength so that perhaps it will come in time.'

'Yes, you are right. This is what I need to hear. I must appear to be some kind of emblem, but now we must go to meet my mediator.'

We stood at a street corner for close to half an hour, Abed asking me every five minutes what time it was. After a while, he stood in a circle of cigarette butts. A man in his fifties, unshaven and pot-bellied, stains down the front of his shirt, approached us.

'He's here.'

'Who?'

'My mediator.'

When the man opened his mouth to speak I saw he could not have had more than half a dozen teeth. I wondered between what forces in the world such a creature could be invited to mediate.

'This man is your mediator!'

'Yes,' Abed cried, 'although surely he is my destroyer. They must see in him a reflection of what I will become.'

'So why can't you find somebody else?'

'It's not my choice. He is married to the sister-in-law of the man I hope will become my father-in-law. Also, he is my mother's cousin. Ghufrān's family owes him a favour for something that happened many years ago. It's all too complicated. You see what he is. He has not worked for ten years. His wife and their sixteen-year-old son support him.'

'Surely, then, he is the worst possible mediator?'

'Yes, of course, but what can I do?'

Abed and his mediator spoke.

'Oh, my God!' Abed translated for me, 'He tells me I'm not the only one seeking her hand. And that her father holds the scales. She, Ghufrān, is in one pan and meanwhile her suitors are piling gold into the other.'

Abed paced back and forth, not wanting to hear any more. The mediator stood about with every appearance of having finished his task but with something still left undone, like a sentence without its full stop. Abed stared at me in panic.

'Please, Sir Marius, give him something. Anything, a few *lira* will do.'

I gave him a crumpled note. The mediator bowed to both of us in a vaguely mocking fashion and went away.

'We are paying him for this service?'

'We are paying for him to go.'

Abed looked despairingly at me.

'Am I not a normal human being?'

A couple of cigarettes later, he spoke again.

'Do I not have green eyes?'

FOUR

The Amazing Adventures of Abū Walīd

Brother Saul, receive thy sight.

Acts 22:13

The Street Called Straight is straight, not straight as a die, say, but straight enough to be deserving of its name. We may detect in a unique turn of phrase a sly dig at exactitude – the street *called* Straight is not quite what it is said to be – it bends just a little. Why else did they put up that arch midway, if not to fool the eye a little? It is roughly at this juncture, where straightness becomes a dead issue, that one goes from the wholly Muslim to the predominantly Christian, once Jewish, quarter. The Arabic name for the street is Souq al-Ṭawīl – literally, 'the long souq'. One comes here rather than to the Souq al-Ḥamīdiyya for a sense of the city's true mercantile life. Tradesmen of all descriptions line both sides of the street. There are broom-makers, woodcarvers, bakers, shops selling cloth, kefiehs, brass – there is even a herbalist where one may purchase a desiccated lizard the consumption of which cures impotence.

The street, the only one to cut right through old Damascus, is considerably narrower than it was two millennia ago, when it was roughly a hundred feet wide. It had four rows of Corinthian pillars tapering into the distance and these in turn formed three parallel avenues, the central one being the main pedestrian thoroughfare. As at Antioch the street had colonnades on either side and backing onto these were houses, constructed on the Greek model, uniformly dull on the outside but containing small paradises within. The immediate impression upon entering Damascus would have been of a city flashing white. What began as marble, however, was gradually displaced by ordinary stone and then, in recent times, stone was replaced by dull concrete. The only thing that survives of the Via Recta of Roman times is part of the aforementioned arch, woefully restored, and at its east end Bāb Sharqī, the third-century Roman Gate of the Sun, with its triple entrance. St Paul, or Saul of Tarsus as he was first called, passed through another, older gate. You would have to squint hard to picture him on this congested thoroughfare. And the world being for him, just then, all sound and smell – the cries of hawkers, a rumble of a passing chariot driven by an exquisite, an occasional smell of camel or horse dung on either side, a swish of leather soles against stone – where would he think himself now, amid buses and choking fumes?

A religious pilgrim might best consider the street a mere template, whose spiritual coordinates are more easily located in the soul than in reality. There's no point getting soppy over concrete; the real action, in spiritual terms, is and has always been elsewhere. Still, it would be a heavy skull that did not care to recollect the scene. As Saul approached Damascus 'suddenly there shined round him a light from heaven' and there, near the village of Kokab, about ten miles from the gates of Damascus, he fell to the ground. 'Saul, Saul,' he heard, 'why persecutest thou me?' It has been remarked many times that the Oriental mind is not historical but artistic, that it juggles facts in order to produce an effective whole; chronology is neither here nor there. We arrive at what is poetically rather than demonstrably true. Sceptical minds have put Saul's sudden blindness down to a summer thunderstorm and his having been struck by lightning – there are suggestions, too, of desert fatigue and even epilepsy. And there are even those, Christians, who speak of a miracle. Paul, as he would soon become, does not strike the reader as being overly impressionable.

What took place on the road to Damascus must surely have been more than a bad tumble, otherwise Christianity would owe its existence to a case of bad nerves. After all, here was a man representing the interests of the Sanhedrin, whose mission it was to stamp out all traces of the new faith. One might go so far as to say he was more than dedicated to his task, that he was enthusiastic even. Unquestionably, there was already blood on his hands and more to come when the heavenly voice addressed him. 'Saul, Saul' – so affectionately ironic that single repetition of his name – 'why persecutest thou me?' When Saul asked who spoke the reply was, 'I am Jesus whom thou persecutest: it is hard for thee to kick against the pricks.' Jesus then commanded him to go into the city where he was to await further instructions. When Saul opened his eyes he was not able to see. His companions led him by the hand over uneven ground, moving, one supposes, as quickly as possible in order to arrive at Damascus before nightfall, when its gates would be closed against them. At the eastern gate they entered what was then the Jewish quarter of the city and from there Saul was taken by his companions down the Street Called Straight to the house of a prominent Jewish figure, Judas, who may have been an elder of the synagogue. For three days he touched neither food nor drink. On the third day, Ananias, who lived nearby, at the bottom of what is now Hanania Street – the cellar, now a chapel, of what was supposedly his house still survives – had a vision or rather Saul had a vision of Ananias having a vision. Artistically, it is a remarkable passage, a double vision: Saul, in his blindness, prays and is answered with a vision of Ananias being told by God that he, Saul, is destined to work among the Gentiles and that it is now the all-important task of Ananias to see to it that the other regain his sight. So Ananias went down the Street Called Straight to the house of Judas and there placed his hands upon Saul who, because of the earlier vision, was already expecting him. Ananias put his hands to the other's brow 'and immediately there fell from his eyes as it had been scales: and he received sight forthwith, and arose, and was baptised' (Acts 9:11). In Christian chronology, this is a decisive moment and, for the purposes of this chapter, should be kept to the front of the mind. Saul rose to his feet, as he was commanded to do, and suddenly he, the scourge of the new faith, became Paul, Christianity's most passionate advocate. He began to eat again, and after a treatment of healing herbs gradually regained his strength, preached in the synagogues, and not long afterwards went into the desert where presumably he worked out the foundations of the new Christian faith. After a period of three years, he went back to Damascus and from there made his famous escape, being lowered down the city wall in a basket, and afterwards journeyed throughout the Middle East and finally to martyrdom in Rome. A tourist will be shown the spots where these events took place.

As I walked down the Street Called Straight, towards Bāb Sharqī, I was approached by an elderly man with a face like a walnut, who moved at tremendous speed for his age. The top of his skull was a squarely clipped hedge of white. After finding out where I was from he cried, 'I love England, if only for Montgomery's sake. I spend fifteen years in Liverpooool.'

A trace of that city was caught in the last syllable.

'Silk brocade – Montgomery very kind to me—'

A story told many times over survived only as a kind of oral shorthand, but within this flotsam of memories one thing seemed solid enough to grab onto.

'Excuse me,' I interrupted, 'but by Montgomery do you mean *Field Marshal* Montgomery?'

'Yes, yes! I loved him.'

'You *knew* him?'

I could scarcely believe my luck, for I had stepped out that morning ripe for a fresh adventure.

'Shall we go for tea somewhere?' I suggested.

'Yes, we go close to here.'

The old man with above forty wrinkles in his deep brown face took me in the direction from whence I had just come, his right arm paddling the air for greater speed. A touch heavy with the sun, I followed him into a carpet shop and, pushing aside a hanging kilim, we slipped into the shop's cooler recesses. Asking me to wait a little, he examined a couple of small carpets, throwing them first one direction and then the other. As every third person in Damascus seemed to be a guide, I half expected him to offer me one at a 'special' price.

'My son, a doctor in Stockholm, say to me, "Please, father, send me a silk carpet", so I come from Aleppo to see my friend here who gives me best price.'

A shop assistant appeared with tea and the old man left the carpets lying where they were, pulled up a chair in front of me and, hands on knees, sat in an expectant pose. I pulled my notebook out. The carpet seller in the corner raised his eyebrows.

'Now, I tell you about Montgomery.'

'Wait, wait,' I said. 'Could we start from the beginning, with your name.'

Ḥasān Muḥammad Alī was born in 1927, in Aleppo. In 1938, when he was eleven, his father took him to India in order to learn the silk trade. There he stayed until he was fourteen, at which point he began to work, in a civilian capacity, for the British Army. In June 1941, in the company of a William Brown-Owen 'also from Liverpooool' young Ḥasān returned to Aleppo.

'Captain Clayton give me a job with passport control at the Turkish border. Any problem, something wrong with the passports – I tell him. Captain Clayton then takes me to see Montgomery who come to Aleppo. "Montgomery," Captain Clayton says to me, "want somebody who speak Urdu to translate for the Gurkhas." I speak Arabic, Urdu and English. I meet Montgomery and Montgomery gives Ḥasān the job.'

'You mean *you*?'

'Yes, Ḥasān!'

Thus began the first of Ḥasān's amazing adventures, one that took him first to Palestine in 1942 and then to Egypt where, in 1943, he was badly wounded at Tobruk. Ḥasān pulled down the collar of his shirt to show me a deep scar across the left side of his neck and running down past his collarbone.

'A bomb hits the hut, kills three British, two Aussies, one Kiwi, one Gurkha. I am the only survivor. You see me now, I'm 71, still run three kilometres a day. I never saw a doctor once, only for my wound when I almost die.'

A critically wounded Ḥasān was taken unconscious to hospital where after ten days he came to. The first thing he remembers is Montgomery patting him on the cheek.

'"Ḥasān, Ḥasān," Montgomery say to me, "it's only a small scratch. Don't be afraid, you will live." You see, he was very kind.'

After a period of convalescence, he then followed Montgomery to Torino. Until 1945 the two remained close, even sharing the same hut at times. Ḥasān would make tea and coffee for Montgomery. When the war finished Ḥasān, with a certain amount of pull from Montgomery, went to Liverpool where he spent the next fifteen years making silk brocade.

'I marry an English woman. She's dead now. She come to Aleppo and she become a Muslim. 1962, she died. I marry another woman, Arab, but she's no good.'

Ḥasān scrunched up his face as though he had just consumed a bad olive.

'My first wife I love very much. I have a son in Stockholm, a doctor. I live near Aleppo, Acterine village. I grow pistachios, my business is pistachios.'

'What else can you tell me about Montgomery?'

'The best man in the world, I call him "Bābā" – he call me "my son". Montgomery was like a father to me. "I had three sons," he jokes, "now I have four." Montgomery very polite, friendly but, you know, with a high nose towards the army. He never talked or laughed with the soldiers, only with me.'

'What did you laugh about?'

'Oh, football. We both like football. We run together in the morning. Montgomery likes poor people, always give money to poor people, beggars, he invite beggars to the camp to feed them.

Once a month he kill a sheep. The Gurkhas catch a sheep, kill it, and Montgomery give the meat to the poor. Montgomery always better at cards than me. All the time I lose. At midnight, we go together on patrol. A very good shot too. We take turns shooting a needle at ten metres. Once, Montgomery he takes a mirror like this, puts an English rifle on his head, and shoots a bird off the telephone wire.'

'Sorry, could you repeat that, please.'

Ḥasān stood up, holding an imaginary mirror in one hand and with the other placed over the top of his skull an imaginary gun pointing it behind him.

'He looks in the mirror, sees the bird behind him on the telephone wire.'

'You mean looking into the mirror he took aim?'

'Yes, yes!' Ḥasān began to be irritated by my pressing him for details. 'He shoot the bird. Once, he shoot at a piece of wood, spelling his and my names.'

'Are you a good shot too?'

'Yes, I can shoot an egg at fifty metres.'

'Anything else?'

'Four years I work for him. He was gentle and kind, but he would get angry if you mention Germans. He did not like Germans. I went to England in 1976, when Montgomery die.'

'You went to the funeral?'

'No, no, I go to visit him in the cemetery. Listen, if you open my heart you will find Montgomery there. I love him. I love all England for his sake.'

Ḥasān lowered his head.

'I wish I died when *he* died.'

A single tear ran down along one of his wrinkles and when it reached the end it dropped onto his pale blue shirt.

'"Ḥasān," he tell me, "always speak the truth, it's better to have your throat cut than not speak the truth."'

We sat in silence for a couple of minutes.

'Anything else?'

Ḥasān raised his hand against me.

'No, enough!'

Admittedly, in the light of all he had just told me, my pushing him for more seemed a bit excessive. After another moment's reflection he then told me about a tourist he met who suffered from asthma. The tourist said he had not been able to find a cure, so Ḥasān asked him for 100 dollars.

'Understand me, I do not need money. The hundred dollars I give to an old Bedouin doctor who lives in a tent, east of Palmyra. This doctor he has the secret of making cures from desert grasses. Only he knows the cures, and when he dies the secret goes to somebody else. There are many kinds of grasses in the desert and he knows which ones cure which diseases. So I give him the hundred dollars and he gives me a bottle of medicine. The tourist is completely cured now. The doctor does not keep the hundred dollars for himself, no, this he gives to his tribe.'

When we parted Ḥasān told me that if I were to come to the shop the following Thursday, just before noon, he would have something for me.

'I bring you from Aleppo a packet of photographs and letters from Montgomery. I will give you my whole life story. I have everything written down.'

'Abed, I had an extraordinary meeting today—'

'Very good,' he replied, with a trace of irony in his voice.

'An elderly man—'

'Stop, I know him!'

'No, wait, Abed, I haven't even told you his name.'

'Yes, yes, I know him – Abū Walīd.'

'Aha, see, you're wrong sometimes. His name is Ḥasān Muḥ ammad Alī.'

'Yes, Abū Walīd, "father of Walīd", Montgomery's translator. I knew it was him right away because not many people of his generation speak English. Speaks Urdu, yes?'

'Alright, Abed, you win.' I began to wonder if Damascus were not a village. 'So what of his story about having been Montgomery's translator, is any of it true?'

'Yes, I believe so. Of course, he tells people this story so he can be their guide or else take them to a shop. I will tell you about how he first became a guide. Some years ago, he took a tourist to a shop, as a favour. The tourist bought a carpet and much to Abū Walīd's surprise he was given a commission much bigger than his regular salary. So he has been doing this ever since.'

'I wasn't offered a carpet, Abed. Also, he told me he grew pistachios outside Aleppo.'

'Yes, maybe, but he brought his wife and children to Damascus.'

'He had an English wife?'

'No, that's not true.'

'You mean he speaks the truth about Montgomery, but lies about having an English wife?'

'The things he speaks of without any change in the details are usually true. Some of what he says is not true. You see, maybe it is more important for him to have an English wife than it is to have known Montgomery. A man covers his pain with lies or else he makes other people think he has what really he'd most like to have. We have a rule in Sufism. When you know someone is lying to you, you should not give the impression you know this to be the case. One refrains from doing so out of compassion, and also in the hope that God will straighten his ways. A good Sufi does not disclose another person's faults and sometimes he will even cover for him. What helps him is that we pretend to believe him. Sometimes, we are rewarded too.'

What Abed told me had its literary parallel elsewhere.

Scheherazade relates the stories of the barber and his six brothers the last of whom, Schacabac, has fallen upon hard times. As a consequence, he seeks how best to gain admittance into the houses of the rich – in other words, he lives by his wits. One day, he stops at a magnificent house which he learns from the porters hanging about outside is the palace of a Barmecide – that is, a member of the wealthy Barmak family – originally from Persia, now domiciled in Baghdad, and renowned for his generosity. The porters invite Schacabac to enter the house and to keep walking until he finds its occupant. The house turns out to be a small palace. After wandering through magnificent gardens he comes to apartments painted gold and azure. There he finds an elderly man with a long white beard who is quite obviously the Barmecide. This man welcomes him and after pleasantries are exchanged asks him what he wants. Schacabac, explaining his plight, says he is hungry. The Barmecide, shocked that a man should go hungry in Baghdad, immediately orders a basin and water to be brought so that they might wash themselves. An extraordinary thing occurs in that although nobody appears with basin and water the Barmecide begins to go through the motions of washing, pouring water over his hands from an invisible ewer. He invites Schacabac to do the same, and Schacabac, knowing that if there is anything to be gained out of this he should defer to a wealthy man's humour, follows suite. Then the Barmecide calls for food to be brought in. Although nothing is brought into their presence he begins to cut whatever sits invisible upon his equally invisible plate, and raising the imagined food to his mouth begins to chew. When he asks Schacabac what he thinks of the bread the other replies he had never eaten any so white and fine. The Barmecide, pleased with this answer, replies that he had hired the woman who baked the bread at huge expense. Again, the Barmecide cries to a boy who is not there to bring the next courses. And so they come, or rather they do so in pantomime. Schacabac devours course after course, beginning with a broth of barley and mutton, this followed by goose in a sweet sauce. The Barmecide cautions Schacabac against eating too much goose, saying it is filling and there is much more to come. A succulent lamb fed on pistachios arrives, and from this, the specialty of the house, the Barmecide takes a morsel and tenderly places it in Schacabac's mouth. This Schacabac eats with great pleasure and exclaims there is surely nothing finer in the world than this table. When the ragout comes, rich with cloves, nutmeg, ginger, pepper and aromatic herbs Schacabac whose jaws begin to ache from chewing so much air protests, saying he can eat nothing more. After such a meal, the Barmecide announces, there is nothing but for them to drink wine. Schacabac has just enough scruples to refuse this and pleads that if he were to drink he might do something foolish. The Barmecide insists, however, saying that the least Schacabac could do is to toast him. The wine arrives in the same manner as the courses that came before. Schacabac raises an invisible glass to his nose and then tasting the wine remarks upon its excellence but says he would prefer a rather stronger vintage. A superb host, the Barmecide orders up an excellent vintage and this they both drink in increasing volume. Then Schacabac, pretending to be drunk, raises his hand and boxes the Barmecide on his ear so hard that the latter falls over. Schacabac is about to hit him again when the Barmecide cries, asking the other if he is mad. Schacabac pretends to come to his senses and says that as he had been good enough to eat he should not have been obliged to drink wine, for such are the consequences; however, he begs forgiveness for his foolish action. Amused, the Barmecide laughs, saying he has longed for one of Schacabac's character; he forgives him, invites him to be friends and offers him a good position in his palace. After applauding Schacabac for having accommodated himself to his humour, the Barmecide then claps his hands and has his servants, his real ones, bring in all the things that he and his guest have just consumed in pantomime. We may gather the meal served is as least as good as the one imagined.

'The Caliph ʿUmar had a saying,' Abed continued, '"The one who deceives us, we are willingly deceived by him." This means we should never call a liar a liar. We should not allow a man to lose face.'

Was not Abū Walīd somebody at whose imagined table one could feast until server and devourer, speaker and listener, were equally rewarded? I asked Abed if he knew any other stories about him.

'One day, in the 1970s, Abū Walīd was walking through the

Souq al-Ḥamīdiyya. There, he came across an elderly American woman in her eighties who was struggling up the stairs to some shop. You saw how small he is, well, Abū Walīd took this woman on his shoulders and carried her up many steps to a shop selling cloth. What Abū Walīd did not realise was that the woman he was carrying was President Ford's sister. When they reached the shop she pointed to the rolls of cloth. "I want all those rolls of cloth," she said. The shopkeeper and Abū Walīd did not think it possible that this small, elderly woman had the means to buy so much. When asked if she were serious she opened her purse. "What would you like, cash?" she asked, pulling out a wad of money. "Or would you prefer traveller's cheques? What about credit cards?" So she bought the cloth and Abū Walīd, of course, was later given a handsome commission. President Ford's sister also gave Abū Walīd money. "Would you like to go to America?" she asked. "What could I do there?" he replied. "I am a farmer, I grow pistachios." She insisted, "You're a farmer, huh? OK, you can come work on my farm in America." She gave Abū Walīd enough money for an air ticket to America but instead of using the money for this purpose he finished paying for the house he had recently purchased in Damascus. When petitioned with letters from America he wrote back saying he was unable to go, never once mentioning that he had a wife and family. At last, President Ford's sister sent Abū Walīd a letter containing just one word – LIAR. This he remembers with much bitterness and shame.'

The following day I went to visit Subhī who worked just off the Souq al-Ḥamīdiyya. I casually mentioned Abū Walīd.

'The Montgomery man?'

Subhī roared with laughter.

'Have you heard his Hitler story?'

My heart sank, for I had been hoping for at least a grain of truth in Abū Walīd's story.

'It goes something like this,' Subhī continued. 'During the war he met, in Aleppo, a German officer. They became friends and the officer took AbūWalīd to Berlin with him. There, he introduced Abū Walīd to the Führer. Abū Walīd presented Hitler with a silk Damascene brocade. "Heil, Hitler!" he said. "Nein!" replied Hitler, "Heil, Abū Walīd!" Hitler spoke warmly to his new Arab friend, saying, "I like you, Abū Walīd. I like the Syrian people, so now you may go home. You will be safe." So you see, Abū Walīd prevented the German invasion of Syria.'

'Yes, and right under Montgomery's nose, too. Do you think everything he says is a lie?'

Subhī smiled.

'Listen. Among his many stories there is probably one that's true. It's for you now to discover which one. Or perhaps each person should pick the story he himself believes to be true.'

It was as a result of Subhī's challenge that I decided to go about collecting the amazing adventures of Abū Walīd. Presumably, if he had approached a French tourist there would be a story about how during the war a French officer took him to meet General de Gaulle. And who knows what he told the Japanese. At every shop I went to I asked the proprietor there if he knew Abū Walīd. Subhī said I would have to conduct the greater part of my investigations in the Christian Quarter. Abū Walīd's 'territory' stretched roughly from the Umayyad Mosque, down the Street Called Straight and then left onto Hanania Street.

'Abū Walīd has a son in South Africa who works in diamonds, another in Holland, who is a surgeon, his wife a psychiatrist.'

'There's a son in Australia – he sent a cow to his son in Australia.'

For every person I spoke to, there was another son in a different place.

'Milan, an engineer.'

'Madrid, owner of the Sultan Restaurant.'

'France, a teacher.'

'New York, another doctor.'

'Tokyo, a son in computers, a maker of robots.'

'Belgium, a tailor.'

'Greece, his son is a friend of the Greek Prime Minister and he owns a ship.'

'Germany, sports teacher.'

'New Zealand, kiwi grower.'

'Helsinki, Helsinki – we do not know what the one in Helsinki does.'

I questioned the merchants perhaps a little too eagerly at times, for some of them became suspicious of my intentions. Others said, yes, they knew him, but apart from vague rumours such as his being a Palestinian or of his having lived in Canada after a stint in the Canadian army or of his having worked on English ships and there was something too about his having been awarded a medal for valour, there was nothing concrete they could tell me.

'It's not us he tells these stories to. We hear them second-hand from the foreigners he speaks to.'

A few days later, a couple of days before our appointed meeting, I came up behind Abū Walīd entertaining a couple of American tourists.

'So Major Moody he take me to Texas, 1942. I stay with his parents two, oh, maybe three weeks.'

I should have kept my distance, for Abū Walīd, catching sight of me out of the corner of his eye, performed a full loop and somehow brought Montgomery back into the picture.

'After the war, Montgomery wants to go into the silk business, so he fix a job in England for me in the silk brocade business. Montgomery had shares, 35 per cent for me, 65 per cent for Montgomery. Very good man.'

'Tell me again about your wife,' I interrupted. The Americans, there on a Bible tour, took this as a cue to make their escape.

'She was not a wife really. Girlfriend, you understand. Scottish. We meet in Liverpool in 1958. I bring her back as my wife to Syria, but at first she does not like Syria. She wants to go home, so I say fine, go home to Scotland. She goes to Scotland,

and then she wants to come back to Aleppo. She gets on a plane, the plane crash near Athens, 1962. June, August – I don't remember exactly. I marry Arab woman, she's no good.'

'Are you a guide?' I asked him.

'When somebody wants to pay me I say, no, I am a *free* guide. In Aleppo, an Australian says to me, "I have lost my hotel." I say, "Which hotel?" So I take him to his hotel. The tourist says, "I will send you a cow from Australia." I say to him, "What will I do with a cow?" We laugh. You see, I like to help people.'

'I will see you on Thursday.'

'Yes, with the photographs, promise.'

Jokingly, he added, 'You must bring 300 dollars for me to choose a carpet for you. But remember, I must choose.'

'Yes, fine.'

At the hotel I met a young woman from Fiji who had met him earlier and she related this story which bore all the hallmarks of a joke Abū Walīd might have heard somewhere.

'Well, this guy Abū Walīd told me he is half Christian, but because he is half Muslim too he decided he must go to Mecca. So he went there. He began to pray there and, forgetting where he was, made the sign of the cross by mistake. A policeman arrested him, saying, "You're Christian!" "No," he answered, "I am Muslim!" Abū Walīd showed them his passport. "So you're Muslim," the policeman said. "Why, then, did you make the sign of the cross?" "I didn't. Oh now, wait a minute! I remember. Look, I was itchy here (scratching his forehead) and here (scratching the middle of his ribcage) and (scratching at both sides of his chest) here and here."'

When I told Abed this story he saw much significance in it.

'Kaʿba is called by the Muslims the house of Allāh. All mosques are called this. What this means is that Allāh is not there Himself because in Islam there is nothing like Him. Anything that you might imagine about Him, what is sure is that He will be different from what you imagine. He has no physical dimensions. The Creator is different from His creatures. Allāh is not like anything, not even His manifestations – every manifestation is different from the other. He never repeats any one manifestation twice, otherwise people will die of boredom. It is a priority for a Muslim of common sense that before visiting the house of God he should know God. The meaning of the Kaʿba is the direction of His manifestation, not Himself. So Abū Walīd did not know where he was going, which is why he became confused there. He crossed himself accidentally which means that in his subconscious he was not yet a believer of Islam. We can derive from his story a good lesson as to how one might go about converting a Christian to Islam. Do not take him to Mecca, thinking you are doing a great thing for him. A poor, ignorant person, he will not realise where he is. You will have spoiled this would-be convert by taking him too soon, by not taking him step by step through the natural processes. If instead of putting oil in a car you put rocket fuel, then you'll have damaged the engine. What you should have done is change the engine, the heart of this man, first and then put rocket oil in. You should have allowed him to taste the sweetness of Islam first.'

I think Abed may have missed the joke.

Subhī, when I told him the story, exclaimed, 'Half Christian! Which half?'

Needless to say, when I returned on Thursday Abū Walīd was not there. I left a message expressing my regrets at not finding him there, but that, *inshallāh*, we would meet again one day.

'Also, could you tell him I brought the money with me.'

Afterwards, I walked down Hanania Street towards the chapel of Ananias when from inside a tourist shop an American-sounding voice called out to me.

'Hey, c'mon in. You want some tea?'

The shopkeeper shoved wads of flatbread and meat into his mouth. 'You want to buy something nice?' I looked in dismay at the plastic-covered jewellery boxes. Khalīl who in his coloured shirt looked as though he had just stepped in off a beach lived in America for twenty years before returning to Damascus.

'Anything you can tell me about Abū Walīd?'

Although I had decided not to push my enquiries any further, I looked upon this as a diversionary tactic to get me to the end of my obligatory third glass of tea without having to excuse myself from making a purchase.

'Abū Walīd!' Khalīl laughed, showing the semi-masticated food in his mouth. 'You kidding me? Yeh, sure I can tell you about Abū Walīd. You see this?'

Khalīl pointed to a calendar hanging on the wall behind him. It bore, beneath a movie still of a devout-looking figure, the legend 'ZDF German television, Director. Heiga Lippert'.

'You see the guy dressed up as St Paul?' he shouted. 'Yeh, that's right, it's me!'

ZDF TV came to Damascus in 1995 in order to shoot a drama documentary about St Paul. Heiga Lippert employed local people to play the various parts.

'And you want to know who the guy was played Ananias?' Khalīl laughed. 'Yessir!'

I had now found Abū Walīd's greatest role, the story Subhī told me I would find sooner or later. Abū Walīd was the instrument employed by God to complete Saul's conversion. 'Brother Saul, receive thy sight.' Abū Walīd, a Muslim, was the hook upon which hung the future of Christianity.

'Abū Walīd got real mad 'cos we gave him only 500 *lira*.' A final hunk of lamb went in as Khalīl spoke. 'We got 250 bucks each, you see, and the German director, she says bring me three people for the part of Ananias. She picked Abū Walīd herself, but left it to us to pay the small parts out of our own pockets.'

'You were subcontracting, you mean?'

'Yeh, that's right.'

Khalīl downed a glass of tea in one and wiped his mouth with the remains of the flatbread.

'Abū Walīd's never spoke to me since.'

I did not expect to see Abū Walīd again, but the next day, the day before my departure back to London, I was rushing down the Street Called Straight when I caught a glimpse of white hair through the window of the carpet shop. When I entered, Abū Walīd barely acknowledged me.

'Why, Ḥasān,' I said, 'I was very disappointed to have missed you yesterday.'

Abū Walīd clutched at his chest in visible pain.

'Ohhh,' he cried, 'I have such bad pains in my head and here.'

Abū Walīd did indeed look terrible.

'The photographs,' he moaned, 'I bring them next week.'

'Thank you, but I must return to England tomorrow.'

A steeliness entered his voice.

'You have 300 dollars?'

'Sorry, Ḥasān, I met two lovely women last night. You know how it is. I spent all the money on them.'

'I make love to fifty women! You go back to England, I will send you the photographs.'

'You are much too kind.'

'Yes, but first you send me brown shoes, expensive, size 42, English shoes. I am going to England in September, so I wear them there. You send me the shoes first, I send you the photographs. When I say "yes" I do not mean "no" – when I say "no" I do not mean "yes". I speak, like Montgomery says, only the truth. Brown. Size 42.'

'It's a deal, Ḥasān.'

As Abū Walīd walked away, furious with victory, the carpet seller who had been laughing all the while turned to me.

'You are writing about this, aren't you?'

'Well, I might be keeping a diary.'

'No, no,' he grinned, 'you are *writing* about him. I think you are a writer. A journalist maybe? Look, Abū Walīd will tell you only one story and, believe me, he will stick to it. Somebody else he tells another story and he will stick to that one too. You should see the faces of the German tourists when he tells them about Hitler. The thing is, he's so believable. I heard he had a Dutch wife once. You must write about him, yes, but when you do please be careful not to destroy his world.'

There is another (always another) story and this one seems to have engendered greater mirth among Damascenes than any of Abū Walīd's historical tales. Subhī, after telling me the Hitler tale, described how one day he and a group of friends were watching a football match on television when Abū Walīd joined them. While they cheered, Abū Walīd watched in brooding silence. 'What's with Abū Walīd,' they asked themselves, 'why this silence?' When the game ended, he told them this story. Abū Walīd said that in his youth he was an excellent footballer, so good in fact that his performance on the playing fields of Aleppo attracted the attention of a visiting German woman. Subhī could not remember being told who she was, but doubtless she was a beautiful Teutonic blonde. She might have been Hitler's favourite niece or even Kaiser Wilhelm's granddaughter or Bismarck's sister. It seemed unlikely that she was just any young Teutonic blonde. She was wealthy, she liked football and she knew a good player when she saw one. Abū Walīd (or, strictly speaking, the young Ḥasān) clearly impressed her. 'You must come back to Germany with me,' she told him. Whether or not they fell in love Subhī did not relate, and besides, football was his main theme. Anyway, Subhī continued, they went to Germany. The German *Fräulein* drove Abū Walīd to a huge stadium. She parked her car outside the main gates. Opening her purse, she searched inside. 'This is my stadium, Abū Walīd,' she said, 'and here is the key. Take it, it's yours. Go, play as much football as you like.' After telling me this, Subhī shook with laughter until he was close to collapse.

And so we leave him on this triumphant note, the young Abū Walīd playing alone, somewhere in Germany, in the year of —? What's certain though, his hair is not yet white. The young Abū Walīd moves with such guile. The ball, if it's there at all, is a moving smudge. As he approaches the empty goal – if we listen carefully enough and if, as the man in the carpet shop advises, we take sufficient care not to destroy his world – what we hear is the roar of an invisible crowd chanting his name.

FIVE

The Green Turban

What is a friend? A single soul dwelling in two bodies.

Aristotle

Autumn falls like a knife in Damascus and the greater number of its inhabitants sicken all at once. There is no cold so cold as that which cuts through a warm climate and each year it seems to take the whole city by surprise. It gets not only into the bones of its people but also into their stomachs and from there seeps into the collective psyche. The vibrancy of the souq was gone; merchants shivered at their stalls; listlessness had settled upon everything and everyone. When I got to Ṣāliḥiyya I found Abed alone. I asked him if Sulaymān too had succumbed to the Damascus plague. Unsmilingly, he clapped his hands several times as if to ward away whatever it was that was tormenting his eyes. Another kind of blade had fallen through his life.

'Sulaymān is leaving Damascus.'

'What, forever?'

'Yes, maybe.'

Quietly I wondered if Sulaymān were not paving a way for the change in Abed's life, if perhaps he realised there was too much dependency in the friendship for either of them to be able to move freely. As it so happened, the timing was pure coincidence. Always Sulaymān had spoken of his desire to travel and now two people, Sufi acquaintances of his, offered to pay his fare to Cyprus where all three would join Shaykh Nāzim whose family home is there and which also is the main

Naqṣhbandī teaching centre. There was talk even that if Shaykh Nāzim were prepared to include Sulaymān among his followers he might find him a wife.

'Tell me, Sir Marius, when I get married will my wife alleviate the pain of his absence? Sulaymān is my only friend here and I am the only one who understands him. What will I do with him gone, even if he assures me that he will see me everywhere?'

Apparently, Sulaymān was not fully decided on the issue, and the two Sufi acquaintances had asked Abed to exert pressure on him to go. Abed was being invited to bring about the event he feared most.

'I must now do so,' he said, 'ours would not be a true friendship otherwise.'

We went to Sulaymān's house. Rashīd, one of the Sufis, was already there. Rashīd struck me as being Sulaymān's opposite, amorphous, pushy, quite lacking in finesse. The day before, he had given Sulaymān forty dollars in order to get himself a visa for Turkey, but this the latter had failed to do. Somehow – he couldn't remember *how* exactly – Sulaymān had managed to spend or give away ten dollars. This was easy enough to imagine. I had already seen him empty his pockets to beggars crowded at the entrance of the mosque or splurge a day's earnings on cakes. If this were thoughtlessness, and the sum involved was not a trifle, it was of species that could never warrant blame. The bookseller Sulaymān was oblivious to the fruits of commerce. With our arrival Rashīd put additional pressure on Sulaymān who in turn became angrier by the minute, accusing the other of insensitivity on so important an issue. I asked Abed why Rashīd was offering to pay Sulaymān's fare.

'You see how he is. Rashīd is not a good Sufi and so in order to win Shaykh Nāzim's acceptance he looks upon Sulaymān as providing him with the right credentials. Sulaymān is everything Rashīd would like to be.'

Rashīd turned in exasperation to Abed, 'You speak to him, then!'

Abed said nothing although with his silence he probably exercised the greater influence of the two people. Clearly all three were at an impasse. After a while, Abed turned to me.

'If Sulaymān were to treat me according to his world, I would not be able to bear his company. And so he gives an impression of normality, something he does even with his parents who at times find him almost impossible to live with.'

'Do his parents not accept him as he is?'

'Yes, they do, but Sulaymān shows them a picture of himself that they are only barely able to live with. There is strong love between them, but their acceptance of him is not quite the same as their understanding of him. If they do so at all it is only within the small area of their own comprehension. They do not see what lies beyond logic.'

Afterwards, when Rashīd and his friend had left in despair, Abed asked Sulaymān if he were still prepared to go to Cyprus.

'I do not wish it to appear as if I'd been forced to go,' was all he said.

'Sulaymān does everything according to his own lights and you see what happened here. Rashīd, by putting pressure on him, perhaps blew the argument.'

Sulaymān put on a tape of Bedouin music – a sound of drums and men's voices chanting verses. The desert spaces seemed to enter this small room, which was as spare as any Bedouin tent. A small reproduction of an Italian Renaissance painting of St George slaying the dragon was mounted on the wall – 'Khiḍr,' said Sulaymān, 'St George.'

I pointed to a mysterious object of about three feet in diameter, wholly comprised of dark green material, a band or perhaps several bands of cloth, with no ends visible, wrapped into a heavy, oblong bale, with a deep cavity at its centre.

'Sulaymān's turban,' Abed said.

A famous *ḥadīth* says the turban signifies dignity for the believer and strength for the Arab, but what of a turban that was not wearable? I asked Abed if it had any special significance.

'This is Sulaymān's own invention. Call it his eccentricity, if you like. Nobody – not his family, not even me – is allowed to touch it. Sometimes, especially when he is in spiritual trouble, he wears it but because it's so heavy he can manage to do so for only half an hour at a time. It took him two years to make. Shaykh ʿAbdullāh ordered him to do so, in a dream.'

The late Shaykh ʿAbdullāh al-Fa'iz ad-Daghestani, thirty-ninth leader in the Naqṣhbandī chain of shaykhs, was the spiritual teacher of his successor, Shaykh Nāzim, and among the various feats for which he is credited was the seven years he spent in isolation, during which time he ate only a fraction of what one normally needs in order to survive.

'Sulaymān saw himself in the dream wearing a turban of the seven colours found on the tomb of Shaykh ʿAbdullāh. As you see, the turban is all green. This is probably only because he was able to buy a large quantity of green cloth at a good price.'

Abed chuckled as he often did at Sulaymān's foibles.

'As soon as he awoke he started making the turban and at that precise moment there was a thunderous explosion or rather it was more like a booming voice. It was not just something one *hears*, but an actual physical force. The power of it broke windows in the neighbouring apartments. A water storage tank fell off the wall. The neighbours came to him, saying, "What have you done?" If it weren't for their testimony I would not have believed any of this. At first Sulaymān suffered from terrible headaches, but soon these were followed by periods of great ecstasy during which time he continued to make the turban. Wrapped inside the folds of cloth are 124,000 slips of paper, on each of which he has written, "There is no God but Allāh, and Muḥammad is His Prophet." 124,000, this number represents the number of prophets who have come to this earth. You can imagine how heavy the turban is. Sulaymān described to me another dream in which he felt his body being injected with strength so that he would have the physical capacity to be able to wear the turban. It brings security, he says, and what he describes as a warm ray of light to his heart.'

Green is the colour of Paradise and also it is said to be

the Prophet's favourite colour although he himself always wore black. The green turban has been associated with his descendants; it is said the angels at Hanain wore green turbans; Naqṣhbandī Sufis wear them; the *sabzpush*, 'he who wears green', inhabits the highest spiritual rank. The turban has suffered of late. Young people tend to go for modern clothes, and even among the older very few wear turbans anymore. Although it was never a religious duty to wear one, it was recommended to do so. It is, after all, the article of dress that distinguishes Muslim from unbeliever. Another *ḥadīth* recommends that it be worn constantly until the ascension of the Pleiades or the beginning of the great heat. There is said to be close to a thousand ways of wrapping a turban but, generally speaking, it should be wound only when standing up and with the right hand folding it to the right around the head. On the Day of Judgement the amount of light a man receives will be measured according to every winding of the cloth about his head. The size of a turban depends upon the rank of the one who wears it, although too large a turban may be considered an extravagance unworthy of a proper religious attitude. A learned man, on the other hand, is liable to be exempt from such strictures. Sulaymān's turban, I discovered later, was not without precedence. While reading through Alexander Russell's history of Aleppo, I came across this passage: 'The Amulett is composed chiefly of certain names of the Deity, verses of the Qur'ān, prayers, or the like, comprehended in small bulk, in a form convenient to be worn. Little slips of paper of this kind rolled up are often concealed in the sash of the Turban.'

Sulaymān brought from out of his wardrobe a huge club, a wooden stick wrapped at the top in the same green cloth as the turban.

'Why the club?' I asked him.

'The club is symbolic of the prophet Moses. Every prophet must have one. Khiḍr commanded me to make this.'

'What's its purpose?'

'I use it to hit people with.'

Abed leaned anxiously on his bicycle. Would I accompany him to the Umayyad Mosque, he asked, where he had a meeting with a Muslim from France, Algerian born, who spoke neither Arabic nor English, and would I translate for him from the French. I suggested that given the rustiness of my French this might be inadvisable.

'A few words will be enough. I met this man a couple of years ago and jokingly said to him that if ever he wanted a Syrian wife he should come to me. There are many such people in Europe, Muslims who do not speak Arabic but who want Muslim wives, and because Arab immigration to Europe is mostly male they must arrange for marriages elsewhere. Now I am being held to my promise. What am I to do?'

We met the francophone Algerian by the visitors' entrance to the mosque and there he solemnly opened our meeting by treating us to freshly squeezed pomegranate juice. The street vendor had barely squeezed his third pomegranate when the Algerian got down to matrimonial business. We were shown an official letter from the French immigration office, confirming that he was to marry a certain 'Mademoiselle Samara, citoyenne syrienne'.

'There's no problem, Abed, he's already got one.'

'Non, non!'

There was something in the Algerian's downcast features that spoke of a snag.

'Je suis arrivé depuis une semaine . . .'

'I arrived a week ago . . .'

'Hélas . . .'

'Alas . . .'

'What's his problem?' asked Abed irritably. The Algerian spoke with pain ballooning in his voice.

'If I understand him correctly our Mademoiselle Samara has gone and married somebody else.'

'Smart girl!'

'Je suis ici pour une autre semaine . . .'

'I am here for another week . . .'

'Il faut que je trouve une femme.'

'Bad news, Abed, he's looking for another fiancée.'

Abed turned to me in desperation.

'What, in one week! Who are these people? They come here and expect me to find them wives while I'm still trying to get one for myself.'

Abed removed from his wallet a folded slip of paper going furry at the edges.

'Alright, give him this. Tell him to go to this address. A Sudanese woman I know is friendly with this girl.'

'But Abed, is she available?'

'Yes, maybe! Just tell him there is a girl . . .'

'Il y a une jeune fille . . .'

'Ah, bon!'

The Algerian pulled from his pocket a gold ring about an inch in diameter, declaring it was for his future bride.

'My God,' Abed whispered to me, 'what's this for, an elephant? Sir Marius, tell me, has this Frenchman got a screw loose?'

'Well, perhaps just one,' I volunteered.

'How many do you suppose he has?'

The Algerian stared at the meaningless Arabic note.

'Où—?'

Just then somebody else appeared, an acquaintance of Abed, who not only spoke French but also, incredibly, was going to the very building where the girl lived.

'Sir Marius, this is most fortunate!'

Quickly Abed passed the responsibility of finding the Algerian a bride to the newcomer. The Algerian began addressing me rapidly, his voice getting higher all the while, but I understood not a word of what he was so urgently trying to tell me.

'Quick,' Abed said, 'let's get out of here!'

We left the Algerian to the uncertain machinations of Abed's acquaintance.

'You see, you must believe in destiny,' Abed told me. 'A man comes along who not only speaks French but is going to the very address I gave.'

A couple of days later Abed and I met for coffee at the Havana Café, a rather pretentious place where artists and writers meet, pay three times the normal price for a cup of coffee, and trade in the latest Western intellectual fashions. Soft muzak played. A painter of some repute, wearing a beret, swanned about from table to table. I wondered if this perhaps was not some Arab conception of Western culture every bit as phoney as our own lapses into doubtful Arabesque. Or perhaps this was something true, fake mirroring fake. Abed reminded me it was my idea, not his, to come here. When he suggested we leave, I said no, we might learn something of use. To be truthful, I was sinking into one of those bouts of despondency many travellers to this part of the world suffer from – also, a virus of some kind was continuing to sap me of my energy.

There was another reason for my dark mood. That morning I had met an American psychologist who chided me for my enthusiasm over holy fools and for the links I suggested there might be between Sufism and early Christian mysticism. I had been addressing my remarks not to him but to a mutual Syrian friend of ours. The American had been in Syria on and off for three years and in his eyes I was a mere rookie. Still, I thought unkindly to myself, in the same way amassed ignorance may be likened to a thickening of the skin where it rubs most against the world so this man could spend aeons here and actually decline in intelligence. Doubtless this was unfair of me, for he was bright enough in the way anything reflecting light from another source produces an occasional gleam. Against any chance of getting a fair hearing from him, I continued to push my case. He then accused me of having fallen into the trap of Orientalism, this presumably being the most lethal weapon in his intellectual arsenal. I asked him if we were supposed to feel guilty for our attraction to Arab culture. This, I realised too late, was a poor defence. The American pounced and I veered a little. And so, masking our mutual loathing, we politely debated the merits of Burton and Layard but there too we soon fell into trouble. I accused him of exaggerating their supposed deficiencies for the sake of contemporary liberal mores. Guilt, I said, was our newest gold, easy to extract and infinitely marketable – academics stake out whole areas of guilt nobody has ever mined before. As he got up to leave, all wobbly with superior intelligence, the American wished me luck in the way one wishes another man a flat tyre on a desert road shadowed by vultures. The Syrian asked me if I had read Edward Saïd, adding that, as far as he could see, the only people to take him seriously were Westerners. I felt only slightly vindicated. I had only just reached the point of thinking I had begun to understand a little only to realise I knew nothing at all – admittedly not the best state of mind in which to write. Also, I understood that this man's politically correct views were yet another obstacle against which I had to write. Sulaymān's green turban seemed to me now symbolic of everything I found unfathomable. I told Abed I was contemplating taking an early flight home.

'Then you must go.'

'Sorry?'

'You must leave tonight, if possible.'

'You would like me to go?'

'Yes, quickly!'

'Well then, I'll stay in that case.'

'Excellent, I was counting on that response. You still have important work here, as my marriage counsellor.'

'Abed, I feel sometimes that Arabs are the only people who understand me.'

'Yes, this is probably true,' he replied. 'You are neither one thing nor the other. Also, you have just the right degree of femininity in you, just enough as any more would undermine your manliness. We respond to your melange.'

A few days later, Sulaymān took us to a Sufi meeting in a tiny mosque, more like a living room really, at the back of which was the tomb of Shaykh ʿAbdullāh, the very one who in the dream or vision had commanded Sulaymān to make his green turban. *Dikhr* was followed by warm buttermilk, biscuits and sweets. Afterwards, we went to a neighbouring house where Sulaymān removed from his bag a towel in which was wrapped a knife of about a foot in length. A man turned his cheek towards him as if readying himself for a shave. Sulaymān pressed the sharp edge of the blade so firmly into the man's flesh I expected blood to appear at any second.

'My God, Abed, what's he up to?'

'This man has a bad toothache and Sulaymān is giving him relief from the pain.'

'You mean he's a dentist, too?'

'No, he can't cure the problem of a bad tooth, but he can relieve the ache.'

I told Sulaymān I had a backache and asked him if he would be able to treat me. Ordering me to lie face down on the floor, he pressed the sharp edge of the blade across the base of my spine. I could hear the sound of his heart, like a steady tapping of a finger against a wooden table. The beating of his heart, particularly at times of great intensity, was clearly audible at a distance of three or four feet, sometimes more. A few minutes later, I felt something like a flash of white heat from the blade and Sulaymān, as though absorbing my pain, made a strange guttural sound and fell over backwards. When I got up the ache had gone.

'Allāh makes the wound, then heals it!'

All was suddenly in Abed's favour. The toothless mediator had brought him good news. The girl's father, he said, had shrunk in size. Now Abed wielded all the power. The father was told that Abed would inherit money enough for him to be his own man – 'a non-mainstreamer' – and that there were plenty of women ready to marry him. The girl had shed bitter tears at her father deciding against Abed, at which the father's brothers ganged up against him. Abed had gone to see her the evening before.

'She looked at me with her honeyed eyes and I had to turn away. I did not know how to return those glances. I've a great problem, however. Sir Marius, you must help me.'

'Well then, how can I be of use?'

'I have never kissed a girl. I have heard that one should go first for the top lip and then attack the bottom one.'

Such difficulties, I suggested, would remedy themselves with practice.

'Also, I understand there is a problem with oxygen intake.'

'Alright Abed, I will try to give you some advice.'

'Wait!'

Abed pulled out his notebook and held his pen at the ready.

'Begin!'

Abed busily took down notes.

'You are writing this in English?'

'Yes, it sounds better in English.'

'Above all,' I continued, 'she must be conquered with language.'

'All that my mother told me,' Abed cried, 'when compared to this is superficial.'

'And, most importantly, under no circumstances are you to join the mainstreamers. You must remain as you are. If she loves you, it will be for your unique qualities.'

'Excellent, this is what I want to hear! I will be able now to make my life here. Whereas only a week ago I might have asked you to support me in my application for a visa, I now wish to be an emblem of Damascene life.'

Only recently I had heard this very word *emblem* on the lips of another person, a merchant born to one of the old Damascene families.

'The old Damascenes whom we consider emblems of our city's dignity and culture make up thirty-five families.'

He showed me his identification card and pointed to a number.

'The number printed here reflects our chronological standing, at least where records are available. The lower the number, the older the family. I am of a family so old we do not know our beginnings. Once upon a time, the old Damascenes would be called upon to act as hosts to visiting dignitaries. Such was our influence, but now we are excluded from all such diplomatic ceremonies. We are no longer given high positions and we are even discouraged from speaking high Arabic. We probably deserve this because every Damascene aspires to be a leader. His ego is gigantic, and before our president came to power there were political coups every other day. The old families dislike each other, which is why even during the Umayyad period the people had to be ruled with a fist of iron. This is a fatal flaw in ourselves, and for our own sakes it may be better that we are forced to live like this. We have had stability now for twenty-five years. We are a resilient people. When the Mongols came nobody believed Damascus would survive, but we acquired the aggressiveness of the Mongol father and the delicacy of the Syrian mother. We are a mixture and because of this interbreeding we are stronger. We are frequently mocked for being a mixed race, but nobody can beat the Damascenes at trade. The Syrian trader is renowned throughout the Arabic world. We have a dark side, however. During the years of greatest oppression many from our Damascene families informed on each other, the result being that scores of innocent people were arrested, not for political reasons, but in order to settle old scores. We have families here who for decades nursed petty grievances, who have been rife with old jealousies. There is no end to the peeling away of the many layers of truth you will find here. Although one cannot hope to arrive at the centre, which is always hidden, there is no wisdom in saying outsiders are to blame. We have been spoiled partly because of our lack of an identity. When you lose hope you degenerate, you drift. We are now a drifting people. Because of our egotism we have allowed ourselves to be marginalised. We say all the faults of the people are summed up in the leader, he being a reflection of their deeds. If he is a good leader, then their deeds are summed up in his personality. We may generalise and say Europeans as a whole are cooperative and that this is reflected in a leader who believes in democracy. An old story best describes our position. Some people approached a saint, saying that the Mongols were about to destroy Damascus. They begged him, "Please help us, you're a saint." This saint had a revelation. He saw an unbelievable thing – St George on a chariot, guiding the Mongolian army. "Why," he asked, "are you leading our enemy?" St George answered, "The Damascene people suffer from too much pride. God put me at the head of this army to give them a lesson." The saint returned to the Damascene people, telling them it was because of their excessive pride that this happened.'

Sulaymān invited me to go back to his house. We sat, just the two of us, at opposite ends of the room. Sulaymān took the green turban and placed it on his head. We watched each other in silence. After about a quarter of an hour, Sulaymān lifted the turban from his head and carrying it across the room placed it on mine. I could hear his heart beating louder and louder as he approached me. Sulaymān went back to his place at the other side of the room and watched me, his eyes growing ever wider in astonishment. I was determined to bear the turban's weight for as long as possible. About ten minutes passed when a knock came at the door, his mother bringing tea. Sulaymān bounded across the room and grabbed the turban. He did not want anyone to see I had been allowed to wear it.

The next day, Abed had already heard the news.

'You were allowed to wear the green turban!'

I wondered if he were not a little jealous.

A rather chimerical figure in Damascus at this time was Ilona Karwinska. A superb photographer, Polish, she lived in London. We met on the rickety stairs of the al-Ḥaramain Hotel and discovered we frequented, although at different times, the same coffee house in London. She had a propensity to giggle. A whole gang of guardian angels must have watched over her, for she had an uncanny ability to get out of scrapes, which was equal only to her ability to get into them. She told me the curious story of a waiter at the Nofara Café, a gruff figure in his sixties, whom I had met on an earlier occasion and whom she later had to flee. This man, either on a hunch or because of my angular features, had addressed me in Polish. Amazed, I asked him where he had learned to speak Polish. 'I lived there for fourteen years,' he said. 'What doing?' I asked. 'A tourist,' he replied. 'What,' I exclaimed, 'for fourteen years!' I got no further response. He was rather more forthcoming with Ilona, and after a couple of meetings told her the story of how he came to speak Polish – *z*'s, *cz*'s, *szcz*'s and all.

Over thirty years ago he had gone to Poland to work and settling there, in a small village, turned his thoughts to marriage. With only 100 American dollars, which in black market terms was a small fortune in the Poland of the 1960s, he bribed the priest of that village to allow him to marry a girl of eleven. As young wine put on the rack might be allowed to mature, so she remained at home; meanwhile, he bought themselves a house in the village and when finally she came of age she bore him his only child, a son. She then moved with him to Syria, a fatal mistake, for she didn't like the place and forthwith returned to Poland; he hadn't seen her since. When I asked Ilona if she knew what became of the son she reminded me of another waiter at the Nofara Café, a tallish man in his late twenties, with blonde hair and blue eyes, who spoke only Arabic. The only thing that seemed to surprise Ilona was my own surprise. I could not believe a priest had sanctioned such a marriage. She said such things happened all the time in Poland, and suddenly it occurred to me that there was something in Syria, not just a fondness for dialogue, which reminded me of Poland, but also a virulent, almost predictable, strain of unlikelihood. When I returned the following year both the waiter and his waiter son had gone, nobody knew where.

Abed called her 'Lady Ilona'.

She had a space between her front teeth and Abed asked her if it were genuine. She had reddish hair and Abed asked her if that, too, were genuine. I could not but admire the boldness that came of inexperience. We spoke of love and friendship or rather Abed sang the praises of one while Ilona hummed the benefits of the other, saying friendship stood neither above nor beneath love. I had to act as referee, for Abed was deeply troubled by her unwillingness to distinguish more decisively between the two. What he wanted more than anything were the proofs of love; anything less was cold-heartedness. On the evening of my departure, which, coincidentally, might or might not have turned out to be that of Sulaymān's as well, Ilona informed us she had found a new café. It was, she claimed, a rather special place. She led us into a covered fruit and vegetable market off the Martyrs' Square and to a hole in the wall that comprised a wobbly table, four rickety chairs, several smudgy glasses and a simmering kettle. I wondered if the proprietor, a man of questionable hygiene, had ever served such a mixed clientele.

'A woman is the seat of creation,' Abed continued from the previous conversation. 'No matter how important I may be, in the presence of a woman I will be annihilated, so this reflects how she is both powerful and useful.'

While Abed circumnavigated the subject of love, I watched a cockroach crawl up Ilona's back. I had never known cockroaches to be so familiar, which suggests they knew the score here, and that we, not they, were the intruders. Just as this one was about to reach the bare nape of her neck I flicked it away. Abed blanched. Ilona appeared not to notice, but then she could be sublimely vague.

'I am sorry for these disturbances,' said Abed. 'I apologise on behalf of the Damascene people.'

The wall was alive with cockroaches.

'Lady Ilona, you must understand I am a raw and defective person. I would like now to compare you with my fiancée.'

'Yes?'

'How many kilograms do you weigh?'

Abed was joking out of a troubled soul, for soon he might be facing a huge vacuum in his life. I glanced at my watch.

'Do you think Sulaymān will actually go?'

'My God,' Abed cried, 'it's almost time!'

If Sulaymān were going to leave it would be from a small bus depot not far from Zenobia Park. We left Ilona to her tea and cockroaches. We were late getting there. We went to the wrong depot and now, in the darkness, Abed started running.

'Don't run,' he cried, 'there's no need.'

Breathless, he laughed at the absurdity of his own words. We arrived with only two minutes to go before the bus departed for Istanbul. Sulaymān was already seated, staring straight ahead, wearing a coat a couple of sizes too big for him. If he were about to leave forever, he did not let it show. I watched the panic rise in Abed's face. Quietly Sulaymān asked him to say goodbye to their mutual friends.

'What friends?' Abed said mockingly. 'We have no friends here!'

They barely said goodbye, much less embrace.

'Goodbye, Sulaymān.'

'Goodbye, Marcie.'

As the bus pulled away Sulaymān did not turn his head once; Abed did not wave. 'Why spoil friendship with tears?' he said. 'We have reached a stage in our friendship where there can be no pain in departure because the world is tiny in comparison to our love. If I ever get to Cyprus it will be like going over to his house.'

We went to Zenobia Park where, approaching midnight, we each smoked a cigarette. When I asked Abed the meaning of his parting words to Sulaymān he said it was in order to give themselves courage at the beginning of their adventures. After a long silence, the dam inside him broke.

'Oh God, I meant to be strong!'

I suggested that perhaps his tears were his strength.

'No, no! I'm weak. It is unmanly for Arab men to weep. With nobody left here, how will I survive? You don't know my tormented life – you have seen only the surface. You have entered our lives perhaps because you, too, feel this pain. There is between us a sweet sadness we instinctively understand and share. God knows if I will ever see him again.'

'Your marriage will give you strength.'

'We must smoke on it, Sir Marius. We have this expression here.'

We smoked another cigarette, and for me who can barely get through one this was the only time in my life I'd ever managed two. We went to a nearby café. After midnight, amid the click-clack of the backgammon boards and the perfumed smell of *nargilehs*, we spoke of the future.

'Sulaymān told me to read Ibn al-ʿArabī, which will be a way of filling his absence. Now that I am about to reach the peak of my happiness, when my sexual frustrations will be put aside, I will be able to read him once more.'

'Do you think Sulaymān will find a wife?'

'Who, then, is this man who dreamed power was his? What kind of man is he who trembles in front of a woman?' Abed asked rhetorically. 'Will he find another wife? No, I don't think so. I fear his will be a life of solitude. The basis of his whole existence is not to receive but to give. This will be his trial. He operates according to some other principle. If he is quite unstoppable, he is not aggressively so. One does not stop him for fear of hurting him, for his is the unstoppability of the gentle. I have been utterly frustrated by him at times, but never so much that I should wish to say anything that would wound him. You see, in the same way he showed me something beyond logic I have kept him from flying into space.'

Later, we stood at the corner of the street that divides old from new Damascus. There was one last thing I wanted to ask Abed, something that had been preying on my thoughts.

'Why did Sulaymān allow me to wear his turban?'

'He doesn't know. He said that when he stared at you he felt pleasure, as if you had understood the whole thing and were living through it with him. Without this understanding you would not bother to be in his company, for he is an outcast. What you have with him is a connection beyond language, something which Ibn al-ʿArabī reiterates. It is what first drew you to him.'

We said our goodbyes.

'It's not forever,' Abed told me.

On the bus to the airport I spoke to an Iraqi Kurd who worked by day as a surgeon and, in order to make ends meet, by night as a singer in a country restaurant. He told me of his escape from Baghdad with his wife and two children and what a close call it had been; they were lucky to be alive. The decision to flee came after he had received an order from Saddam Hussein to surgically remove the ears of those who sought to escape military service. Who could do such a thing, he said, and continue to call himself a doctor? Any contact with his relatives in Iraq was impossible for fear of what might happen to them if the authorities found out. The bus driver stopped without being asked to and this regular passenger who was both doctor and singer got off and walked down a dark lane to the restaurant hidden behind a row of trees.

'Despite all evidence to the contrary, flesh is more permanent than stone. We should not but for flesh contemplate stone.' I stare at this entry in my notebook, not remembering who its author was, whether it was me or somebody else.

Part Two

SIX

Man with a Yellow Face

You can't prevent the birds of sorrow from flying over your head, but you can stop them from nesting in your hair.

Arabic proverb

A flick from the level of the table, and the Marlboro sailed like a guided missile through the air towards Abed's mouth. We were getting off to an uneasy start, one of deadly silences and wooden phrases. I had feared this. What would Damascus be without Abed's friendship and, admittedly, with a certain amount of self-interest now entering the picture, his guidance? This was the corner I had gradually worked myself into. The book had become almost too much his, perhaps rightly so, otherwise I might have gone on to write a book dealing only with the matters I have excluded from this one. Also, I had begun to distrust the very idea of travel literature. A friend, Jarosław Anders, wrote to me: 'Wherever I am in a place that actually has some effect on me, I almost never take notes. It seems so corny and artificial – that studied pose of a thoughtful traveller with his leather-bound scrapbook. Travel writing is a very paradoxical enterprise, both reductive and expansive. It is ostensibly about the surface, the skin of the world, yet asks to be taken as something much more. It can be done neither from *here* nor from *there*, but from some purely imaginary point in between. Finally, it often takes a talent for self-dramatisation, or simply lying through your teeth.' Worthy Pole that he is, gloomy diviner of my silences, he went straight for the demon snapping at my ankles. What I would have to do was write something else – a spiritual yarn, a chronicle – anything but *travel literature*.

The cigarette bounced off Abed's nose. He flailed wildly in his attempt to stop the precious weed from breaking in the middle, which is precisely what happened. In the two years since I last saw him the boyishness had fled his face and his left leg shook uncontrollably as he spoke of the 'vicissis*i*tudes' in his life.

Over the period between his first and last letters to me I had been able to observe a downward curve in his fortunes. The engagement with Ghufrān proceeded merrily enough, with indications that Abed had acted on my earlier advice. 'Oxygen is very scarce over here. I do hope sincerely that you will suffer this lack of oxygen.' I did wonder, however, at the mention of his prospective father-in-law drawing him into the family business, which involved the importing from Europe of 'certain machines'. Would Abed finally become a *mainstreamer*? Would the street philosopher trade his dreams for wares? A few weeks later, he wrote, 'Sir Marius, I really miss our adventures in the small coffee shop in the fruit market. The famous cockroach walked on Lady Ilona's neck: and in doing so it expressed its love, a love that knows no obstacles. It believes in the religion of love, its heart is open and ready for all kinds and manifestations of love; its heart has become a church, a synagogue and a mosque. The cockroach's attitude towards life is similar to mine.'

One day, perhaps, the Arabs will perish of hyperbole.

A month later, another letter arrived. 'Three weeks ago, I broke my engagement. I had no harmony of any sort with her. I need a girl who can feed me with compassion and elevated ideas. After four months of engagement I realised she is neither compassionate nor intelligent. So I took my priceless life from her hands and ran away. So now let us talk of my general situation. I am longing to leave Syria, as soon as possible, because I am increasingly ostracized by my society, and because I have lost contact with its mentality. The people I would care to be with are artists and people who have suffered, who know what beauty and sorrow is.' Doubtless the situation he described was true, but there had to be another side. A girl of Ghufrān's age could not but have entered a set of expectations, the very least of which being that Abed would provide for her. Abed's predicament seemed clear enough, even to an outsider like myself. He wanted an old-fashioned marriage to a girl immured in traditional values, 'pure of heart and face', and whom he would hide from the gaze of the world; at the same time, he hoped for someone who would respond, as only a free woman might, to his ideas, who could talk philosophy with him – in short, a girl of modern European sensibilities tucked behind a veil. It was more than a girl of sixteen, unschooled in anything other than how to cook aubergines, would have been able to give him.

Sulaymān, meanwhile, had returned to Damascus soon after his departure to Cyprus, but what the circumstances behind this were Abed had not told me. 'It is nothing new to you,' he wrote, 'that Sulaymān and I have spent our years seeking knowledge at the loss of riches. This search has been our secret preoccupation. Though we suffer distortion and satire for being poor, we feel absorbed by this secret preoccupation and their satire will not spoil our confidential enjoyment. On the contrary, we are actually filled with pride and are shocked at their ignorance. This, our extraordinary and pathetic survival, makes me badly in need of a relationship, mysterious and romantic enough to kindle the raptures of love.' There was a gap of several months in our correspondence. Then, just as I was about to return to Damascus, another letter came, saying their friendship was over, that Sulaymā n's dreams had taken a turn for the worse and, in what I took to be a purely metaphorical turn of phrase, that he imagined himself capable of making gold. The letter was not signed and was strangely abrupt in tone. Such was the mood in which I now found Abed who was busy trying to straighten his cigarette.

'I was afraid you would judge me over my split with Sulaymān. In fact, I had contemplated not meeting you.'

I was in no position to judge, I said, and, in any case, both he and Sulaymān remained firmly, if now separately, in my affections. Abed nodded his approval, saying he had no wish to blacken the other's name, but that there was considerably more to the break in their friendship than he was at liberty to tell me.

'A man's goodness is measured by his not being influenced by rumour and gossip. Anyway, from what I hear, Sulaymān seems to have found his buoyancy. There have been rumours about him. I heard that he applied for a British visa, was turned down and went mad with disappointment. There was talk even that he had ended up in a mental asylum. I have not seen him for eight months. If it's true and he did slip from the path he appears now to be fixing his position. If I say anything critical of him you must understand I do not wish to. I regret it, for I mean only to relate some of the circumstances that led to our moving apart. There are other reasons I would rather not give. Sulaymān is a good man.'

Abed caught the next cigarette.

'There's somebody I knew once who fell in love with a married woman. She reciprocated his love though not sexually, I believe. This went on for a year and then one day he phoned her and she told him in the rudest terms that everything was finished between them. "Why did you make me love you, then?" he asked. She mocked him. Obsessed, his dignity crushed, he turned to black magic – we have such people here, black magicians – in order to make her love him. He did not sleep for days at a time, walked the streets constantly, and even spoke of killing her. There is an analogy here in my relationship with Sulaymān. I felt rejected by him at a time when I was overwhelmingly dependent on him. He had taken me into a world so very different from mine. For all his compassion, however, Sulaymān can be cruel. There are times, of course, when cruelty is beneficial. Although Sulaymān did not intend this, God did. On my side there was envy and prejudice and when rejected I become cruel. Sulaymān has this power of hypnotizing people and of making them love him. After seven years of friendship, what I saw as Sulaymā n's mission with regard to myself was finished. There is a Sufi rule – a person is attached to his guru, then he is elevated from the presence of his guru into the presence of the Prophet Muḥ ammad, blessed be his name. Such is the target of life in Sufism, to be annihilated first in the presence of one's shaykh, then to be raised into the presence of the Prophet Muḥammad and then to be finally annihilated in his presence. Our target is God. We say blessed is the man who leaves his shaykh when he should do so, but here, you see, politeness is all-important. One must be polite in one's departure.'

I suggested that perhaps Sulaymān pushed him away for his own good, that when friendship turns to possessiveness, as quite obviously theirs had, it becomes destructive.

'Yes, probably. Also, he pushed me away because of my despair. A philosopher, either Plato or Socrates, said, "A good woman makes your life comfortable – a bad woman makes you a philosopher." Sulaymān had been the greatest boon in my life, in that I was able to correct my own faults through his. He spurred me to think out of bitterness. For seven years he tormented me. My family pleaded with me, "Why do you waste your life on him? What kind of hypnosis is this? You have lost your chances of any profession by staying with him. You are destroying your future." But were it not for his defects I would not have been able to correct my own. I have become a philosopher because of Sulaymān, just as this bad woman made Plato one. God wanted this chain broken, and perḥaps the 10,000 *lira* was His means of breaking a vicious circle.'

Another factor, a financial one of which I knew nothing, had entered and which I decided best not to pursue. All the same, although I had no doubt that what Abed said was true, there seemed to be an element of one argument, a spiritual one, being used to fudge over another more cruelly rooted in the temporal world.

'It is written in the Qur'ān that those who *say* they are inspired by God but in reality are not will go to hell.'

A bitterness entered Abed's voice.

'What is the main defect of Sulaymān? The problem with him is that he has a superego that is fed by many people. He is a victim. This is reinforced by what went on before. He imagined he and I would go through the world, to many countries, where we would be applauded by all the peoples of those countries according to their customs. In Africa, for example, they would beat drums and dance for us. And for some reason, because of Sulaymān's green turban, nobody would know where we'd come from. This sudden awareness I had of his ego wounded me deeply. Also, part of the problem between us was a vicious competition, one having always to be better than the other. Then there is the matter of his turning copper to gold. His family watched day by day to see if anything would come of it. Actually, he did once produce something that looked like gold.'

Abed laughed, and in that laugh I sensed affection. A laugh, when it comes from deep enough inside, is often the sturdiest of bridges. I felt the gap that was there at the beginning of our meeting was beginning to close.

'The cruelty of the shaykh is to quell this ego. Sulaymān refused to have a shaykh. He wanted to be a great Sufi, but by reading the great Sufi books of knowledge he took upon himself too great a burden. He wanted to be an exception but the truth is, a Sufi should be as simple as possible. If God wants to make an exception then He will do so. One should not wish for it, however, otherwise he will be burdened. There is a very important verse, "God never burdens a person more than he can endure." The pace towards God should be as subtle and slow as that of the ant's. An ant going from here to Mecca might require twenty years to make the voyage. One should have that patience. The problem with many Sufis, and Sulaymān is one of them, is that they want to rush. They read the great books, wanting to be like their authors. As a consequence they are poisoned, they lose their target, they drift. So instead of reading they should be busy defeating their enemies – the ego and Satan. We have a problem here. Shaykh Nāzim uses the analogy of a baby who drinks milk first, and then, after acquiring teeth, eats meat. Many Sufis, like Sulaymān, want to eat meat before drinking milk. In Sufism, one must have a shaykh in order to be annihilated by him. Egotism blinded and deafened Sulaymān. The ego equals arrogance and pride and is a catastrophe in the path towards God. This is why Sulaymān has been so important to me. He kept telling me, "I have saved you." A great Sufi teacher, al-Rifāʿī, said, "May I be doomed if I have said that I am a guru or teacher to even one of you." The more the ego shrinks, the greater a Sufi one becomes. Sulaymān takes only what he likes from Shaykh Nāzim. A Sufi attributes all his glories to God. I discovered this defect in him and it saddened me deeply, but out of love and because he was my ideal in life I coped with it. I was hypnotised. I worship beauty, and for every fault I discovered in Sulaymān I found a beautiful aspect, one that he might not have been aware of himself. He likes commerce too, so how does one reconcile the two? Me, I would like to be a philosopher, whereas he wants to be a successful businessman. All my life I have wrestled with ideas, trying to find solutions in them. I would rather have a solution to a philosophical problem than have two hundred dollars.'

'So, then,' I interrupted, 'what happened when he went to Cyprus? Was there something in his going there that signalled the end of your friendship?'

Abed laughed. 'Sulaymān never got there!'

I reminded him of our running to catch the bus.

'This was partly a problem of pride, his inability to take advice. He was supposed to have obtained a double transit visa, but whereas the other two people got them Sulaymān thought he would do things *his* way. The first time he went to get a visa he went to the Turkish embassy – this secular place, you understand – wearing his pointed turban, his Sufi clothes. There he got into an argument with the Syrian guards in front of the embassy. They chased him away. On the second attempt he shaved, cut his hair. And after securing the first visa, which is only a single transit one, he was so enthused by this success he did not bother with the second one. "I want to see Turkey," he said to them at the border, instead of stating he had somewhere specific to go to in Cyprus. What is this success that is also failure? God pays more attention to the fool than He does to saints. Why? A fool is vulnerable. I have witnessed this with my own eyes. I saw how Sulaymān was going to be in a mess because of his own foolishness. God understood this. Sulaymān spends money that is not his. Why, then, does he escape the punishment of those from whom he takes money? A holy fool is protected, that's why. This is one of the reasons many Muslims criticise Sufis, because they revere fools.'

A fresh tenderness entered Abed's voice.

'When you see him you must play upon his strings. He has this obsession about going to England, even of marrying one of your daughters.'

'Will I be able to see him?'

Abed who understood that any such meeting would have to take place through his good offices went silent for a minute.

'We shall go to his house, but I'll be there only as your interpreter.'

Walking through the souq we saw a man of indeterminate age, completely bald, with a yellow, babyish face. A walking mountain of rags dwarfing the man inside them, he moved among people yet appeared not to be *of* them. He had small eyes, like currants, that seemed not to see, parched lips, and his feet were badly splayed, covered with running sores. Wandering aimlessly, he made pitiful, blubbering cries.

'He is always in pain,' explained Abed, 'but although unable to speak he occasionally breaks into beautiful songs praising God.'

The medieval physician, Ibn Sīnā, better known to the Western world as Avicenna, describes the physical symptoms of lycanthropy – dryness, a marked yellowishness of the flesh, running sores – and the mental – the sufferer is a fugitive from life, exceedingly wary of people and often seeks the relative peace of cemeteries. Doubtless, the animal cries often made by sufferers gave rise to the legend of men who became wolves. Originally, lycanthropy was a medical term, derived from the

Greeks, which described a particular form of melancholia. The condition, a hereditary one, was thought to have been caused by black bile and was almost impossible to cure. Such treatment as there was often involved bleeding the sufferer until he lost consciousness, then moistening him by internal and external means, applying purges, scents to inhale, sometimes opium, and, if all else failed, physical beatings and cauterisation to the head.

We took a taxi to the edge of Ṣāliḥiyya. There was no reply when we got to Sulaymān's house, so we decided to find a local café, spend an hour there and try our luck again. It was then I learned that in order to help Sulaymān to get to England Abed persuaded his mother to sell some of her jewellery. This was the 10,000 *lira* by which means God would break a terrible cycle. Abed's father had resolved to take Sulaymān to court, a move that for Abed would only bring bitterness to the sweet memory of friendship. It was a matter of pride for his father, Abed told me, but behind this I suspected there was an ulterior motive, to once and for all sever the ties between his son and the friend who had wrecked his life. The key witness against Sulaymān would be Abed himself.

'I must leave this place.'

'What would you do?'

'I could become a computer operator.'

Abed plucked the idea out of the air. If, indeed, his aim were to become a computer operator and make plenty of money then I told him go, take his chances, but that the philosopher he wanted to be would surely fall upon hard times. The main destinations in Abed's thoughts on that bright day in April were England, France, Norway and Canada. As I contemplated them in turn perhaps two of those destinations made sense, a third might have made some kind of sense, and even a fourth though not in terms I could imagine, but as valid options the four together made no sense at all. Sulaymān had tried to go to England but failed, absurdly in Abed's eyes, and now Abed was claiming to have learned from his old friend's mistakes.

'Sulaymān believed he could go to England and get by with mime. He said that language is a burden. You see, he is full of nice ideas.'

Although it was true that Abed was more grounded in the real world than Sulaymān, I couldn't help but feel this other reality would quickly remove the glint from his eyes. Sulaymān, for all his eccentricities, might be kept afloat by his sublime madness for a while. Abed would surely crash.

'You would go to Norway?'

'Yes, maybe.'

'Can you ski?'

'So now we can eliminate Norway, perhaps Canada too.'

Already he had hatched up a scheme to go, with a friend, to London via Istanbul, the details of which he said were too complicated to go into, which, to my ears, probably meant there were no details at all to speak of. I asked him how he planned to survive there.

'Look, I will not be any kind of burden to you.'

The question never once arose in my thoughts. Without a work permit, I explained, he might have to work as a waiter, a cleaner, some such position that would not necessarily rob him of his pride, but which might, on the other hand, wreck his dreams. (One slips so easily into flowery language.) Could he see himself doing this? Also I knew that although he was always mentally engaged, he was physically idle.

'So where can I go?'

Abed tore a piece of paper into five strips and wrote on four of them the names of the aforementioned countries. On the fifth he wrote, 'No place'. He repeatedly folded the five strips of paper and then shook them in his cupped hands for the longest time.

'In the name of God I pick—'

Abed unfolded the bit of paper.

No place.

Abed tried again and got the same response.

'It's getting interesting, yes?'

Again, *No place*.

'Forget it!'

Abed threw the bits of paper on the ground. When we returned to Sulaymān's house there was only silence. We agreed to meet the following evening at a specific place.

'I'll be there, *inshallāh*, unless I have an accident.'

The Damascus I loved had become oppressive. There is a passage in Marmaduke Pickthall's remarkable novel, *Saïd the Fisherman,* which contains a passage describing a dream that the main protagonist has when he first arrives in Damascus.

> When at length he fell asleep it was to dream that the whole city had become solid, of a single stone, and that he was immured in a little cavity in the midst of it. The stone was populous, swarming with human beings who gave no heed to his cries. There were endless tunnels thronged with wayfarers, all bearing lanterns – a nation which had never seen the sun. The weight of the whole stone was somehow upon him. He called to Allāh for relief; but the thickness of that stone was inconceivable, and Allāh very far away.

The city as it appears in his dream reflected perfectly my state of mind just then. Curiously, this was for many years, long before I had read the book, a recurring dream of mine. My city of stone was not Damascus, however, but one I discovered down a small country lane not far from where I grew up. I knew the only thing that could possibly lift the weight hanging inside me would be to effect some reconciliation between Abed and Sulaymān, even if only a partial one. I would play upon Abed's strings as he had asked me to play upon Sulaymān's.

There was a thick dressing across the bridge of Abed's nose.

'Do you remember I said I would be here unless I had an accident. As you see, I had one. After we said goodbye last night, I tripped and my nose hit the pavement.'

Something in Abed's eyes told me the reason was otherwise. He had had a couple of stitches put in.

'What do you propose I do, then?'

'You could try plastic surgery.'

'No, no, I mean about my leaving Damascus.'

'Do you remember what you told me last time, that you would like to be an emblem of Damascene society, even if you were to be on the outside of it? And he who is on the outside frequently preserves what historically was on the inside; he holds dear what modern society has pushed down the chute. You and Sulaymān may be the only true Damascenes.'

'Yes, this is true, but there is another important aspect. The main Sufi doctrine is that God has created everything, including our deeds. Though this may sound illogical it is known and revealed by one's spiritual experiences and by God's manifestations through one. So we attribute our glory, deeds and successes to God and have no hand in them. The final stage in Sufism is when, due to God's manifestations, one reaches a stage whereby he forgets himself *and forgets that he is forgetting himself* because if he knows that he is forgetting himself then he is not forgetting himself, is he? One does not see oneself or other things, only God and His deeds. Ibn al-ʿArabī says this creates a dilemma in that one says one may achieve this state but also that it is God who creates this state. It is as if God is saying, "Do this and this, but I create what you are going to do; everything you do is preordained and I am ordering you." Our will is a drop in the ocean of God's will. This creates many problems for Muslims, and the solutions to those problems are understood not by the mind, but by the soul. As Ibn al-ʿArabī says, those who limit their knowledge to the brain only are pathetic because much vital information can be reached only by the soul. In the Qur'ān there is a verse: "God knows an atom and less than an atom and is capable of everything." At the time of the Prophet this did not make sense because the smallest thing discussed then was the atom. All scientists said there is nothing smaller than an atom, but now, in the twentieth century, scientists discover there are subatomic particles. This verse that contradicts Greek philosophy reflects an endless and ultimate God whose powers one's brain cannot grasp. Sufism is the direct personal treatment between a man and God. A Sufi has no spare time, for he is always busy thinking of God's wonders. A Sufi uses every breath, each action of his, every word – he uses all those things to bring himself closer to God. He thinks of the greatness of God's creatures, so that when he sleeps his heart does not sleep. In Sufism we do not judge people by their miracles because, after all, the devil can fly; we judge them by their behaviour. God might test a Sufi by creating something miraculous to see whether the man wants Him or the miracle. One famous teacher, al-Junayd, says that if only once you think you're better than anyone in the world then you are not even close to Sufism. According to Ibn al-ʿArabī, "If I despise you, I despise the deeds of God because all is God's deed." We should not take for granted that the Qur'ān comes from God or that Muḥammad is a prophet – we should be *convinced*.'

'So how does this answer our question?'

'Well, don't you see? Only after all this may I become an emblem.'

Whitish blood seeped from beneath the dressing.

'I did not tell you the truth earlier. I was in a fight.'

'Well, then,' I volunteered, 'we'll find the man who punched you and I will take revenge.'

'That's what I like, a Bedouin from London. The fact is, I'm to blame. What really happened was this. I love old magazines. I like to steal from them, take lines from them that later I pass off as my own. Sometimes I slip them into the letters I write you. This morning I bought from a street vendor an old magazine, out of which fell a packet of stamps. All of them were over twenty years old. Quite obviously, God had sent me these rarities so that their sale might pay my way to France. Only two weeks ago, I dreamed I would be going to France. A few months ago, I met a French girl who did not reject my compliments and she went so far as to give me her telephone number. We spoke for no more than five minutes, but I think my future may be with this girl. When I get to Paris what I'll do is phone her, saying I am in Damascus. If her response is positive then I will ring again a few days later, saying I am now in Paris; if it is negative then I will have been spared the humiliation of having to face her excuses.'

'A lie too soon,' I told him, 'and, besides, a man should not build his pyramids upside down.'

'What do you mean?'

'You are building your future on a single point rather than on a broad base.'

'Will you repeat this line, slowly please, so I might translate it into Arabic.'

Abed entered into his notebook the proverb I coined right there and then, for which henceforth I will demand royalties.

'So who bopped you on the nose?'

'Yes, I'm getting there. Anyway, I took the stamps to a philatelist who mockingly told me they were worthless. This news put me in such a state that I neglected to go for prayers at the mosque. This terrible oversight of mine resulted in a broken nose. Anguished and humiliated, tormented with the thought of this French girl and the stamps, I went to my friend's shop where I got into a boxing match with his eighteen-year-old helper. It was not serious to begin with, but because I was feeling wired I began to throw a few strong punches. Our play got out of hand. The other fellow smashed me in the nose and the scar from this will last forever so as to remind me of my folly.'

I told Abed that he was 10 per cent holy fool, 60 per cent philosopher and 30 per cent idle although perhaps I was being kind in not reversing the second and third percentages. When Abed was not being morose or spiritually inclined he buzzed with an exuberance bordering on madness. The following evening we went to a small restaurant I often went to, where the owner, the cook and the waiter all knew me. We always shook hands, both on arrival and on departure. Abed, for fun, addressed the waiter in a poor, heavily accented, Arabic. Whispering to me, he said nobody would be able to determine his nationality.

'Where am I from?'

'Yugoslavia?' answered the waiter. 'You have a European face.'

'You see!'

'Very good, Abed, very good.'

'What happens if I go to Greece, Sir Marius, and I see a woman naked on the beach? What will I do, then?'

'You are going to Greece?'

'Yes, maybe I will stay in a monastery there.'

'A Muslim in a monastery?'

'Yes, why not?'

'And the naked woman, where does she come from?'

'She'll be on the beach.'

'Which is nowhere near the monastery, I hope.'

Abed searching for his lighter shouted an order to the waiter to give him one. The waiter's face froze. Abed, in his excitement, did not notice.

'Okay, so the beach is one mile away. Will that be far enough?'

The waiter whispered something to the owner who then slowly got up from his table.

'Abed, what's going on here?'

The waiter flicked his lighter, pulling it back a little as Abed leaned to with his cigarette. As Abed continued to lean further forward the waiter kept withdrawing the flame.

'Oh my God, I forgot!'

'What did you forget?'

'I asked him for a lighter. A foreigner could never have mastered that sentence.'

'You're Arab!' the waiter said.

'Quick, Sir Marius, slip me your passport under the table.'

'You're crazy!'

'Hurry!'

I managed to retrieve the passport from my jacket pocket without anyone noticing. All eyes, even those at the neighbouring tables, were now turned on Abed.

'C'mon, how much do you want to bet I'm not a foreigner? 500 *lira*! Shake on it.'

Abed was becoming aggressive.

'Alright,' said the waiter, 'I'll bet with you.'

'Right, there you go.' Abed flashed my passport under the other's nose. 'Give me 500 *lira* now.'

'Abed, for Christ's sake!'

'Show me the passport then.'

The waiter made a grab for my passport while Abed quickly withdrew it, burying it under his jacket.

'First, the money!'

The owner glared at me. A question was written all over his face: *Who were we and what was our game?*

'Listen,' I whispered, 'I'll pay now, then we quietly leave.'

We slipped away without the usual handshakes and smiles. A silly prank might have remained so anywhere else, but here we were pulling from the same river the same floating books of magical symbols; the Praetorian Guard was everywhere. *The whole city was in a tremble*. The darkness was not dark enough to hide the luminous white dressing over Abed's nose.

'That was close,' he said, the seriousness of the situation only beginning to settle upon him. We went for tea at a nearby café and for the rest of the evening he barely spoke.

A few tables away, sucking at an unlit *nargileh*, sat the man with the yellow face. What was he doing here? The pretending to smoke seemed to be his one stab at intelligence. A waiter brought him tea free of charge. At another table, a couple of youths made taunting jibes. Compassion was *not* universal, then, not even here in Damascus. The youths had the mean and vacant faces one might find anywhere. Abed asked them to stop but they continued to torment the poor unfortunate. Occasionally, the man with the yellow face would respond with hideous, rasping cries, not directly at them or at anything in particular. And then, curling his lips like an elderly baby, he began to dribble. I wished then he would sing beautifully Allāh's praises.

SEVEN

A Desert Father

All clarity has come to us from the desert.

Edmond Jabés

The monastery of Deir Mar Mūsā is situated in the al-Jabal al-Sharqī, about fifteen kilometres east of Nabyk and, as the hoopoe flies, some eighty kilometres north of Damascus. A bumpy car ride brought me from Nabyk, a dreary town where seemingly few people smile, over winding dirt track to the edge of the Jabal escarpment, after which I walked for a couple of kilometres over a mountain of mostly pinkish limestone. The world just then was this salmon hue, the skies azure. If not exactly spectacular, the scenery accorded well with one's fledgling notions of a biblical landscape. Its character quickly entered the bloodstream so that even now, as I write, the memory of it enfolds me. One hears of the loopiness that affects religious pilgrims to this part of the world and while it is not difficult to empathise with or even to wince at them one thinks surely it must have been always so, for those who lived here, the saints and the prophets and, of course, 'the fools for Christ's sake'. As the scholar Peter Brown points out, the Syrian desert was particularly conducive to the monastic life, for here there were none of the extremes of the Egyptian desert where to live was to survive. There was just enough water and vegetation to eke out an existence. This area became home to odd nomadic figures, fools and 'grazers' who fed like beasts upon the sparse vegetation and, if they had to, they could easily make their escape. There is something in the physical here that *is* the spiritual landscape. Would it be folly to suppose that without these particular stones and these particular skies, monotheism would never have caught on? Why, otherwise, should three of the world's religions, all of them monotheistic, have fought over this arid zone?

As I approached Deir Mar Mūsā Father Paolo Dall'Oglio was coming towards me, his right arm in a black sling that looked well against his grey robes. A gladiatorial figure, physically built for wrestling both angels *and* antelopes, this permanently unshaven Jesuit certainly was one of God's athletes. Born in Rome in 1954, Father Paolo set upon his priestly vocation in 1974, and three years later came to Lebanon in order to study Arabic. In 1981, he studied Islam and Arabic at the University of Damascus, continued his studies at the Oriental Institute in Naples, there studied the Qur'ān in depth, and, in 1989, obtained his doctorate in Rome. After a number of visits he settled in Syria full-time, embarking, in 1992, upon the venture that in the annals of Eastern monasticism will forever link his name to Deir Mar Mūsā. Such is the affection he inspires in people, even in his critics, that to them he is simply 'Paolo' and as such I shall address him here. With him was Jens, the Swiss postulant whom I had met before.

'Are you the doctor?' were Paolo's first words to me.

'Yes, perhaps,' I replied, 'but not the one you're looking for.'

When Jens reminded him who I was, Paolo cracked a joke, something to do with poetry being a cure. Actually, I was relieved he appeared not to remember me. When we first met, two years previously, we had got off to a bad start, whereas now any wrong-footedness seemed to be of a rather more mundane nature. The previous evening, Paolo, while rounding up the goats, had slipped down a rocky slope into a crevice, fell hard upon his shoulder, and now after a sleepless night was on his way to the hospital in Nabyk.

'Go, Ḥudā is waiting to speak to you.'

Ḥudā, I remembered, was the frowning female novice with freckles.

The only entrance to the monastery complex is at ground level, through a narrow door three feet high, proof enough that self-protection was a major issue. The monastery, dramatically perched on a rocky promontory, was built on the foundation of a second-century Roman tower and still looks better made for defence than prayer. A fortress may well be the most appropriate setting for one of the Jesuit discipline. St Ignatius of Loyola (1491–1556), founder of the Society of Jesus, began his adult life as a soldier, suffered a broken leg as one, and brought a certain military rigour to the order he created. The view from the courtyard is very much as Richard Burton described it when he visited Deir Mar Mūsā on 28 September 1870. The mountains have contrived to stay in one place, and in the Jayrūd plain below the only difference he would notice is the presence of a couple of army camps, barely visible to the naked eye. On the far side of the plain are more mountains and beyond them the empty spaces which one born to a motorless age would need to cross in order to reach Palmyra. A couple of years before, Paolo and I stood on this spot, in darkness, quite unable to communicate.

So what had gone so badly wrong then? Firstly, I had arrived with *Lady* Ilona, who was evidently much younger than me. I was most definitely *not* involved with her, but then only rarely do facts accord with appearances. Whether intentionally or not, or perhaps led by the same imp of the perverse that would later guide me, Paolo, in his evening sermon, raised the subject of adultery, in English, for the benefit of the only two Anglophones there. As it was, my companion could barely suppress her giggles. Later, matters took a turn for the worse when, in the presence of a roomful of people, I told Paolo that it was my understanding that he was under investigation by the Bishop of Homs. 'You are in possession of more information than I am,' he muttered.

'Well,' I answered, 'such is the word on the streets of Damascus.'

I had been remarkably insensitive, though not, I believe, deliberately so. It was more a case of jangled nerves. Quite understandably, Paolo was evasive during the rest of my short stay there, not so much spinning circles around my questions as skilfully running forays in between the words themselves and then skewering them where they lay in sun-baked, waterless isolation. Clearly he was a victim of various misunderstandings and innuendoes. The question is whether a man who is constantly misunderstood is not to some degree a man who speaks in riddles or if he sees deeper into the empyrean than most people. When I asked him if he were seeking to create a new order, Paolo closed his eyes, breathed deeply, and, as though sucking every last trace of oxygen from my question, replied, 'Orders come from the West. In the East there are no orders.' I did not believe this to be wholly true, but the effect was dramatic enough to forestall any further enquiries. A full moon, suspended between mountains on either side, flooded the desert below with ghostly light, so that the world seemed to have but a single purpose, to be moonlight's fragile receptacle. This was Leopardi's moon, the one of 'Night Song of the Nomadic Shepherd in Asia'; it was also the setting moon of the last poem he ever wrote, containing that untranslatable line, *Scende la luna; e si scolora il mondo*, which, mirroring the dying poet's own hopes, roughly means that as the moon descends the earth becomes deathly pale, although one needs even more words in English to describe exactly how the earth is robbed of colour, how it blanches, as when blood drains from a face; the colour of Leopardi's poetry is the bleached white of bone. Paolo and I stood in that bright darkness, he, after some minutes of silence, adding to what he'd said earlier, 'For me there is no East or West', before quietly taking his leave.

As was my arrival now, my departure then was marked by a joke. The inner wall of the well, only recently constructed at huge expense, had collapsed. This was a deeply serious matter, for a monastery without water is a monastery doomed. 'I wish you well,' I said, waving Paolo goodbye. 'Wish me water,' he replied. I returned now to Deir Mar Mūsā, filled with memories of its haunting frescoes, the beauty of the Syrian Catholic Mass, the joyous laughter of some girls from Damascus who'd arrived the night before my departure, the melancholy words of Father Zygmund, the Polish Jesuit priest who brought them there, who, mustering phrases in a language not his, said that people because they are alone go with whatever befriends them, hence many of the world's troubles.

Ḥudā appeared and seemed to me disburdened of whatever it was made her frown so much last time. She glowed when she told me she was soon to take her vows. She would be only the second nun here. Ḥudā took me into the depths of the monastery, into a museum where, beneath a light bulb of the weakest wattage ever devised, I squinted at odd bits of leather, pottery, a fragment of Syriac manuscript and, most oddly, ancient wax from candles. She then took me into a deeper level which houses a library of between two or three thousand volumes, reminding me of what was once one of the monastery's major functions, to produce manuscripts. Afterwards, we left the main building and walked along the precipice to the dairy, Ḥudā's domain, where each day she made fresh yoghurt and goat's cheese. The smell had a sharp, pleasant edge. The monastery chores she told me were divided among people according to their talents and their physical capabilities. They awoke at six in the morning to milk the goats, of which there were approximately thirty. After an hour of prayer they had breakfast at nine, then did the daily chores until two-thirty, which was when the main meal of the day was served. The afternoon was reserved for free time, meditation or prayer, and then, at six o'clock, the goats again, followed by an hour's meditation in the church, Mass, a light meal, and, finally, bed. One day of the week was devoted to spiritual exercises, fasting and silence. This was organised on a rota basis, so as not to break the work routine. Ḥudā spoke to me of her early life in Damascus, of how, as a Greek Catholic, she was brought up quite separately from the Muslims, so that they seemed as strangers to her, something that struck me as incredible. Was it possible to avoid, and at so great a loss, the Muslim presence? She applauded Paolo's efforts in trying to bridge that cultural and religious divide. When she first came here it was only for a short visit. The simplicity of the monastic life attracted her, and she left her job as an agronomist or rather she brought her experience as one to bear upon this place. And looking at the barren landscape, both so lovely and so merciless, I asked her if she were prepared to spend her whole life here. She was. And yes, she would die here too.

The earliest evidence for when the monastery was founded is in the British Library, a Syriac manuscript, dated AD 575. The text, by St John Chrystostom, was written by Abbot Mar Georgias, Bishop of Palmyra, and a note states this was the property of 'the convent of Moses, on the hill called the Great Head', the name whose Arabic form, *al-Mudakhbkhana*, is still in use. Also, during excavations, some Byzantine coins were found, one of them dated AD 570, which, if not precisely pointing to that date, puts us in the right time frame. The present church was, according to a chiselled inscription, completed in 1058, and presumably stands on the site of others destroyed by sectarian violence. In the surrounding hills are numerous caves where the early ascetics lived, prayed and died. Burton found a number of skeletons 'placed within loculi of cut slabs, after the ancient custom of the country . . . and mostly sitting, still in the ecclesiastical position. One skeleton was wrapped in the Mas'h, a coarse canvas which touches the flesh, with silk outside.' Burton took measurements of the skulls, and, most intriguingly, concluded that at least some of them were those of women. Ḥudā, when I told her this, would have liked nothing better than a sisterly precedence. Although Burton's findings are inconclusive, it is not entirely impossible. Prior to the Maronite synod of 1746, there had been an Eastern monastic tradition that at times included both sexes, whose living quarters were frequently in close enough proximity to enable their inhabitants to pray together in the same church and to receive spiritual guidance from the same sources. In the frescoes of Deir Mar Mūsā monks and nuns are seen ascending to heaven together, and this may well explain other kinds of anxieties, descending to hell too.

Burton found little to admire in the frescoes, of which only a few would have been visible to him; the rest, until recently, were concealed beneath white plaster. 'The vilest of daubs,' he called them, the church itself being 'in the rudest Graeco-Syrian style.' Although their primitive style may not have been to Victorian tastes it appeals to modern sensibilities. Our palate jaded perhaps by too much formal beauty craves the imperfection of the naïve. The frescoes, mostly dating from between the mid-eleventh and twelfth centuries, comprise one of the earliest examples of Syriac Christian art in Syria and Palestine and it is certainly the most complete. Stylistically, there are elements here of an Oriental style that would seem to have developed independently of both Byzantine and Crusader influences. According to some art historians, the frescoes of Deir Mar Mūsā provide a valuable link between the early school of Aleppo art and the developed Christian style of the fourteenth and fifteenth centuries.

The six riding saints that adorn both sides of the nave, even if fragmentary, suggest how striking the whole must have been. St George we know only through his absence. A corner of gold saddle, the white belly of his horse, its tail, forelocks and leg muscles streaked with red and, beneath the hooves, a river filled with small pink fish are all that survive, but we know it is St George's white charger because the same image is found complete in the Krak des Chevaliers. The legend it depicts is of a youth from Lesbos seized by pirates who were now taking him to Algeria as a slave. St George upon hearing himself summoned in the boy's prayers descended on his charger, seized him, and returned him to his mother in Lesbos.

An impressive Last Judgement covers almost the whole of the west wall, its symbolic play of red and blue representing the fires of hell and the blue of heaven. A cross stands upon a golden throne inlaid with jewels, and either side of this are the four evangelists and six apostles. Beneath this, centrally placed, are Adam and Eve who act as intercessors for the souls of the saved. To the left of them sit the patriarchs Jacob, Isaac, Abraham and with them, as never depicted before or since, the Virgin Mary, all four holding in their laps the souls of the saved while to the right of them are four heretical bishops with black crosses stitched onto their white chasubles, against a background of leaping flames. The misery beneath them gets increasingly worse. Artistically, the damned get the best pictures. The most starkly powerful images are of two rows of sinners, the first depicting the wrongdoers with the objects of their crimes, a pair of scales, a knife, a couple of coins; immediately below, the figures have snakes crawling in at their ears, mouths and eyes. The mathematical sense visually conveyed here is that for every virtue there is a sin and that on Judgement Day they would find themselves confronting each other, as they do in the frescoes. Spilling over onto the nave are some stylish women, wearing costumes similar to what Bedouin women still wear, with red tears streaking their faces.

These frescoes alone are worth the journey to Deir Mar Mū sā, although they should not be allowed to outweigh in importance the church they fill with their message. It is with thanks to Paolo's zeal, his having raised money for their restoration, from both European and Syrian sources, that they have survived at all. It is ironic, of course, that this outstanding achievement should also be the cause of much censure. As we shall see, this helped create a climate of criticism in which it was argued that the monastery had become more important to Paolo than anything else, that when he was supposed to maintain a balance between his own desires and the strictures of the Church, he had become too attached to the place, even possessive of it. But Paolo, in returning to God what was originally done in His name, has made this a living church rather than a museum. If the community he founded were to be disbanded this could only be with tragic consequences. The world would be left with one more husk emptied of all significance.

Burton mentions a silver casket containing the thumb of St Moses the Ethiopian. Women wishing to bear children or to provide their husbands with male issue would come here, he wrote, and kiss the casket, which, I learned, is now in the Church of the Virgin in Nabyk and reportedly continues to feed the same hopes. What of the man whose thumb this was? My preliminary researches put me on the trail of a gigantic Negro slave who, after being turned out of service for bad conduct, took to a life of brigandage. St Moses made the frontiers of Egypt a hazardous place. Some time after, he took refuge among the Desert Fathers, and so impressed he was by their example he converted and became a hermit himself, one of many, in the desert of Scete. Later, he was ordained to the priesthood by the Patriarch Theophilus of Alexandria. Moses had a deep understanding, based on much experience, of man's nature. In the *Apopthegmata*, one of the most valuable sources for the history of the Desert Fathers, there is a story of a monk being tried by his brethren for some crime. Moses burst in upon the assembly lugging behind him a basket of sand that spilled out through the holes. 'My sins are running out behind me, and I do not see them,' he cried, 'and today I come to judge the sins of another!' According to another source, he was so tormented with sexual desire that he spent his nights carrying water to more distant cells. So despairing he was of overcoming his violent passions he consulted St Isidore who at dawn took him up onto the roof of a house. 'See,' Isidore told him, 'the light only gradually drives away the darkness. So it is with the soul.' Moses was later murdered, in 395, by infidels, probably Berbers, and was buried *not* at Deir Mar Mūsā, as I had been first led to believe, but at the monastery of Deir al-Barā mūs in Egypt. I had the wrong Ethiopian, the wrong Moses, the wrong century and the wrong place. I had confused St Moses the Ethiopian with *another* St Moses the Ethiopian.

Father Metri Haji Athanasiou, a Greek Catholic priest in Damascus and author of a five-volume history of Christianity in Syria, spoke to me of this other Moses, whose story, patchy though it is, has come down through the Syrian Orthodox tradition. What he said was later substantiated and added to by Paolo. This Moses was born towards the end of the sixth century, and, as opposed to the humble origins of the other, was the son of an Ethiopian king. Soon after his marriage, which he did not consummate, he determined to become a monk. Why did he decide to do so at this stage, rather than before? What horrors did the marriage bed hold for him? Or, perhaps being indecisive by nature, did he allow himself to be cowed into marriage? Father Metri, who considers his scholarly role to be merely to analyse what is put before him, said to me, with a shrug of his shoulders and not a little irritation in his voice, 'What can we know for sure? There is a sash in the church at Homs said to be the Virgin Mary's. Would you like some Nescafé?' The courtyard which his cell window looked onto filled with calls to prayer from the neighbouring mosques, and, because of the ricocheting effects of the enclosure they soon became a cacophony of meaningless sound that drowned out the birdsong and the gentle rustling of leaves. A few minutes later, he spoke pessimistically, along purely demographic lines, on the future of Christianity in this part of the world. Whereas now the number of Christians in Syria comprises roughly ten per cent of the population, by the year 2040 it will have shrunk to a mere one per cent.

And so, to return to our story, Moses, with the agreement of his wife, had the marriage annulled and, rejecting the responsibilities to which he was born, fled to Egypt, which was then the main centre of monastic activities. From there, we are told, he went to Jerusalem. This, according to Paolo, is interesting because east of Jerusalem there are a number of monasteries that closely resemble Deir Mar Mū sā, whose organisation, the *laura* or 'little footpath', comprises separate grottoes, where monks prayed and lived alone, dispersed around a central core of buildings that included church, kitchen and storerooms, all of which were connected by a network of constructed paths. Very few monasteries in Syria followed this semi-cenobitic pattern. From there, the story continues, Moses came to Kara, an important monastery not far from here, associated with St James the Cut. 'The Cut?' I asked Father Metri. 'In French', he replied, 'we say *intersice* which sounds better, no?' Father Metri took a historical detour here, describing to me, in vivid detail, the martyrdom of St James who, having forsaken his friendship with the Persian king, Bahrām, for the kingdom of heaven, was made to pay for his disloyalty by being slowly cut to pieces. Father Metri told me what was said by St James as his fingers were removed one by one, until finally he cried, 'I sing to you, O my Lord, on the ten strings of the oud, and I bless you because you found me worthy of losing my fingers, one for each of your Ten Commandments.' And so the butchery continued until he lay in many pieces beside the Euphrates. While his head went to Rome and some of his bones to Braga in Portugal the torso, we believe, went to Kara where a monastery named after him was built, and where, two centuries later, St Moses the Ethiopian makes an appearance. Moses left Kara, afraid of finding worldly glory even there, and came to these mountains to become a hermit. Presumably, there were soon enough hermits gathered here, as gather they do, for him to be able to establish another monastery. According to tradition, he was killed during the reign of the Byzantine emperor Heraclius, who, after waging war against the Persians, came to this area and massacred the monks of the Monophysite creed. If so, this does not accord with what we know of that heroic and ultimately tragic figure, and perhaps what Burton relates is true after all, that Heraclius had the monastery built over the remains of Moses. At some point the two traditions converged because both St Moses the Ethiopian I *and* St Moses the Ethiopian II share the same feast day, 28 August. To add further confusion the epithet 'Ethiopian' appeared only in the sixteenth century, and may have originated with a group of Ethiopian monks in Lebanon at that time. There still is, in a couple of Lebanese villages, a strong cult surrounding Moses.

There are many miracle stories of local vintage, especially relating to the issue of male children. Women, Christian and Muslim, still go into the gorge beneath the monastery and eat the figs of a certain tree. Also, there are miracles of a pastoral nature, relating to the safeguarding of the monastery and its possessions. There are tales of people who stealing grapes from the vines are unable to find their way out of this place until the stolen produce has been returned. The area surrounding and including the monastery was considered a divinely protected zone, but if so, what of the monks who, on several occasions, met with violence? What, I asked Paolo later, if his immediate neighbours were to rise against him?

As I sat in the courtyard outside the church waiting for Paolo to arrive, a turtle Ḥudā had earlier introduced me to, Gwendalina, consumed a leaf of lettuce.

Paolo returned from the hospital in Nabyk and was proudly displaying X-rays of his fracture, when suddenly we heard the sound of bells in the surrounding hills. The goats were coming from all directions, of their own accord, as though in penance for their earlier crime. 'A miracle!' said Jens, and on this Paolo, Ḥudā and everybody else agreed, yes, a small miracle.

'If only they would now milk themselves.'

If, in a moment of selfishness, I feared that Paolo's broken shoulder might prove a further obstacle to communication I was soon proved wrong. Although evidently in pain he had me follow him to a secluded spot in the valley where, amid stone and beneath blue skies, the only other living thing was a fly that flew about our heads in noisy, invisible circles. Later, when I listened to the recording I made, its sound occasionally sliced through our dialogue, like a circular saw ripping through plywood, obliterating a phrase here and there.

The French Jewish Egyptian poet, Edmond Jabés, spoke of the desert as the privileged place of his depersonalisation. And so it must have been for the early Christian monks who lived here, their consciousness slowly burned by the silences. I wondered whether Paolo, if not quite so rigid as they were, felt any particular affinity for them. 'Why the desert?' I asked him. 'Why make your vocation among stones?'

Paolo gazed into the distance.

'When I go back, in my weak memory, I see myself, aged

six, being taken to the hermitage of St Francis. I remember seeing there, at Assisi, this incredible stone upon which, I was told, the saint slept. This fascinated me. And then there was another holy place in Italy, Sacro Speco, the cave where St Benedict lived, where he spent three years in solitary prayer. So you see, these two acts, Franciscan and Benedictine, which contained within them the deeply religious, monastic life of Italy and Europe, began with stone. Again, when I was on my pilgrimage in the Holy Land, I spent twenty-four hours in a grotto beneath the Mount of Temptation. I was very young at that time, nineteen. I said to myself, in that grotto, "If life in this place, a life of constant prayer, is without any meaning, then the life of everyone is without meaning." It was as simple as that. I am still on this path, and although I put my enthusiasm into many things and activities it is with the conviction that this is a real life. And then, in 1981, I visited Deir Simʿān, the place where St Simeon's column was, and once again I was so deeply touched by the stone. Always this stone, this wish in me to make stone fly. Although I can say to you I was weighed by a desire to withdraw to this place, to Deir Mar Mūsā, these matters are difficult to express. But being where we are now, on this very rock, brings back certain early impressions. I came here many times, alone, at a time when the monastery was still in ruins and when there was little difference between it and the surrounding grottoes. When I first came here, in 1982, for ten days of spiritual exercises, I had to remove worms from the dirty water before cooking with it. Later, in 1984, I spent one week in a grotto beneath the mountain, in a closed cell where I was not too greatly troubled by flies. I broke my leg there. It was dark inside, and I could stay silent for a long time without seeing the monastery and without being affected by its condition and the desire to see it restored. I was looking to be close to God but also I saw the destruction of the monastery as a symbol of the destruction of the capacity of the Church to be present and to be able to speak to this generation. I had to accept this failure. I had to understand that human strength alone couldn't bring change and that it has to be with the active presence of God and the Holy Spirit. And so the end of these exercises took another form, in a desire given to me from on high to restore this place. Also, I had to fight my own activity and put it in the passive attitude before the greater activity of God. It was not always possible to remain at that level, when there were so many tensions and difficulties. So many questions too. Yet these questions of one's relationship to God were more interesting to me than those relating to modernity and ideology. You walk with something you do not know and from this you are called to something which is transparent, clear, without its being imposing, obligatory or authoritative.'

Transparency, clarity.

The American poet George Oppen wrote, 'Clarity. In the sense of transparence. Clarity in the sense of silence', and again, 'Clarity, clarity, surely clarity is the most beautiful thing in the world. A limited, limiting clarity.' When Paolo spoke of transparency I remembered being told on several occasions that Bedouins speak the best Arabic, which was why the poet al-Mutanabbī went among them, in order that he might purify his language. I remembered a Bedouin in Palmyra explaining to me how the desert air, the harsh way of life, the stars, everything in his existence, went towards a refining of the sensibilities. And it was for this reason, he told me, that poetic response is built into the Bedouin's everyday language. And now, listening to Paolo, I began to understand what this landscape meant to him in terms of language. Was this clarity not fought for among these same stones? And was it not so for the early Christians who lived here? And for the Jews before them, who, in the Book of Job and in the Songs of Solomon, gave us some of the world's greatest riches? Paolo leapt at this parallel, the desert as being a place for both the sharpening of faith and of language. I asked him if he remembered the precise moment when he decided this valley would become his home.

'In fact, it didn't happen quite like that, although my sense of belonging here was so powerful it would have been scandalous to leave. It was seven years before I could say what my conscience demanded of me, before I could freely decide to come to this place, with the conviction that somebody had to do so and that I was the one. I saw from the very beginning the possibilities of this place, the cultural and spiritual possibilities, the interreligious possibilities. This valley was so incredibly meaningful for me, represented a great synthesis of deep needs within me, and, as I understood it, the needs of this country and its population. So, in 1982, although I understood it would be very good if somebody came here to do this, I was in an important religious order. I could not do as I liked, as well as there being many years of study ahead of me.'

This led Paolo to the subject of what would be the most painful dilemma of his life. Although he did not wish it to be so he found himself in conflict with the Jesuit order, with whom he had recently taken his vow of obedience.

'I do not want to go too deeply into this question, and I thank you that you'll be so kind as to put it in a way so that any Jesuit reading these pages will not be hurt, that they will not feel I am a vain man and they are stupid people. They were faced with a huge problem. First of all, to what extent could they accept a man saying he had a mission from the Lord while still pretending to be in an organised, soldierly group? This was understandable. To what extent was it an answer, in modern society, to go into the desert? Was this what we needed, when we had so many pastoral needs to attend to? This, too, was understandable. And to what extent was it necessary to underline interreligious dialogue to such a level when even the Church appeared to be in danger of an earthquake? What do we say to this man who is too enthusiastic, who is *not* so very holy? Can he be called upon by God? The answer for a while was *no*, and this I accepted although with much pain. I found myself alone with my convictions. But, and this was most important, the dialogue did not stop, which was why, in the end, we understood each other much better. When you write of these matters remember there was love for the Church from both sides, love for our religious Society from both sides, love for each other from both sides. The conflicts were also with the local church, and, oh, there were so many conflicts. One was because of my bad character. Also, we touched upon nervous points but in fact there was also much effort in dialogue, not only from my side but from all sides, the Jesuits of this region, the local church and because of this we were able to clarify many points.

'The anguish was of two kinds. Firstly, when you feel something deeply in your prayers and the rest of the community does not think as you do, this is very difficult. I remember, God bless his soul, Bishop Edaby of Aleppo, a very important man for the Church in Syria, an open-minded, deeply cultivated man, and spiritual in the traditional sense. I went to him to express my anguish, and he, after shedding some tears, said, "I've never said this to anyone, but because of the inspiration of the Holy Spirit I want to tell you to go ahead." This was a great moment for me, confirmation from an authority who stood on the line of the apostles, on the line of the Church.

'The second anguish was of an even more violent nature, penetrating to the very depths of my soul. It was the strong reaction of part of the Christian population of this area, one that continues to this day. In restoring the monastery we probably committed a crime. We destroyed a symbol. The symbol is a destroyed monastery, a lost monastery. A symbol of what? At one time we were the most important religion in this country. At one time we were the majority. There was a time when we were the people in power. We have lost all this, which is why the monastery was in ruins. Yet there remains something of this feeling of power, which people, in terms of property, family and relationships, try their best to preserve. They still are attached to these images of power. So when you come and create, when you work in another mentality, what you do is destroy this symbol because a restored monastery becomes a symbol of something else. In many ways, my understanding of the whole issue is symbolical. The fact is, the monastery went out of their control, to somebody else with other ideas.'

This surely, I suggested, was something Christians would desire.

'It was not enough, not when my attitudes towards the Muslims were so different from theirs. The ecumenical aspect was not well received by those who insisted upon strict solidarity, a closed community, one that divides people into those on the inside and those on the outside, this pattern they have. We found ourselves in tension with them, but probably if we look at the larger pattern we will find those tensions wherever, in this and in many other churches.'

'And so for the time being you have been accepted,' I said. 'There's been a big change over the past two years, but isn't one of the main problems your having men and women in the one place?'

'Not so, not so!' Paolo answered in a voice that sounded like musical chimes. 'There are many such attempts being made in the Catholic Church today, although we have to organise things in such a way so as to not create scandal. I feel that the change of the male/female relationship that happened in this century has changed everything, including the monastic life and even, if possible, the hermit's life. Women are no longer a source of fear and danger. Some people feared something that was hidden in many of the best pages of the history of spirituality and culture over the centuries. There are many examples in history of monastic life, of women hiding themselves in monasteries just to be able to lead the same existence – Pelagia, a famous actress and courtesan, who converted, dressed as a man, and lived as a monk on the Mount of Olives; Mary the Egyptian, a prostitute from Alexandria, who spent forty-seven years wandering about the desert – there are many others. So there was already something of this in early Eastern monasticism, but in this century something new happened, with many bad things too. Humanity changed. There was a deep anthropological change, both in our understanding of the male and female aspects of life and in our discovery of what is common in the person, *before* we are men and women. As for our critics, it's another idea of women that they have. Although we are dressed more strictly than their daughters, they feel we are working on some other level, without a paternalistic structure. I am *very* paternalistic. This is my character, my ideology.'

'I can understand the Church must be fearful of allowing too much freedom, too much open-mindedness. Would you call yourself a liberation theologian?'

'You know, for me liberation is very important! Also, in terms of my spirituality, the Society is as important to me as these rocks and stones. There is nothing truly important that is not embodied in our Society. So for me, the story of Christendom is one of liberation, but to be open-minded in a philosophical way that expels from our symbolic word the presence of the spirit, the presence of God, this for me is not open-minded. This is perhaps *modern*, this is perhaps *illuministic*, this is perhaps deeply *atheistic* although one who says so can still remain a priest or bishop, but to expel transcendence from our life and to live out of good sentiment alone? I am scandalised by the attitude of European Christians who try to protect God from all accusation. "God is not responsible for our pain," they say, "God is not responsible for our worries; He does not gaze at the questions of everyday life; the problem between me and my wife is our problem alone, not God's; if a child is born sick this is not God's problem, etcetera, etcetera", so finally He is merely a symbol of very distant hopes, and is removed from the struggle.'

'So would you describe this as a new order?' I asked, wondering how Paolo's response would differ from last time.

'I do not like the word "order" because it is so very occidental. I have nothing against it, but look, this is a community. A community has a personality and is held together by a vow to agree to stay together in a certain way. Afterwards, it may spread, there will be other communities. It is not exactly the Western point of view, in which the community *is* the order and nothing else but a work instrument.'

'Presumably you would like to see this place continue beyond your own lifetime, but is there not some danger that without the rules that constitute an order the community can become whatever it likes?'

'I wrote some pages, more a description really of our intentions and desires, which concern our identity, which say, look, we started with an idea and now we must try to be faithful to it. We understand ourselves on three main points. Firstly, we spend time and heart in the relationship with God, to realise the fundamental and central aspect of our vocation as monks and as human beings. Secondly, there is our relationship to the earth, the material world and the importance that we, as an organisation, give to work. Thirdly, and I am strict on this question – some individuals have had enormous difficulty with this – we are here for the Muslims and for Islam. We must not be against them. We are here *for* them.'

'Do the Muslims appreciate this?'

'Some of them, yes, although we cannot say this is always the case. We do not pretend to have more truth than them, only that we have to be faithful to what God is doing with us, in making us attentive and pleased to look at and to understand something about Islam; at the same time He confirms us in our Christian faith, to be disposed towards Jesus, the one from Nazareth, once again this person, this man, this very particular reality. It is important for the Muslims too. There is a mystery in the Islamic religion, belief and symbols that is based upon Jesus coming back at the end of the world.'

'If, according to the Qur'ān, everything is contained within its pages, thereby making it a closed book, what possibility is there of dialogue with Islam?'

'When I speak of this I find myself between two points. The first is, what pushed me towards dialogue? It was a deep desire to be in touch with God and his truth. At the same time, this so deeply pushed me into trying to understand Islam that I can no longer say it confronts me. Islam is too much inside me, it is too much a part of my culture now, a part of my way of thinking and of looking towards the Word. So, in fact, the real dialogue is to be no longer as foreigners to each other but to be close, to understand each other as one would one's friends. So you can understand the opinions, ideas and feelings of the other, even without speaking. This is a good historical moment to pursue this. For the Church Islam is a big question mark. Somebody had to go into this question so deeply as to be within himself a kind of answer. I came to the East many years ago and started then, at the beginning of my formation, to pay attention to the Islamic world. I am not really sure if I understand myself any more. Am I just a Westerner, a foreigner, as people here sometimes sharply remind me? Yet I feel this valley has been my home, from before creation.'

'You have no desire to make converts of Muslims?'

'I hope that everybody connects to God, and then, I believe, God will show his mystery. In this respect, I understand the Muslims are out of this, but some of this mystery is seeded in Islamic spirituality, and what is needed is to be faithful. When the Jews reacted against Christianity that reaction was needed. The Islamic reaction is needed and will be until Christ returns. But there are the personal stories, another question altogether, in which everyone is free to go along the silk thread of his life. These people who convert from Islam to Christianity, from Christianity to Islam, this has to be respected. Each individual must be free to go his own way. I believe in this freedom.'

'I imagine you have been misinterpreted here.'

'A journalist said I was more Muslim than Christian, and he said, too, that I was seeking to create a mixture of both the Islamic and Christian faiths. What I actually said was on one level, the reactions to what I supposedly said on another. Although I gave my own opinions the good journalist put them down according to his own understanding. I had some explaining to do. I said to myself, when I read his article, "Somebody, if he is scandalised, will come and ask me about this." This is to say I consent to your questions, I give you these things freely, as I would speaking to people inside a church. You are free to go home and write whatever you like, but in a sense to interpret is always to misunderstand. I accept the game, but I

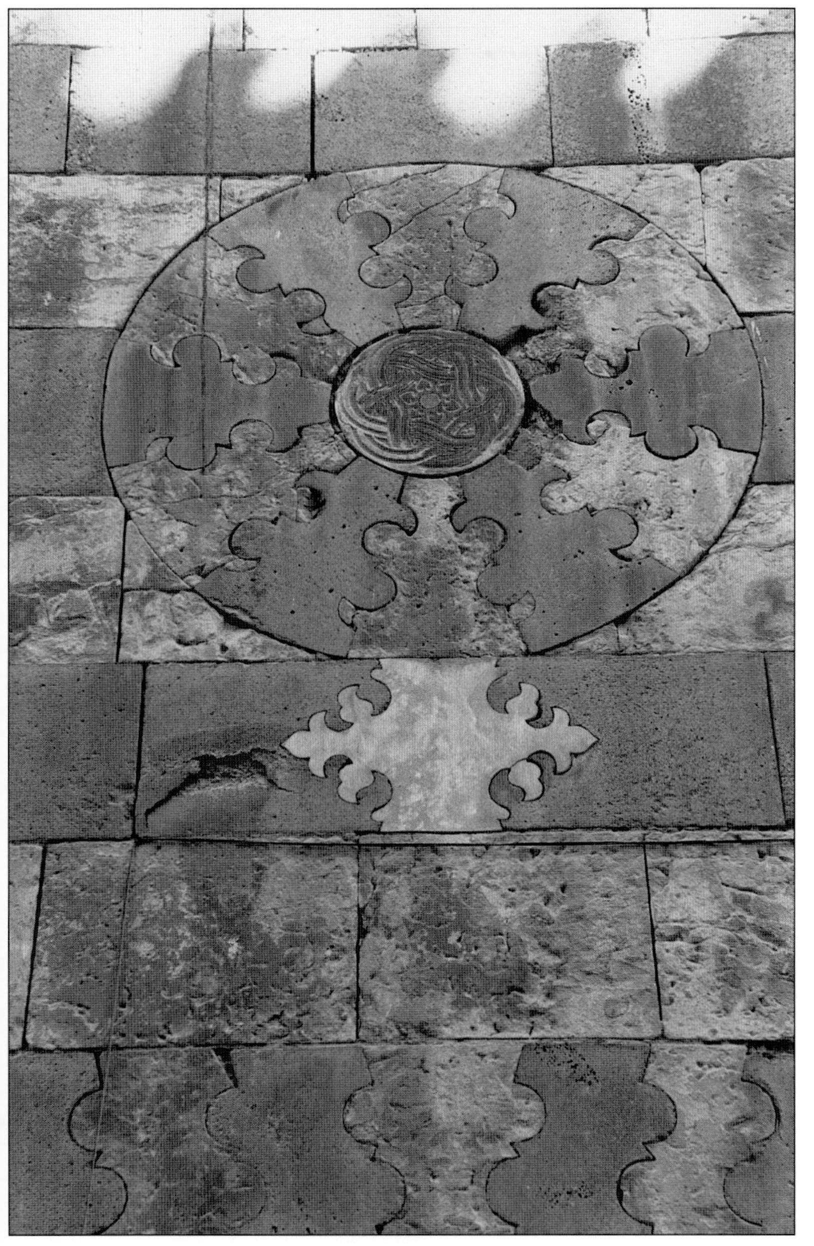

Wall, Damascus

Māristān Arghūn al-Kamilī, Aleppo

Citadel door, Aleppo

Damascus

Father Paolo Dall'Oglio

Detail of fresco, Deir Mar Mūsā

Deir Mar Mūsā

Saint Simeon

Ummayad Mosque, Damascus

Spinner, Damascus

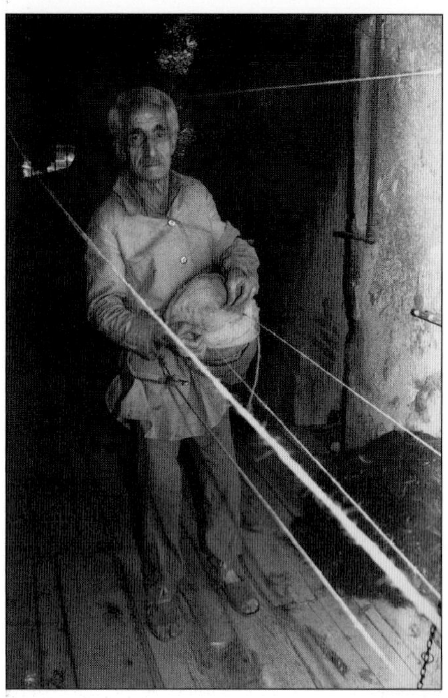

Abū Walīd

Muhammad al-Māghūt

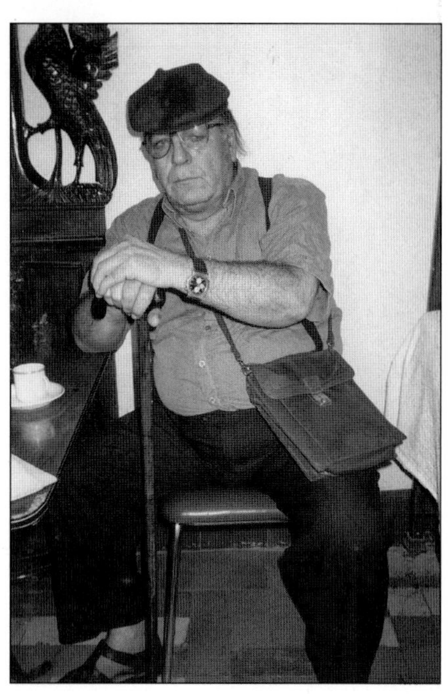

Nouri ʿAjamī

Left: Entrance to house, Ezra'
Below: 'The smell of gold bei
made . . .'

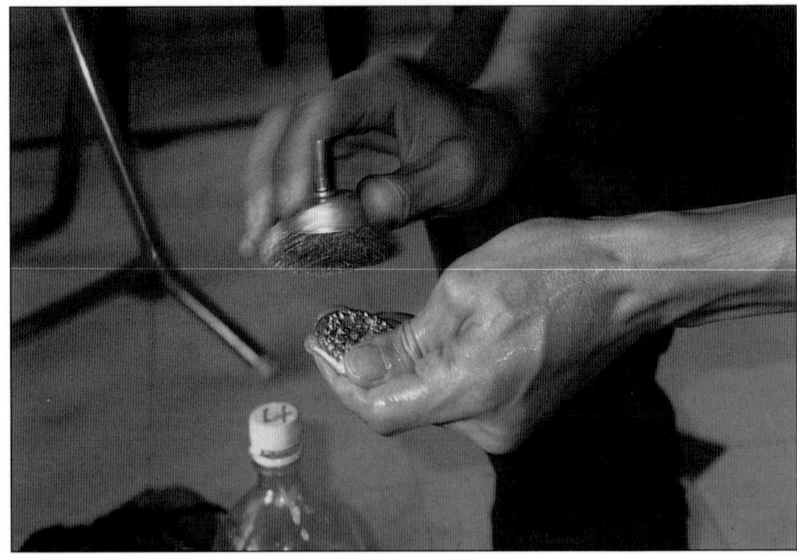

hope people will understand that what is written is not exactly the man, that there is always something more.'

'You are not afraid the Muslim inhabitants of Nabyk will one night rise up against you?'

Paolo laughed, somewhat nervously it seemed to me.

'It could happen if things were to suddenly change, if these people were pushed by others to misunderstand our intentions, or if we were to enter an occidental pattern of anti-Islamic attitudes.'

'There is, I believe, an important link between early Christianity and Sufism. When I read of the Desert Fathers and when I meet Sufis they seem to occupy much the same position. The Sufis are, of course, a bit outside the mainstream of Islam. The one thing that particularly interests me is the image of the holy fool who, although no longer a stock figure of Christianity, is still important in Sufism. I am wondering to what degree Sufism might have drawn from early Christianity.'

'You have opened a big question. Certainly, there is a relationship between Sufism and early Christianity but the Sufi way is very much based on the experience of Muḥammad although his was rooted in Christian and Jewish elements and also the Bedouin culture of that time. Even if not all aspects of Sufism are accepted in Islam, it is, generally speaking, looked upon as the very soul of Islam. As regards the matter of revelation, however, and of dynamic confrontation, yes, it was very much the same in early Christianity.'

'You said earlier that you cannot conceive of a spirituality that is outside the material world, but isn't that what Simeon Stylites believed he could find?'

'Simeon raised the material world up. He was not just flying, he was sitting upon stone. It is difficult to love without a body.'

'And yet the early Christians almost destroyed their bodies in order to communicate with God?'

'They felt heaviness was the product of sin. If the stones are heavy, are unable to fly any more, it is because of sin. So they fought against heaviness. The old monks fought, some of them for forty years, against temptation, bodily temptations, and only in a night of grace did God free them from their anguish. In fact, God showed them this was a bad way, but so generous were their efforts that really they are our fathers in these experiences. As we know, to fight bad ideas is so tiring and so useless, whereas to go with good ideas is more interesting. St Paul said, "Fight evil with good." This doesn't mean you do not have to be prudent. There is a time for everything. There are times when you are violently attacked, when it is necessary to be violent in return, but you have to know this is not the right way, only a strategic moment.'

'Would you say Simeon Stylites was wrong in his approach?'

'No, no! I am not judging him. He was trying to say to people, look, a free man standing on a column is more interesting than an emperor or a pagan idol.'

'And so he made stone fly?'

'Yes, in my opinion, he was consequential with his deep desire. He was not judging people, not telling them to get onto columns themselves. He was just showing himself. As with the artist we do not say he lacks humility because he wants to show his work. The desire to show comes out of the excitation born of the unity with truth. This has to be shown, this has to be made known, this must appear to everybody, like a couple kissing on top of the Eiffel Tower, saying "Our love has to be known by everybody!"'

'My friends in Damascus tell me that every action, every event, is somehow determined by God. Would you say, Father Paolo, that in early Christianity there was a much closer dialogue with God than there is now?'

'More passionate perhaps, in that men tried to understand and interpret all that was around them. They looked upon all that happened as being part of a greater pattern. It is like a family in which the love between a man and a woman is always the present element, in the choices they make, what to cook, whether or not to invite this or that guest. The love is always present and is the main element in decisions and choices.'

'What about spiritual healing?'

'There is another monastery, at Deir Mar Eliān near Qaryatayn, in the desert about an hour's drive east of here. The monks were taking the body of St Eliān for burial and where the animals pulling his coffin stopped the monastery was built in that place. To this day, mentally sick people, Bedouins mostly, attach themselves to the column of this church, hoping to be healed by this man in the night. You see, there is a parallel between the monastic life and spiritual/psychological health, and I believe that here we touch upon the question of fools for Christ's sake. Many who embark upon monastic lives come not from the spiritual life but from being psychologically weak. We come now to the source of this sickness, which is the lack of spiritual depth in our own society, our families, our relationships. This makes not only people but also a whole society crazy. Many weak people come here. We wish to do more for them, but first this will require building strength within ourselves. We hope to spread our activities to Deir Mar Eliān, and then, who knows, to Palestine, Kurdistan, Iran and Pakistan. To dream is for free.'

'How important to you are holy fools?'

'Many people tell me we are fools,' Paolo laughed, 'so they must be important. We accept that spiritual experience may take one out of what is normally correct behaviour. You may have seen we have an icon of a Holy Fool in the church, Saint Basil of Russia, who walked naked.'

'So you are a community of fools?'

'Yes, yes! On this we are all agreed. We have come to accept this. I mean everybody, in Nabyk particularly, is agreed on this.'

There was another question nagging at me. What precisely is the nature of happiness? Was not the great error of this century to believe that happiness may be grasped and held on to? What solution, if any, was to be found at Deir Mar Mūsā?

'I think the big misunderstanding of this age is the urge to *realise* yourself. In this monastery I try to teach myself and to impress upon others that there is a spiritual level at which you must give up even your own spiritual happiness for a deeper feeling that is not even the happiness of others, but rather to be consequential with your choices, to stay on the line of your life, to go to the end of your aim. That is the answer, to express the desire of God, although I think "happiness" is too weak a word for His desire. How do we imagine happiness, which is all in the desire to make others happy? God is happy to create happiness for others and to pay the bill. This bill may be high, especially when one refuses happiness. A psychological equilibrium is very important. Spiritual happiness, spiritual health, is very sweet, but you will never enjoy it if you are not able to give it up for something deeper. The realisation of your material or intellectual capacity, to be recognised for your gifts and your attitudes, is very sweet, but will never be realised if you are not able to give it up for something deeper. Your relationship with friends and loves is very important, very sweet, but will never be wholly so unless you are able to give it up for something more essential. And only when this being with God, in His essence and His desire, is at the centre of all of your desires, decisions and choices, only then will many things be realised, and will be far better and far deeper than you were ever able to imagine. The organisation of society, arts, culture, taking care of people, social assistance, all these are marvellous, worthy aims but you will never be able to do anything really interesting without this essence.'

As we reached the end of our conversation the sun had already sunk behind the mountain, its descent deepening the pink of the surrounding stone. Jens and the others would have finished milking the goats by now, and soon it would be time for meditation and then Mass, by which point all this would be in silhouette. Wishing to conclude as we had begun, I told Paolo that in old Damascus when people spoke to me of their love for the city, almost invariably they would mention its stone.

'You want to hear from me more about stones?' Paolo laughed. 'When the young people come here and they say to me, Father, teach us to pray, I say to them, look, choose a very nice rock in the mountains and seat yourself there. That rock will teach you everything.'

The following day the monastery was besieged with visitors, most of them on a day's outing, this being Martyr's Day, in remembrance of those who gave their lives for Syria, fighting against the Turks, against the French, against 'the Zionist forces occupying Palestine'. A busload of children arrived, a French class from Damascus, together with their teachers who were even noisier than they were. Later, Paolo spoke to the children in the church, in French, giving them a history of the monastery and its frescoes. I could not help but notice his young audience was visibly enthralled. This priest was not trying to speak their language, but in speaking his own, with sufficient conviction, was able to reach them. When they dispersed, still more people arrived. A Protestant couple unpacked sandwiches. Gwendalina backed inside her shell, ignoring the scraps of manna that fell from her heaven.

As I walked up the mountain towards Nabyk I waved goodbye to Paolo in the distance, but, with day trippers milling about him, he stood abstracted like a traffic policeman in Rome. A strong sun pushed the colour of stone towards white rather than rose. What would I take away from here? Apart from a memory of stone, would there be a slight softening of my critical attitude? When people say it is wrong to judge other people, usually they are judging whoever they're saying this to. I used to judge people by their words; as of late, however, I had begun to move in the direction of observing what people actually do. A man may easily lose his centre fighting the world, says Ezra Pound who fought with words until they fought him back into silence. As I looked back at the monastery, which Paolo's detractors say may be less God's than his, which only recently was a symbol of loss but is now a symbol of victory, I understood that sometimes, just occasionally, it indeed is better to follow a good idea rather than to fight a bad one, that a green shoot breaking through arid soil makes the best sense of all. As the crest of the mountain rose behind me and Deir Mar Mūsā sank from view I waved again, but Paolo who wears glasses did not see me.

EIGHT

The Prince of Fools

The one who cares about fools has seen the world.

Abū al-Ṭālib

When a fool dies Abū al-Ṭālib goes to his funeral because when they die fools are often alone. What he does is take care of fools; he feeds and even bathes them. And because he does not think of them as imbeciles, choosing instead to see in them something superior to what he has, shyly, surely, the fools of Damascus come to him. Perhaps they understand this man's kindness will not suffocate them, and besides, al-Ṭā lib does not make a show of his generosity. Ideally, according to the Qur'ān, one should give alms secretively, for only then are such acts free of pride. There may be one reward in store for Abū al-Ṭālib – he believes when he dies all the fools in Damascus will go to his funeral.

'He is something of a fool himself though not completely so,' Abed told me, 'but then everybody inside the walls of old Damascus is at least partly one.'

An observation often made about Muslims is that they become more beautiful with age. The elderly are a photographer's paradise. When I asked al-Ṭālib, who is not old but appears considerably older, if I could take his photograph he replied, 'If you were to do so now, at this moment, you might steal the beauty from my face.' As I put the cap back on my lens he added, 'But you can always ask me later.' Al-Ṭālib has quite the most extraordinary nose, a couple of sizes too large for his face and with a slow boulder-like curve. He is quick to point out that many great people, poets and kings, have this feature in their noses. If al-Ṭālib looks seventy rather than fifty doubtless it is because he spent many years in considerable hardship. As Abed would say, he has graduated from the University of Pain.

Abū al-Ṭālib looks after not only fools but cats as well, 150 of them, he claims. Each day he scatters pieces of raw meat over the ground outside his shop and any discussion with him is continually interrupted with asides to whichever cat has just made an entrance.

'Where are your children?' he asks one.

'Where is your husband? No, no, please, do not bring them here!'

Alertness fills his eyes. If a bird were to fly from a distant tree he would use this sooner or later in order to illustrate some point or other, for in his 'pills', as he calls them, what we might call parables, he continually draws from the natural world around him. A man more formally educated might have had all this burned out of him at an early stage. Al-Ṭālib has, if not exactly a mistrust of books, a deep scepticism in the faith other people place in them. A dismissive wave of the hand puts centuries of learning in the shade. There is a side to him that is quite unreasonable, but if we measure a man not by what he says but by what he does then al-Ṭālib is indeed wise.

Ibn Khaldūn, the fourteenth-century scholar, is careful to distinguish between those who are born fools and those who become so. The insane, he writes in his *Muqaddimah*, are those whose rational souls are corrupted and are but weakly connected to the body and the senses. The imbecile (*ahmaq*) and the possessed (*majnūn*) are deprived of sensual perception, but even though their condition destroys and enslaves them they do at times glimpse the world of their soul. The soul, corrupted though it is, may receive information that, in turn, the imagination transforms into utterance. 'Statements concerning supernatural things are also placed upon the tongues of the insane,' he writes, 'who are thus able to give information about [supernatural things].' Such perceptions as they have are a mixture of truth and falsehood. The old proverb, 'If you want to know the truth ask a child or a fool', remains true to this very day among certain people of Damascus, Sufis especially. The Persian mystical poet ʿAṭṭār, whose verses are filled with madmen communing with God, spoke of there being a special relationship between the madman and God, and that one should strive to understand the talk between them. Ibn al-ʿArabī who was much acquainted with fools and sought to learn from them said that God speaks through the lunatic, placing revelation (*tajallī*) in his heart and wisdom on his tongue and the fool being so absorbed is robbed of reason – 'They possess understanding without reason.' Scholars, poets and mystics frequently visited hospitals, believing they could find spiritual insight in the incoherent ramblings of the insane. Also, those with epilepsy, the 'prophetic madness', could tell the future. Of this Ibn Khaldūn writes, 'Lower than prophecy, soothsaying is a particular quality of the human soul . . . but the revelation he receives is inspired by devils or affected by foreign notions. . . . His imperfect contact with the supernatural results in a jumble of truth and falsehood.'

When Abed meets a fool in the street he asks him a question. 'What will happen in two weeks' time?' 'Should I follow this course?' 'Will she love me?' Usually, the question relates to particulars rather than to universal matters. Although the response he gets may be nonsensical when read in conjunction with the answers of other fools it may be seen to form a coherent picture. An observer may ask: Who imposes the pattern, the one asking the question, the fool answering it, or God?

When I asked Abed about his attitude towards such people, he replied, 'We remove from the madman his commitments. We do not, for example, expect from him a commitment to prayer. He is not judged because he moves in a limited framework of life. One must seek his weakness, and if he is to be treated you must respect the shock he has had in his life.

What corroborates our theory regarding fools are the endless miracles they have performed. We have the story of a fool who spat into a communal bowl containing beans, *ful*.'

Abed smiled at his own pun.

'People were disgusted, of course, and threw the contents onto the ground. A poisonous scorpion was then discovered in the bowl. The Sufi says a fool takes his knowledge and directions from God's throne – by comparison, we take our information from the ego. We take from the gutter, they from God's throne.'

The holy fool (*majdhūb*) is a person who has become so by choice or because there is something in his nature that draws him involuntarily towards God. An Arabic proverb makes the distinction quite nicely, 'The wise man understands the fool for he was once a fool himself, but the fool does not understand the wise man because he was never wise.' If, according to Ibn Khaldū n, the insane are lost and have no devotion a holy fool, on the other hand, may be devoted to God though not necessarily in orthodox ways. He is, on account of his folly, not subject to religious jurisprudence. Ibn Khaldūn writes:

> Among the adepts of mysticism are fools and imbeciles who are more like insane persons than like rational beings. . . . The information they give about the supernatural is remarkable. They are not bound by anything. They speak absolutely freely about it and tell remarkable things. When jurists see they are not legally responsible, they frequently deny that they have attained any mystical station, since sainthood can be obtained only through divine worship. This is an error. 'God bestows His grace upon whomever He wants to.'

If any of this seems exotic it is so only to the extent that we have removed the holy fool from our own lives. Long before the advent of Islam the Christian Middle East was a scene of holy mania. 'The prophet is a fool,' so says Hosea 9:7, 'the man of the spirit is mad, because of your great iniquity and great hatred.' The 'fool for Christ's sake', as coined by St Paul (I Corinthians, 4:10), was infused with divine madness and, after all, had not Christ himself favoured the simple in heart and for all his ignorance was not the fool thought, at times, to be the mouthpiece of God? According to Corinthians, 1:26, 'God chose what is foolish in the world to shame the wise.' The good insanity of which Plato speaks, the gift that comes from the gods, would become in both the Christian and Islamic worlds, to use Michael Dols's memorable phrase, 'the privileged mania of the holy man'. St Paul, in his Epistles, said that men should become fools for Christ's sake and in words that seem to span irony and spiritual truth declared, 'Let no man deceive himself. If any man among you seemeth to be wise in this world, let him become a fool, that he may be wise.' (II Corinthians, 3:18). St Paul was not, of course, a holy fool, but he did recognise how his words might appear as foolishness to the sophisticated Corinthians. It was for this reason that in the Middle Ages the fool was thought to be under the special protection of God. A man might willingly become a fool, of course, and appropriate the licence of the fool who had been made so by nature. Among the Sufis, for example, the appearance of lunacy is merely a disguise for deep religious discipline. It is beyond doubt that the early Muslims were well acquainted with the varieties of religious experience found among Christians – we may assume Muslim spirituality absorbed certain elements from Christian, but this is not readily demonstrable. We know, for instance, that the Arab tribes gathered about Simeon Stylites on his pillar. We know, too, that the eighth-century Sufi, Ibrāhīm ibn Adham, prince of Bakh, withdrew to the desert and was instructed there by a Christian monk. The Desert Fathers exhorted their followers to reject worldly wisdom as being a barrier to the truth of God's mysteries.

Although there is evidence of early Sufis having lived with and learned from Christian monks what they took from them was soon reshaped according to Muslim belief. While it would be folly to overstate the case, it surely is fair to say that adherents to both Islam and Christianity shared the same spiritual landscape. The Sufi ideal is not at all remote from the early Christian one, which is not to suggest that Christianity has somehow gone to seed but that the world it inhabits has changed rather more dramatically than the Muslim one. The fact that in recent times Islam has been forced, mainly from outside, into a political dimension may soon enough render it unrecognisable to itself. The holy fool is always news. What both religions shared, in the purest sense, was a desire to conquer pride and to renounce selfhood and as such the mad mystics of both Christianity and Islam frequently gave voice to the struggles of the poor, the sick and the crazed. The holy fool lived with them and to a great extent shared their fate. What protected him were his childishness, the purity and simplicity of his motives. Whereas the holy fool has largely vanished from Christian hagiography he remains to a strong degree an important figure in mystical Islam. Certainly he was a familiar figure in medieval Islamic society and Sufism was particularly tolerant in its attitudes, to the extent that a wide range of religious experience was commendable. 'Everything is folly in this world,' wrote Leopardi, 'except to play the fool.' (*Zilbadone*, II, 820, 1823). The artificial fool of court and theatre was able to mock with impunity the accepted order of things, but this, in a sense, was his apotheosis. As Enid Welsford writes, in her masterwork, *The Fool: His Social and Literary History*, the development of the idea of the fool 'is one of the products of that uneasy time of transition when the great medieval synthesis was shattered and the new order (if order it was) had not yet been established'. The fool has not fared so well since. He has been marginalised by Western society and, in many cases, is fodder for psychiatric care.

Abed spoke at length of the man he had come to revere.

'After my break with Sulaymān I came to look upon Abū al-Ṭālib as my teacher, even though he can be volatile at times. The other night he threw some people out of his shop. They were in despair, he said, and despair in others is something he will not tolerate. "Get out of here," he shouted, "and don't ever come back." Of course, they do. They *always* do.'

I rather suspected Abed had been one of those asked to leave.

Whatever constitutes a happy childhood Abū al-Ṭālib may be said to have had one. The environment he was born into was comfortable enough, there was sufficient food and clothing – but these are the woolly parameters beloved to makers of thumbnail sketches, which in the end may help produce some kind of portrait but say nothing of the subject's inner life. We know nothing of the details, the overlooked, sometimes unreasonable, pleasures and fears that go into the making of any life. The only irregularity in the fuzzy pattern we have, one that many people in this part of the world believe augurs a life of some importance, is that up to the age of five al-Ṭālib barely spoke. When he was eleven suddenly his world crashed – his mother whom he revered died.

'When Abū al-Ṭālib speaks of this, people listening to him weep,' Abed told me. 'I know, I wept too. "Your mother has died," they told him, but still the meaning of those words was not clear. It seemed as though she would return soon. The young boy pressed his hands to the door to block the passage of the coffin from the house. "Where are you taking my mother?" he cried. Only then did he begin to understand that the luxury of his childhood had come to an end.'

This was only the beginning of what al-Ṭālib would regularly refer to as his seven years of torture. Soon after, his father remarried. Al-Ṭālib's stepmother imposed every punishment on him, especially hunger. An unreasonable woman, she punished if not the imagined then the *want* of a crime. She kept the food locked away in cupboards, so that the boy would have to go to the market looking for scraps. After some years he met a girl, married her, and for a while they lived in his father's house, but because his stepmother made things impossible for the young couple they were forced to move. This resulted in divorce, for his mother-in-law would not allow her daughter to live in a rented house. Al-Ṭālib returned home. Although he was allowed a small room in his family house his father cut him off in every other respect. They did not speak for three years. Later, he met another woman, married her and together they produced five children. During this period, al-Ṭālib suffered another catastrophe. Abed, like so many Arabs (if one may so generalise), has an obsessive interest in the workings of fate, for there is nothing in this world that God does not determine.

'When Abū al-Ṭālib was doing military service he was involved in a terrible accident. He and a friend got into the front seat of a taxi. You've seen how they drive like Bedouins here. First, the friend sat in the middle, beside the driver. Then, for some reason, the friend decided he wanted to change places. Al-Ṭālib sat in the middle. A few minutes later, the car crashed and the people sitting on either side of him died instantly. Al-Ṭālib, badly injured, spent many months in hospital unable to move.'

It was during those seven years of torture that his shaykh embraced him. Up to that point al-Ṭālib had not been particularly religious. It was under the guidance of this shaykh that he set upon the extraordinary path that has made him 'prince of fools'.

'Abū al-Ṭālib goes to mental asylums, taking with him clothing, food and cigarettes for the people there. Sometimes he feeds them by hand, straight to their mouths. Among them was a victim of formaldehyde, with only two fingers, one on each hand. Al-Ṭālib fed him meatballs that he swallowed whole. The poor man would swallow one, then another, until finally he had consumed thirty-six meatballs. All this time al-Ṭālib was weeping. The nurses told him this man would go on storing meatballs forever, like a camel storing water. Why did he swallow them whole? It was because the nurses who fed him did not have the patience to give him time enough to chew.

'Abū al-Ṭālib has an obsessive love of Damascus, says the area from the Umayyad Mosque to his house which is only a few hundred yards, has the purest air in the world. The stones are a part of him, he says, as is every object here. The worst thing about prison, he imagines, would be if one were to forget the stone. Also, he is a man of many fears and phobias, some of them foolish in nature. Among his phobias are English people, who he fears will bring him ill fortune.'

'Will you tell him, in that case, a Pole would like to speak to him.'

Abed said he would try to arrange a meeting for me, with the man whose very name means 'kind-hearted one'. We went to see him. When I asked al-Ṭālib to tell me about fools he answered quick as a flash, 'The one who cares about fools has seen the world.' I asked Abed if those really were the words he spoke.

'Abū al-Ṭālib never says the same thing twice.'

'Abed, this is a line worthy of Rimbaud!'

'Yes, or Oscar Wilde!'

Al-Ṭālib took Abed aside.

'You are about to be put to the test,' Abed warned me. 'Abū al-Ṭālib has set a question for you. If you had three children two of whom were perfect but the third simple, to whom would you show the greatest love?'

The answer seemed obvious, yet I suspected it would not be so.

'I would say, to the one who is simple but not so that the others would notice and be made imperfect themselves, by what they would imagine to be an unequal sharing out of love.'

Al-Ṭālib winced.

Abed had warned me earlier not to complicate matters. 'With him you get what you get,' he said. 'Always remember, his is not the academic way but a vendor's, a man who knows the weight of things and their values.'

'God makes the fool because He loves him most,' al-Ṭālib explained. 'I would naturally love the third more. God loves all His creatures, and God loves the people who are generous to His creatures. If someone makes fun of a fool he will lose God's approval. The one who is generous to a fool ranks highly in His eyes. God, you see, has created certain people to serve His fools.'

I felt slightly admonished although not wholly persuaded. Who but a fool would measure love?

'Can you tell me any stories of fools you have known?'

Al-Ṭālib told me about how he went out once with his seven-year-old daughter. She had a twisted thumb, a distortion of the muscle tissues that required much gentle manipulation and for which apparently there was no cure. They bumped into a well-known fool called Baī who, pointing to the girl, asked, 'Is this your mother?' Al-Ṭālib did not find the question strange because he, too, has a funny nature. 'Yes, this is my mother,' he replied. Suddenly, without so much as looking at the girl, Baī grabbed her by the wrist and twisted her finger very violently. She started crying that God might curse him. Then she touched her finger and saw that it had healed perfectly. The tears on her face were now those of laughter. 'Father,' she cried, 'my finger is cured!'

Al-Ṭālib then told me another story about Baī. There were two business partners having a quarrel in a closed room. They agreed finally to part company when Baī arrived unannounced. 'Do not break up this business between yourselves,' he said to them. They were amazed, for how did Baī know what they were talking about? Naturally, for otherwise the story would be without a moral, the two men followed the fool's advice.

'What is the funeral of a fool like?'

'You find the atmosphere more serene and more calm than that surrounding an important man's funeral.'

'God loves the man who loves fools,' al-Ṭālib told me, signalling that our conversation had come to an end. When Abed asked if I could speak to him at greater length he said he would have to consider the matter.

Abed and I sat at the Nofara, drinking coffee.

'Everyone has a path in his life,' said Abed. 'What makes Abū al-Ṭālib's worthy? A sign of very elevated people is that their speech follows their hearts rather than their hearts follow their speech. In other words, you get fresh information from them, coming from the heart, which is the house of God. Prophet

Muḥammad, peace be upon him, says heaven and earth cannot contain me, but the heart of a believer does. That's why if you remind al-Ṭālib of something he said the day before he will have forgotten already. Everything comes fresh to him and is right for the time, in that place, in those circumstances, while in a different place and in different circumstances he'll have new things to say. With him there is never any repetition or boredom. You never get the feeling he is teaching you. This quality on its own requires much elevation for it means that for him the ego is finished. Once, when al-Ṭālib was a street vendor, he said, "Please God, I want a shop", not knowing when he made this prayer that the building closest to him would be his. Al-Ṭālib is a poet who does not write.'

'Is his Arabic eloquent?'

'Sometimes eloquence is a sign of a destroyed inner personality, of there being nothing there, whereas informal speech can be a sign of a refined inner personality. We have a proverb: "Give the baker dough although he might eat half the bread." That is, go to the expert on any subject, for if you try to do it on your own you might lose all of it. I am not a baker. Go to al-Ṭālib, even at the expense of his volatile nature, but from him you will get the bread. You might be exposed to insults but through him you will reach God. This too is Sufism. If, however, you stay in your seat of self-esteem you will remain where you are. Sufism is humility. If you do not smell a sense of humility at a Sufi meeting then you will know they are not true Sufis. Abū al-Ṭālib has been a follower of al-Rifāʿī for perhaps twenty years. Al-Rifāʿī said, "I have knocked at all the doors of God and I have found them busy. Then I found a door where there was nobody. I went through that door, which is the door of being humiliated for the sake of God. May I be damned if I say I am the teacher of any one of you." Which means he is not here, he is completely with God. What I mean by humility is that I am humble before you, before God who is in you. It is humility for the sake of God. I might be an emblem of Damascus, my glories may surpass those of other people, but I have no hand in those glories. God has given them to me. The one who is able to give them to me is also able to remove them in the blink of an eye.'

A couple of days later, Abed came to me with the news that al-Ṭālib had agreed to my request for another interview or, rather, he was prepared to impart knowledge.

'At dawn, he said, your silhouette came to him and the idea of what he would talk about exploded in his mind. It would be the summation of thirty-five years of his life, the intercourse of those years between the soul, the body and God. He says of this "pill" he's going to give you that if you were to drink three and a half litres of milk a day for the next 300 days this pill would be an equivalent. You will be spared time, exhaustion and routine. You will be given a lesson about "the prince of fools". Al-Ṭālib told me I would need 100 years of learning to be able to give a lesson such as the one he is about to give. But first, as Ibn al-ʿArabī says, "You who come from the mountain bring me a stone from there."'

'Which means?'

'You should take him a gift.'

'Any idea what he would like?'

'I did hear him mention some weeks ago that he would like a pen.'

Abed and I went in search of a pen, one which I insisted had to be worthy of the man it was being given to. The shop where Abed took me was closed for an hour so we slipped into the courtyard of the nearby Madrasa ʿĀdiliyya, where, until recently, the manuscript collection of the National Library was housed and in another part of which is the burial chamber of Saladin's brother, Sultan al-ʿĀdil Sayf al-Dīn or, as he was known to the Crusaders, Saphadin. This was the man of whom Richard the Lion-Heart said was his 'brother and friend', for they were the best of enemies. A considerable diplomat, it was he, not Saladin, who negotiated peace terms and who bluntly refused Richard's offer to take Palestine and it was he, Saladin's spiritual heir, who after his brother's death held the crumbling

Ayyūbid dynasty together. In what must be one of the more comical episodes of the Crusades, Richard offered him his sister Queen Joan's hand in marriage, promising that they should jointly rule over Palestine. A somewhat bemused Saphadin informed Saladin who upon hearing this exclaimed *Naʿam* (yes) three times, treating the idea as a magnificent joke. Meanwhile, and we can well imagine the scene, Joan flew into a rage with her brother, saying she would never become the wife of an infidel. Richard then asked Saphadin if he would consider becoming Christian. The suggestion was politely declined. Richard had ulterior political motives, of course, but these ought not to diminish our understanding of his affection for Saphadin. The times were passionate.

A turtle was wandering about the courtyard. Abed asked the attendant if the turtle had a name and when he found out it had none he gave it one. A turtle bearing my name now traverses the courtyard of the Madrasa ʿĀdiliyya.

A Frenchwoman by the name of Isabel accompanied Abed and me to al-Ṭālib's shop. Earlier, I had planned to take her elsewhere as an interpreter, for she spoke Arabic, but now there was this sudden change of plan. She, too, wished to meet 'the prince of fools'. She had a most engaging smile, though later Abed, always quick to spot the sadness in other people, would say, 'She does not smile from the bottom of her heart, but only from her face.'

Al-Ṭālib, blinking merrily, asked what her favourite number was.

'*Khamsa*,' she replied in Arabic.

Al-Ṭālib turned in bitter disappointment to Abed.

'*Khamsa?*'

They discussed the matter for a minute or two. There was a slight look of panic in Abed's eyes as he translated for me.

'Why five, Abū al-Ṭālib asks, when his favourite is six?'

Then al-Ṭālib asked Isabel what her favourite colour was.

'*Aswad*.'

This answer intrigued him.

'Black is the president of colours. It is, especially in dreams, a sign of leadership. The Prophet Muḥammad, peace be upon him, wore black.'

Suddenly, al-Ṭālib slammed shut the drawer of his desk.

'Five, why five?'

I saw now what Abed meant by his being occasionally volatile. Quite honestly, I feared Isabel's answer might dissolve al-Ṭālib's 'pill'. Instead, he bought some cakes and led us to his house. On the way Abed spoke to him of the turtle at the Madrasa ʿĀdiliyya, a detail that would alter the course of al-Ṭālib's talk, for the one he gave cannot have been the one he prepared, equal to 1,050 litres of milk. I remembered later what Abed had told me with respect to al-Ṭālib's unpredictability, his continually fresh approach to things.

'You have been chosen, otherwise you would not be able to speak to me,' al-Ṭālib began. 'The focus of this lesson is love, like that of the turtle which lays her eggs on a beach.'

We sat in a high white room with blue doors and frames. Al-Ṭālib's children crawled all over him as he spoke. A boy of about five snatched the turban from his head.

'This action you see is also included in this focus,' he said, 'for out of a son's love for his father he felt I would be too hot.'

Cigarette smoke spiralled above his magnificent, hawkish profile.

'The turtle digs in the sand and puts her eggs into a hole which she then covers and leaves. After twenty-four days, which is the time of incubation, the eggs hatch. So here, then, is the meat of our subject. She looks at the baby turtles in their shells, and in doing so she projects pure warmth and love. It is a giving which is both selfless and complete and for which she expects no reward. The eggs themselves are weak, vulnerable. They can do nothing on their own – they are the very essence of weakness. From this we may make an analogy. When you see weak, vulnerable men you will look upon them the way the turtle looks at its young. And by looking at people's eyes you get the knowledge you will not find in books. The eye discloses. Whatever one may try to hide in his heart the eyes will disclose.'

Abū al-Ṭālib got up and gathered some dishes. Ceremoniously, he put the cakes out and arranged tea glasses. I wondered if he were not stalling a little, working out in his mind the next stage of his lesson.

'So now back to the turtle. The turtle looks at the eggs from a distance. The rays of the turtle's eyes penetrate the soil and the shells of the eggs. This is proven to be scientifically true. When a hen has an egg which is ready to hatch she uses her beak to peck it open and life goes simultaneously to the chick inside. The chick uses the same hole in order to break the shell open. Once the chick breaks through the shell the mother hen looks at it with the same kind of warmth as the turtle does. But who breaks the eggs of the turtle? You see, both the mother and the eggs are weak and vulnerable. Remember, the eggs are buried in soil. So it is not the sun that hatches them either. God looks at the turtle and the power of His look is manifested there.'

Al-Ṭālib laughed, evidently pleased with his own improvisation. He poured the tea.

'This manifestation is light from God that goes to the turtle and which is then utilised in the look of the turtle. So the shells break open. The mother is so overwhelmed with happiness she forgets even her own existence. She is annihilated. The joy of crying is similar to the joy of laughing. A single tear can be the forgetting of one's existence. We think of the happiness in our own lives, but what she experiences is like the accumulation of all happinesses. When you feel the joy of a great love do you not lose contact with your own body? Have you never felt this?'

Al-Ṭālib was addressing Isabel who shaking her head said no, she had never experienced such a separation but then perhaps she had never been deeply in love. Al-Ṭālib's hands froze in a single gesture. The very air froze. Abed glanced nervously at me.

'Anyway, this is the feeling the turtle has,' he continued and soon a note of anger entered his voice. 'What makes me sad is that some people come and deprive the turtle of such love. They dig and remove the turtle's eggs for the sake of "environmental conservation", placing them in an incubation machine. The scientist hurts the mother's feelings and, as we shall see, the baby turtles' feelings, too. So now, they hatch inside this machine. What they miss is the look of their mother's love. The tragedy is that when the baby goes to the water's edge it grows up with a bad personality. It wants warmth and love, but is unable to differentiate between itself, its brother, sister and neighbour. Its character is to go to the water by any means, whether good or bad. As you know, a human being is two-thirds bad and one-third good. Our turtle has lost the balance. And so it is with us.

'What makes a fool? This depends on the amount of time God looks at him during the first four months he is in his mother's womb. If, during pregnancy, the look from God is provided for by the mother and especially the father then the good in him will be developed and the bad will shrink. The fool is someone who has taken a huge share of God's gaze. Because God looks at him for a long time he becomes, like the turtle's egg, very fragile. God uses the fool to feed other people. When one helps a fool he takes or steals from him good energy. As the good increases you yourself are being hatched. The one who helps a fool will enter a world quite different from that of his peers. It is one where the ego shrinks and good develops. The shell is broken. One sees a poor man, strange and unkempt, uncared for by people who have yet to be hatched from their shells. One who has been hatched sees beauty in everyone. And the greater the burden of the fool, the more disturbed or obnoxious he is, the greater the good will be in one who helps him.'

I asked Abū al-Ṭālib about those he has personally helped. Abed looked nervously at me, clearly desiring me not to interrupt with questions.

'You are greedy for knowledge, but this, I think, is a pleasant greed,' al-Ṭālib continued. 'Fools have no bathrooms. I met a fool once with splayed legs and who had probably never bathed in his whole life, who stank like one hundred toilets together, the essence of all bad smells since the day I was born. I had never smelled anything so terrible. I love perfume and I adore fresh air more than food and drink. The air of the old city is the finest in the whole world. This area was called the Valley of Figs long before the Umayyad Mosque was here. As a consequence of this man's smell I have never been troubled by any other smell since. It's as if you were to eat two kilos of sugar and then drink a cup of tea. You will not taste the sugar in the tea. Also, as a result of this experience I acquired a talent for bearing the problems of other people. And so it is with one who lives with fools. By comparison, he finds other problems in his life simple. When we entered the *ḥammām* my temperature rose and at the same time I felt a frozen line, a million degrees below zero, right down the middle of my forehead. When I removed this fool's trousers they were so stiff with dirt they stood up on their own. Can you imagine, they actually stood on their own! When I finished washing him the fool who normally did not speak clearly thanked me.

'The one who leads my kind of life will understand animals and see them all as beautiful and will be able to have a dialogue with them. Once, when I was very poor, I saw a cat between two parked cars trying to rip open a plastic bag. I asked her, "What's up?" She answered, "Please, open the bag." What do you expect from a bag lying in the street? Suppose it contained nothing but more rubbish? "Alright," I said, "I'll open the bag." I gave her a warm look and likewise God looked at me. A look like that of the turtle's. A weak man opens a bag and a weak creature waits to see what is inside. Such was the position in which we found ourselves. What I found inside was a whole leg of chicken, some bones and two pieces of bread. A cat does not eat bread, so I said to her, "The meat is for you, the bread for me." This happened during the seven years when I was collecting old bread in the streets. I would gather the pieces, dry them in the sun, and then sell them to farmers to use as feed for their cattle. Perhaps I exaggerate? When speaking to one who leads a very different life, for whom some of these stories are outside his reality, the one who speaks of such matters develops a habit for exaggeration. He tends to exaggerate so that he can get as much benefit as possible from the object he is dealing with, by which he means this life. So when I exaggerate in my love for you my heart is extended.'

'Are there fools you are unable to reach?'

'They live in another world. When I opened the bag I had but two seconds of this love. The turtle with a single look penetrates seventy centimetres of soil. So what is it like for the fool who gets a continuous look from God? Who knows what he is thinking? It is very difficult to reach him, for although he is physically with you he is not with you. If you wish to reach even a slight bit of his heart you must acquire some of his temperament. You must avoid him in the same way he avoids you. Why? So as not to make him feel you are a burden on him. Usually, fools do not look at other people, but stare at the ground. They begin to pick you out and then an intimacy develops. If you manage to enter his heart just a little then it will be easy to enter the hearts of other fools. And it will be even easier to enter a normal man's heart. But because most people want to receive rather than to give they do not give. The one who takes a lot, although he might think he is gaining, is really a loser. Fools give and never take because they are busy with the Giver, God. They are drunk with the wine of God. There is a poem, "The wine we drink is not of worldly grapes; it is the wine of God." So here we have the drunkard, the fool, who leads his life in ecstasy. How can a person who is not himself drunk deal with such a figure? What should I do in order to communicate with him? Although I may have not tasted the wine I pretend I am drunk too, that is, drunk in a spiritual sense. This is all one need do in order to communicate with a fool. As a result one develops a stealing nature. I steal from other people's knowledge. When you help fools and are warm and tender to them, God, looking at the fool, will look at you and so you too will become a fool. You will be as distracted as the fool is, with spiritual wine. The fool will feel this, so instead of you interfering with him he will come and interfere with you. I became a fool by my continual contact with them. So, you see, God takes care of the one who takes care of fools.'

What, I wanted to ask, of those fools who are not in ecstasy but in constant pain, who fill the air with their cries? I was thinking of the man with the yellow face. As though forestalling me, al-Ṭālib moved his hand through the air and brought it down heavily on his knee.

'Now the subject is closed.'

Abū al-Ṭālib had given much and I wanted more.

We must beware of the small coffins words make. If we should not romanticise the unfortunate, neither should we push him beyond the reach of our imaginative sympathies. A healthy society has a place for the fool, sometimes, as in many Mediterranean countries, at the head of the parade. If, for the sake of convenience, we hide away those whom we would rather not face we do so at a cost to ourselves. We lose the connection to the fool in ourselves. The painter Cecil Collins, a prince of fools if ever there was one, in his essay *The Vision of the Fool* writes:

> Where a real civilization exists there also exists some degree of reverence for the Fool in men, and an understanding of the vocation of the Fool, by allowing him to live and move through society, clad in the ironic beauty of his devotion and compassion to the heart of man. . . . A society that has lost its reverence for poetic imagination has in reality lost its creative pride in life; with this gone, it has dropped into the universal welter of a vulgar search for mechanical pleasures of an incredible stupidity, and has forgotten the immortal goal of life. Soon everything will be cancelled out. Our disillusionment will be complete. And from complete

> disillusionment there can come only two things; final decay and death, or the birth of a faith. . . . The artist is a fool, and Art is a cosmic folly by which purity of consciousness can be attained. For the Fool, the artist, and the priest, are the victims of the radiance of life. The true priest is a fool whose purity of spirit is the folly by which the world grows and becomes enlightened. But modern society, by its concentration upon Science to the point when it threatens to sterilize the growth and life of the human psyche, has outlawed the priest, the artist and the Fool; and has consequently outlawed an entire field of human vision.

A few days later, Abed met me in the street, full of some fresh enthusiasm.

'Sir Marius, we are going to Latakia!'

'When?'

'Tomorrow. You are going to be an actor.'

'A what?'

'I am in an acting troupe that a friend of mine has just put together. We have a guaranteed audience of 500 people. You are going to act as well.'

'As what?'

'We have yet to write the play. You can play the British ambassador. There's still plenty of time.'

'When's the play?'

'Tomorrow afternoon, at four o'clock.'

'You're crazy, Abed, I've never acted in my life.'

We went to the Nofara Café where together we worked out a scenario. Abed said that in the role of ambassador I would be in charge of giving out visas. Slow down, I said, was that not playing just a little too close to the bone? What about a Buster Keaton routine instead? I'd be a foreigner trying to figure out how to make my *nargileh* work. First, I would take it to pieces. And then try to put it back together again. I would put a match under the *nargileh*. Abed looked doubtful, as though this would be tampering with sacred knowledge.

'Now we must go to see the director.'

On the way to see him we encountered a fool whose eyes were rolled upwards. Anything Abed said to him elicited a giggle.

'Abū ʿAmr. He's very shy, very pleasant. Abū al-Ṭālib loves him. Only those people who know their value may ask fools questions. Last week, he saw a sign on me, a signal from God that I would go to Europe. I hadn't even asked him. The information volunteered by a fool is more valuable that the information asked for. Abū ʿAmr believes there is a role for me in Europe. You may ask him any question you like.'

I asked him whether I should go to Latakia. The fool gazed towards heaven and whispered his answer.

'Really!' Abed was thrown by the fool's response. 'Are you absolutely sure?'

Abed looked uneasily at me.

'Permission is denied. Allāh does not want you to go.'

'Perhaps He knows my presence would wreck the play.'

Abed and I sat down in a small clearing beside the Umayyad mosque.

'Well then, that decides it. You are not going to Latakia after all.'

A crescent moon hung above Saladin's tomb. The air was alive with the flight of a hundred swallows, a hundred darting silhouettes, their sound like the humming of a hundred gently struck steel cables.

NINE

Our Lady of Soufanieh

Vision is the art of seeing things invisible.

Jonathan Swift, *Thoughts on Various Subjects*

'Do you believe in miracles, Abed?' 'I remember asking myself once if I were not too restricted by logic,' he replied, 'and soon I realised many things beyond logic remain tangible. You ask me about strange occurrences of which there are many in this country and I hesitate in telling you about them because we should not focus on miracles but rather on what is tangible. This is the way of true Sufis – they focus on the miracle of persuasion. They bring, by means of logic, an infidel or someone who is adrift towards the truth. You hear of Sufis who run themselves through with spears or knives and of others who walk through fire. This is trickery, we know how it's done. Somebody asked Shaykh Nāzim once, "Why don't you fly?" He answered, "The devil flies. Are you telling me that if you saw the devil fly you would believe in *his* religion?" Shaykh Nāzim then said to this person, "No, my son, you must try to use your mind and be convinced by the ideas I present you with because the ability to fly is very trivial when compared to the power of the mind." So you see, the quest always is to be a perfect servant, not to perform miracles.'

Mr and Mrs Nazzour are perfectly ordinary people. When I first met them Nicolas, with the silent *s* in his name, was dressed in a white tracksuit and had about him the peculiar buoyancy of a basketball coach. The only thing missing was a whistle. Nicolas wore a wristwatch with a picture of the Virgin Mary on its face. Myrna was smartly dressed, somewhat distant, perhaps a touch on the shy side. Nicolas is older than she is, perhaps by a couple of decades. Of the three perfectly ordinary children they have, the two I saw were watching television. It's truly amazing just how much like you and me the Nazzours are, a fact that they themselves like to emphasise. I say this, knowing perfectly well how extraordinary, when properly revealed, most people's lives are.

Nicolas was, until recently, a goldsmith but this he gave up in order to become the manager of a medical and charitable centre, Oasis of Hope, where poor people, Muslim and Christian, may learn the skills whereby they might improve their lives. Myrna, born in 1964 Mary Kourbet Al-Akras, is a housewife; she washes the floors, gets the three children ready for school, prepares the meals and irons the clothes. She is a busy young mother and he a busy older father, both of them a little bemused at times, I imagine, by the normality they have had thrust upon them by rather odd circumstances. As I said before, Mr and Mrs Nazzour are perfectly ordinary people but they are so with a difference. Myrna is a stigmatic, she has conversed with the Virgin Mary several times, regularly emits pure olive oil from her hands and eyes, and the perfectly ordinary house where she and her husband live, in the Soufanieh district, a few minutes away from Bāb Tūmā, has become a regular place of pilgrimage. The door is continually open to people who come from miles around, from all over the world in fact, sometimes busloads of them at a time, in order to pray (in what was once the living room, but now a chapel) before the icon of Our Lady of Soufanieh, although surely many of them come to set eyes, perhaps hopes, upon the lady of the house. Were it not for the events that took place there and the added bonus of having in attendance the very person through whom such amazing things have manifested themselves, how many people would come? A public chapel inside a private house would be merely eccentric otherwise. If this is normal life, as both Nicolas and Myrna would have me believe, then I do not know what normality is.

Initially, I had resisted the idea of meeting Myrna, bearing in mind the words of a novelist friend of mine, a Catholic, that meeting a stigmatic in Croydon would not be the perfect introduction to an understanding of life in London. Also, I feel uncomfortable with such phenomena, finding in them and in people who dip their fingers into wounds of their fellows something repulsive. Yes, I might agree with this author and his Croydon principle were it not that in the context of Damascus, where so much seems strange, the story of Myrna seems perfectly plausible. So often in Syria things make perfect sense when seen close up and make hardly any sense at all when seen from a distance.

I approached Myrna by slow degrees, first asking people I met in shops and on the streets of the Christian Quarter what their opinion of her was. There was only one dissenting voice – 'a fake, lazy too' – and only a couple of people reckless enough to confer sainthood upon her. The greater number of people I spoke to said she was genuine enough and, yes, although they had seen the blood with their own eyes or had touched the oil with their own fingers they did not necessarily put their faith in miracles. They believed in God in any case and needed nothing more to support their faith, but a deeper analysis shows that underlying these events and yet to be fully addressed is an ecumenical matter of some importance. The responses of most people were by and large refreshingly sane, although sometimes madness and hysteria gnawed at the edges of this calm picture. After all, what is more vulnerable than a woman who is said to have performed miracles and whose address is available to the world at large? I had heard reports of near hysteria, when people overly keen to witness a miracle saw one where blatantly there was none, and whose frantic response, Myrna's husband told me, brought tears of bewilderment to her eyes.

I gathered the following statements from people in all walks of life.

'My uncle can't walk,' a young Catholic man told me, 'because of a deterioration of the muscles. Some people said to him, "Go, maybe Myrna will help you", and my uncle, only human in that he wants a cure, went to Mass at her house. The room was full of people – it was hot and stuffy in there. "Get me out of here," he said to the two friends who brought him, "I can't breathe." They got on either side of him and helped him up in such a way so as to not make too much of a spectacle of his departure. "Look," somebody screamed, "he walks, a miracle!" My uncle was barely able to escape. You see, I am Catholic, a Christian, but I do not need or even *want* miracles. She is a good woman, Myrna, but without meaning to she can do harm.'

'Myrna?' said a man selling pistachios, 'Yes, sure, she's for real.'

'I did not believe it was true,' a young woman told me, 'because the first I heard of it was when a *mukhābarāt* living in our apartment building told me.'

'Did he believe it was true?'

'Oh yes, he's Christian.'

A priest explained, 'God is saying through her we must pray together, especially at Easter, not as many Christian faiths but as one.'

'Our children go to school with hers,' said a mother of three. 'Our daughter plays at Myrna's house. We've seen everything, the blood too. She was asleep and nothing could wake her. A doctor tried to by pulling her fingernail away from the flesh. She felt pain only much later, after she awoke. She could remember nothing.'

'Two weeks ago, in the village of Heine,' a grocer told me, 'a silver icon of the Virgin began to shed tears of blood. There was a wound at her neck as well. Many people saw this. Such things happen in our country.'

'The Muslims believe in Myrna more than the Protestants do. In fact, many Muslims go to pray at her house.'

'If I insisted on understanding I would not believe.'

The Catholic Church's position on stigmata is cautious in the extreme. It has never defined their origin or nature, and never has stigmata been accepted as evidence of sanctity, although, of the several hundred stigmatics noted since the thirteenth century, St Francis of Assisi being the first recorded case, sixty-one have been canonised. The problem is rather more complex in this case in that although Myrna is Catholic, Nicolas is Orthodox and therefore, in the eyes of the Church, the house must be considered Orthodox as well. The Catholics of Syria, however, seem to have rather less difficulty with this than do those of Rome. Also, Myrna's is the first recorded instance of stigmata in the Middle East. Although stigmatics the world over have in common the wounds of Christ there are many differences in detail and in Myrna's case much falls outside the normal pattern. She is married, whereas stigmatics, the majority of whom are women, tend to be single; she has no history of a troubled childhood or of eating disorders; she was an outgoing girl who liked to dance and go to parties; she enjoyed tormenting her father a little, and was religious only to the degree that she did not disbelieve. Frequently, I heard her described as being *more* than normal, although really I can think of few conditions more alarming than a surfeit of normality.

I spoke to a number of clerics.

At Deir Mar Mūsā, Paolo told me that when he feels troubled he goes to Myrna's house. When I asked him whether the stigmata and oil were miracles or phenomena he repeated the question to himself, turning it over once, then twice.

'A miracle is always a phenomenon.'

'But is not a phenomenon something inexplicable that occurs in nature,' I asked Paolo, 'whereas a miracle is a definite sign from God?'

'All right, I accept this very orthodox definition. Whatever it is, it is always touched with meaning for the one to whom it happens. When I first went to see Myrna, I found a normal woman washing the floors and taking care of the children – a family, a home – in short, a good place for God to visit. The fact that pure olive oil really comes from out of her hands and her eyes is, in the end, a strong confirmation in itself, strong enough to create meaning, one that comes from the complex meaning of oil in our country. Olive oil is such a marvellous sign of abundance, a symbol of light, food, medicine, holiness, the oil with which Christ was anointed. What better sign can there be? Oil comes from her hands, *oil*, not something else – not *butter*, for instance – but *oil* which is so full of meaning for this place. When I first spoke to Myrna and again, in 1992, when she visited here, on both occasions oil came from her hands. Some pages of my diary still have oil on them. From that time on, prayer for me is oil – oil of prayer that comes from the heart, oil of prayer that comes from the hands, oil of prayer that comes from the eyes.'

'So you have no doubt this is a miracle?'

Paolo laughed irritably.

'Once again you address this matter in a way that is not mine. For me, the miracle is that we are speaking here together and feeling that God is with us. This is the real miracle.'

Father Elias Zahlaoui who sees Myrna most days and who holds Mass at her house is in no doubt whatsoever that this is a miracle. A kindly and warm man, he struck me as being simple in his faith, almost too much so to silence the doubter in me. While I do not question his integrity, and, after all, he has been closer to the situation and for longer than most people, I cannot help but wonder if his always being close to her is not a bar to objectivity. What must be said in his defence is that at the beginning he was deeply mistrustful of such manifestations. Father Zahlaoui was unsparing in his efforts to help me and was happy to verify many of the answers the Nazzours gave to my questions.

Father Metri Haji Athanasiou, on the other hand, was sceptical enough to make a believer of me. A man who wears solemnity like a cape, he pauses before such matters as if before a powerful cheese. When his credulity was strained or when he spoke of human foibles, such as those a wayward faith can produce, sudden merriment filled his eyes. 'They had, in the ninth and tenth centuries, this big enthusiasm for collecting relics, the bones of saints, the shoes of Our Lord, and even,' he roared with laughter, 'relics of the angels themselves.' Father Metri was nothing if not blunt.

I presented him with a copy of my book of poetry.

'Dear me,' he said, shying away from the offending object, 'there are two things I could never digest, canon law and poetry. When I was thirteen, in school, we had to write an Arabic verse.' The memory of this drew painful lines across his face. 'Please, please give it to somebody else.'

Haji can mean either 'saint' or 'pilgrim'. Father Metri's grandfather, a Greek, worked as a conductor on the train between Istanbul and Palestine. He met his Syrian wife in Damascus and settled there. He went on a pilgrimage to Jerusalem, and when he returned was given the surname Haji, 'one who has been on pilgrimage', a name shared by Muslims and Christians alike. So it would appear Father Metri, a Greek Catholic, was born a pilgrim. Also, he is one of the country's leading religious authorities and has written a five-volume work on the history of Christianity in Syria. A man pressed for time, he offered me glimpses of Eastern Christian life that we, in the West, have tended to ignore. There is little room, for instance, for the Eastern saints in our hagiographies. A number of them, such as Simeon Stylites, for example, present difficulties. We have little time for those who spiritually annihilate themselves, choosing instead those who have been physically tormented by outside forces. Father Metri skimmed through the pages of one of the books he wrote, showing me photographs and drawings of strange markings in stone.

'These are the marks hermits left behind in their caves. Each of them means something. I could tell you more, but you must understand I am very selfish with my time.'

In fact, he demonstrated the opposite. We spoke of many things – St Moses the Ethiopian, holy fools, Sufism and the future of Christianity in Syria. The subject of Myrna arose.

'We must not talk of holiness here, only phenomena. We are not talking about the lady, you understand. The oil is definitely genuine. You cannot deny reality. As a doctor of medicine, a physician, you can say there is something strange here that cannot be explained by scientific knowledge. There is something strange, yes, but now we must take that word "strange" and extend it to God's word. As a man of both faith and science, trying to be both objective and religious, I cannot deny reality. As for the stigmata, I was not against its being scientifically analysed.'

'What about the conversations with the Virgin Mary,' I asked, 'do we accept these or take them on trust?'

'Look, we have all the texts of those conversations, in Arabic and translated into French. The first thing we do is analyse these messages. If there is anything in them that goes against faith we can say they are false, but up to now in all of these teachings or sayings which, according to Myrna, were told her by the Virgin Mary there's been nothing against faith.'

'The problem must be that people want miracles and sometimes in their pursuit of them forget God.'

'Yes, of course!'

'Would you not say Myrna poses a danger to the religious community?'

'Look, for people who are aware of their faith, if it is strong and open, there is no danger, but for people who look for miracles only, without relating them to God, there can be deviation. I do not rely on miracles. If there is a miracle the Church must analyse and then judge it. There are many miracles in the history of the Church. Recently, I translated a book from French into Arabic about Lourdes. Of the 5,000 or so miracles that are said to have happened there, after analysis and after the judgement of the National Medical Board, the Church agrees upon only fifty-five.'

'Does the Vatican know about Myrna?'

'Sure, sure. But there is a critical problem. As you know, her husband is Orthodox. She is Greek Catholic. According to our law and tradition when a girl marries into an Orthodox family she must follow her husband's faith. Since these phenomena are occurring in an Orthodox house there is some sensitivity, a problem of protocol. The Vatican cannot give its judgement. Unfortunately, the Orthodox Church here in Syria is still not very enthusiastic for these phenomena or for the lady herself. According to my analysis, some Catholic priests have interfered in the problem and are generating publicity. As a consequence they have *baked* the phenomenon of Myrna.'

'You mean for their own ends?'

'No, there is nothing in helping this phenomenon along that will gain them influence. The problem is, the Orthodox authorities are not very enthusiastic because Catholic priests are putting their fingers into this matter. A Catholic priest used to go to Myrna's every day for prayer, to preach and to collect information. This, for them, is not a matter of jealousy or special goals. It is about reality – about truth more or less.'

'Could this result in a split in the religious community?'

'There is already a gap between the Orthodox authorities and the Orthodox lay people. Many feel indifferent towards their own authorities and go to the Catholic Church, to meetings with Myrna and so forth. For them the difference between Orthodox and Catholic is not a problem, whereas with the Orthodox authorities there is a move to become more orthodox, more fanatical. You ask whether a split is possible. If the Greek Orthodox authorities find enough determination to take against Myrna they may be subject to strong criticism, but I don't think there will be any split. Anyway, it is a good phenomenon for Christians, for Damascenes, not necessarily in a deep way but in a popular one.'

'If the main import of the Virgin Mary's messages is for there to be unity among the churches,' I asked, 'what of those who resist change?'

'What did I say to you earlier about Muslims and Christians? It is about the same for the churches in the Middle East. If we do not want this, then it is not yet time – it is not the right climate. Only if there is holiness, spiritual truth and spiritual detachment can we arrive at something, but not if we continue to be like this. If the Virgin demands penance, we must ask *what kind of penance.* A union of some sort between the churches could happen, not necessarily now or even in ten years, but only if there is holiness and determination on all sides and if they allow the Holy Spirit to work upon themselves. The problem is not with her nor is it with the phenomena. The whole problem of Myrna is finished for me. During the first six months I would visit her every day, sometimes twice. I collected information. Then I noticed the enthusiasm of several other priests who went to her regularly, so I said to myself, "I have my own work to do, let them pursue the problem." After those first six months, I never went again. I do not need to any more. I have my books and I need my time. I have heard the message, but for me it is finished. I have had to take the conclusions, the fruits, for my life.'

Nicolas was very much Myrna's spokesman, she, for the most part, confirming answers to questions that must already have been asked of her thousands of times. The story he related and which Father Zahlaoui's testimony and various documents and articles have supplemented is as follows. When Nicolas went to Sofia, Bulgaria in July 1980 he bought at the Alexander Nevsky Orthodox church a cheap icon of Our Lady of Kazan, framed in plastic and measuring 2.4 by 3.2 inches. The original icon of Our Lady of Kazan was venerated first in Moscow, in a cathedral that stood where Red Square now is, and when St Petersburg was made the new capital it was moved there. After the Revolution it vanished and was found again in 1970 in a sale. It is now at the Byzantine Chapel in Fatima. On 27 November 1982, six months and eighteen days after the Nazzour's marriage and on the eve of the first Sunday of Advent, this cheap replica began to leak olive oil. The Nazzours were frightened and confused. They stood the icon over a plate which the oil filled to brimming – precisely 150 millilitres. When Nicolas went to fetch some family members Myrna, left alone, heard a woman's voice, telling her not to be afraid and not to deprive anybody of the import of this event. Soon the first visitors began to come. Rumour spreads like wildfire in Damascus, and by the following day State Security had already heard of the situation. A police officer called Akram Abboud came, took photographs and made a report. Later, that same afternoon, he returned with three *mukhābarāt* and a government doctor, Ṣalība ʿAbd al-Aḥad. Myrna was given a bar of soap and told to wash her hands in front of them. She was then given a tissue, supplied by the police, and told to pray. Oil flowed from her hands. They ripped the icon from its frame to see if there was a hidden oil supply there. They took a hammer and smashed the corner off the icon. The oil continued to come. The agent said a quick prayer and since that day the authorities have left the Nazzours alone. The Minister of Defence, a Muslim, after having the oil tested in the army laboratory and in France and Germany said no scientific explanation could be found. It was 100 per cent pure olive oil, of a quality not found in the markets of Damascus.

'How did this affect your relationship?'

'I was afraid to touch her as my wife. She had become something holy, so how could I touch her? We began then to sleep separately.'

Nicolas spoke unabashedly of this troubled period in their lives.

'Father Zahlaoui saw there was something wrong. I told him, "I can't touch her", and his response was, "If God wanted Myrna to be single He would have appeared to her in her own house, when she was a virgin, but God wanted to place her within a family. This is a message for the unity of the family." We then resumed a normal life, but were unable to have children. After four years of marriage, on May the first, Myrna was in ecstasy and saw the Virgin who said to her, "I will give you a gift." We never thought this would mean a child. Our first daughter, Myriam, was a gift from God.'

Myrna sat on the sofa in silence.

'Would you like the stigmata to return?' I asked her.

'Yes,' she replied, longingly.

'Why?'

'Jesus promised to return when the Eastern churches are unified.'

'Did you feel ecstasy before the stigmata or after?'

'First, the Virgin appeared upstairs on the terrace, then I felt ecstasy, then the stigmata. The pain was terrible.'

'Did you feel the pain coming from inside your flesh or from outside?'

'It went from inside to outside.'

'Yes,' Nicolas added, 'something the doctors noted too.'

'Even though Christ would have felt the pain from the outside?'

'Yes,' said Myrna. 'I had pain all over my head, back and front. It was too painful to describe.'

'When you had the stigmata was there a smell, like flowers or perfume?'

'Like flowers. The oil smelled like perfume.'

'When the stigmata went did it leave a scar?'

'A very small red one, but unfortunately it disappeared within a few hours.'

'Do you think having these signs of God is in any way dangerous to the soul?'

'God is love, so there can be no danger to myself.'

'What do the soil and the stigmata mean to you?'

'The oil is a sign from heaven, to lead people towards belief. The blood is being at one with Jesus in His suffering. It happens only on Holy Thursday afternoon, and only when Catholic and Orthodox celebrate Easter at the same time. When they worship separately nothing happens. So this is a sign for unity.'

'What is your role?'

'I am only a messenger.'

The Virgin Mary made her first appearance on the horizontal branch of a eucalyptus tree at the edge of a small park opposite the house. A globe of light appeared and then a blue crescent high above. When that disappeared the Virgin appeared. At first She was sitting on the branch and then She stood up and walked through the air and through the iron railing of the terrace. She held in her right hand, between the index and annular fingers, a crystal rosary. When the apparition came to an end She moved backwards through the air towards the tree, and when back on the branch disappeared. A globe of light remained for a while afterwards.

'Tell me about your visions. Did you see the Virgin physically? What was She like?'

'Really, description is hard. She was wearing a head-cloth of white, a shawl over her right shoulder, a sash of blue. There was a strong light behind her. She was very pretty, oriental in appearance, dark eyes. In Europe, they always give her blue eyes.'

'Did She look like you expected her to?' I wondered how vulnerable to suggestion Myrna might be. 'Were you able to recognise her from any icons or pictures, one that you might have?'

'I did not expect to see her. When I first saw her I ran away. I was crying. Later, I saw her four more times. She did not resemble any pictures I have seen of her.'

'When She speaks, is it in Arabic?'

'Yes.'

'Does She speak a beautiful Arabic?'

'Yes, high Arabic.'

'She studied well at school,' interjected Nicolas, laughing.

'Did you hear the voice coming from her or from inside yourself?'

'Yes, this is important. The voice came not only from her, but from all around.'

'What were the intervals between seeing her?'

'The last appearance was on 24th March 1983. On 26 November 1984 I lost my sight for three days. After fasting for two days, on the third I vomited oil, then I felt ecstasy. Since then I have had thirty-three periods of ecstasy, the last time being in 1990. I have had the stigmata three times in fifteen years, and only when Catholic and Orthodox celebrated together. There has been no oil on the icon since 1990. In her last message the Virgin said there would be no more oil from that source, no more appearances and no more ecstasies until the Eastern churches have unified.'

'Were you together with Myrna when she had the visions?'

'The first time, no,' said Nicolas. 'The second time, I, *all* the people, watched Myrna. It happened at precisely the same time, before midnight, at 11.35. There was a light in her face. She walked upstairs to the terrace. We followed. We saw nothing, of course.'

'Did Myrna see the Virgin in the tree opposite the house?'

'Yes, She came from the tree. Myrna saw a ball of light and the Virgin emerged from this, came through the air, *through* not *over* the railing of the terrace.'

'Do people want only miracles?'

'Some people believe in miracles more than they do in God. This is something that happens in our society and in this house too. People expect always to see the oil, but sometimes it is not there.'

'Are they disappointed, Myrna?'

'Yes, sometimes. When it does come people run towards me to take oil from my hands. They leave God and follow the oil instead. This hurts me.'

I asked Nicolas if there were any danger of a cult developing.

'Something like this happened in Lebanon. And here, in Damascus, at the beginning of Myrna's experiences many people claimed to have similar visions, but those quickly disappeared. Now, everything is calmer. The important thing is that from her fruits comes the tree.'

'Do you get weary of all this attention, Myrna?'

'Yes, sometimes I want to be alone.'

'So do you ever consider this a burden from God?'

'Yes.'

'Are you ever angry with Him for giving you such a burden?'

'No.'

'Did you have a happy childhood?'

'As you see!'

'No eating disorders?'

'No.'

'Some people would say this is psychological in nature.'

'Yes, many doctors say this,' said Nicolas. 'A well-known psychiatrist from California spent four hours alone with Myrna. Afterwards, the door opened and he came out crying. *He* needs a doctor now!'

'So you do not think it possible that it is the unconscious working on the body?'

'No, no. Anything like that I would have seen long ago, even from before our marriage. My brother married her sister, so I knew her for three or four years before marrying her.'

'Did you think you would get yourself into such trouble, Nicolas?'

'No, but what beautiful trouble!'

Myrna announced she had to go to buy vegetables.

There was something in me that did not want to know about miracles. I had heard things, of course. A paralysed child walked; a young man carried his paralysed father to the house from which he then walked; a young woman was cured of blindness. I remembered what Abed told me, that the devil can fly too.

'Do you think these things, which some people call miracles, qualify Myrna for sainthood?'

'Oh, no!' said Nicolas. 'I would run away for sure. That would be enough for me! Myrna would never think like that. Here, in Syria, we have very poor people, simple people, especially in the villages. They come to visit Myrna. They call her "saint" and this makes her cry. You cannot give anybody this name, nobody can.'

'She does not want fame?'

'No, she is *more* than normal. See, she has gone to buy vegetables. I will tell you something. At the beginning, there were two old ladies who used to come here. One day they found Myrna mopping the floor. They were very angry. They cried, "How can you put your hands, those holy hands, amid dirty things? How can you do this?" Myrna replied, "I do not think the Virgin Mary has any servants in her house."'

'And in *this* house one senses a strange combination of the domestic and the holy.'

'A normal life, as you see. I wish all people could lead such lives. If everyone put God in his heart we would have no wars, no troubles, we would live in peace. The important thing for me is that after fifteen years I have peace in my heart. I used to be very worried about my future. I feared God would give me a handicapped son. This idea obsessed me. Now, the peace I feel inside is my capital. I found somebody to carry my burden with me. I no longer carry it alone.'

As I left the house a large group of pilgrims was enthusiastically making its approach. I wondered what Myrna would think when she got home to find a full house and what they would think when they saw her carrying a basket of vegetables.

I returned the following day to attend Mass. A boy of seventeen or eighteen stood beside Father Zahlaoui. At first, I thought he was severely palsied. I learned afterwards that when he was still in the womb his mother suffered an electric shock and when she collapsed damaged the foetus. The boy made strange guttural noises. When hymns were sung he would join in, spasmodically waving his arms. Later, when people queued up to take communion he assisted Father Zahlaoui by holding the silver plate for him. I was the only person who did not join the queue. When everyone was done there was one piece left on the plate. The boy came towards me beckoning me to take it, and when I declined the look in his face was one of deep puzzlement. Again he tried and again I refused.

A couple of days later, I got up early and walked through a still shuttered Damascus towards Soufanieh. As I passed through the Bāb Tūmā I turned right, towards a white domed building that contains the remains of Shaykh Aḥmad al-Hārūn of whom I shall write more. At the Nazzour house I had seen on the wall of the chapel a framed article, in English, probably dating from the end of the last century. According to this article a short stroll from Bāb Tūmā brought one to the Soufanieh gardens, which were beautiful beyond description:

> You almost feel that you walk on enchanted ground, the cool waters of the Abāna gurgling and glinting their way, while overhead the branches of the trees interlace and cast flashing shadows below. The poet [Shaykh Arslan] wrote: 'This region surely is not of earth;/Was it not dropped from heaven?'

The distance from heaven to earth has greatly increased. The gardens are now separated from the mosque by a noisy traffic circle, which took me several minutes to get across. What survives of the gardens has been subdivided by roads, paved paths and rail fences. A Ferris wheel and, most bizarrely of all, a blue aeroplane, a real one, fill most of what is now a children's playground. The aeroplane looked more like something dreamed than actual.

It was too early yet to descend on the Nazzour house. I sat in the small triangle of green, which is all that remains of the garden's former glories. There was only one other person who sat on a neighbouring bench and, to my eyes, seemed not to belong there. A row of huge eucalyptus trees stood between the house and myself. The Virgin Mary, I recalled, had stood on the branch of the one nearest to me and sailed through the air onto the terrace opposite, where now, among various articles of clothing, Nicolas's white tracksuit, as though a cotton ghost of himself, swayed on a washing-line. A pleasant breeze thinned the surrounding traffic fumes. Swallows dived in circles. The man on the bench kept looking over at me, although perhaps he was only returning my own suspicious glances. I, feeling more the spy than I imagined him to be, watched a couple of women enter the Nazzour house. I wrote some passages in my notebook, and recently when I went looking for them I discovered only a ragged edge where the page was. I have no recollection of removing that page. What those passages contained, I believe, was the description of a struggle, about whether or not I should go to the house and that if I were to do so, I would be punished in some way. Sometimes, as I was about to learn, pushing a degree too far into other people's lives makes one feel badly inside. There are people, of course, who are so habitually used to probing other people's silences they lose all contact with themselves, or rather, their own consciences. The conscience, if spirit terms may be translated into physical ones, has about the same consistency as soapstone, durable enough, except it can be carved into with the smallest of penknives. Always we run the risk of disfiguring our own consciences, but the good news is, that if done with sufficient thoughtlessness the discomfort we may feel soon becomes a small twinge and after a while is not there at all. We are then free to slay whomever we like. When I looked again, the man on the bench was gone. As I got up to leave, intending to retrace my steps to the Bāb Tu¯ mā, I turned instead towards the Nazzour house.

The older woman of the two I had seen enter the house a few minutes before now stood in front of the icon of Our Lady of Soufanieh. She began to shake. Suddenly, she covered her face with her hands and gave a low wail that rapidly swelled in size. The younger woman tried to console her. When the weeping woman came to sit on the bench beside me I gave her a tissue. Myrna appeared in a somewhat dishevelled state, pulling her dressing gown about her. She embraced and kissed the older woman. She then whispered to me, explaining that the woman was her brother's mother-in-law and that her husband with whom she always used to come here had just recently died. After a while, Myrna and the woman's niece managed to make the other laugh through her tears a little. When the two women left, my voice, for I believe it was mine, asked Myrna if I could take a photograph of her.

'What, looking like this?' she snapped. 'Another time.'

TEN

Sulaymān's Dream

Cease to boast of your reason and learning;
Here reason is a shackle, and learning is a folly.

Jāmī (trans. R.A. Nicholson)

At first I did not recognise him, sans turban, clean-shaven, in blue jeans and sweatshirt. Abed had told me to turn the corner of the street where I would find somebody waiting for me. 'Marcie!' Sulaymān embraced me, so tightly I could feel his heart knocking against me. We went back to his house in Ṣāliḥiyya, Abed following at a slight distance, stepping cautiously through the ruins of their old friendship. I presented Sulaymān with a piece of amethyst I'd bought for him in London. I couldn't think of anything else to give him, this man who possessed so little. Squeezing the stone tightly in his fist, he said he could feel its pulse. Abed, ever one to read significance into things, said he had recently encountered the English word 'amethyst' for the first time, in a poem by Oscar Wilde, and only now did he understand why it seemed important to him at the time.

Sulaymān told me he recently had a dream about me.

'You were sitting on the edge of my bed reading a book and in order to test my spirituality you kept hiding the book in different places, asking me where it was.'

I asked him if the rumours were true, that after his application for a British visa failed he had a nervous collapse.

'I went back home. The crisis started, waves upon waves of heavy pressure. At three in the morning I could no longer stay at home. I started walking the streets. I became insensate, could no longer feel my body. After four days of this, I was taken to hospital where I was given sedatives. I was there for one day only. The others always inflate details.'

Was it true, I asked, that he had found a means of making gold.

'Gold brings suffering into people's lives, so the quantities must be slight and used only for good causes. The only thing that might change for me is that I might get a new sweater or a car.'

'Is this not entering a world of illusions?'

'No, it is a sign of perfection to be able to make gold. An angel takes part in the process. The goal is not to make gold, but to reach this point of perfection. Then I will do something else. Anyway, it requires three days' work in order to be able to make one hundred grams, so not only is it tiring – it's not commercially viable.'

'Something tells me you're making a mistake.'

'It is folly only if one is looking for worldly pleasure, but I am not after this.'

'You might step onto a fatal path though.'

'A knife can be fatal, but you kill a sheep with it in order to feed people. I will use gold to benefit others.'

'I'm still trying to decide whether you're completely mad or sane.'

'I've told you many times, madness and sanity are the same. How can you reach truth unless you're crazy? Ibn al-ʿArabī once said, "See this *imam*. You think he is sane, but he is the craziest person on earth. He is a holy fool." Not every fool is a holy fool, of course, just as not every king is a king – there are different types, different statuses. God creates you the way He wants you to be.'

I remarked that I rather missed his Sufi clothes.

'I will wear them for you if you like, but I feel more comfortable in casual clothes. Also, I have reason to look as inconspicuous as possible.'

If what Sulaymān was about to tell me made sense at the time, the notes I made, when I looked at them later, were a meaningless tangle. I had problems enough absorbing the tenets of Sufism without having to go down some of its odder tributaries. Our discussion revolved around the Malāmatiyya, a mystical sect whose origins are unclear, but whose name is rooted in the word *malāma,* 'blame'. The object of blame was to be found in the Malāmatiyya themselves. Although they were Sufis they differed from others in that they sought to conceal their spiritual progress. Accordingly, the self was to be subdued, humiliated and punished; the Malāmatiyya even invited upon themselves the disapprobation of other people, so that while being despised by men they could completely lose themselves in God. Any demonstration of piety, including participation in public *dhikr*, any virtuous action or even the wearing of Sufi clothes, could be interpreted as ostentatious behaviour and so, although purity was to be preserved in the heart, the Malāmatiyya frequently became antisocial figures. A parallel can be found in the lives of many early Christian ascetics who went to great lengths, some of them becoming actors or rope-dancers, in order to conceal a deeply religious nature. This creates problems, of course. One Sufi writer, Ḥudjwīrī, although he believed the Malāmatiyya were sincere, saw in their desire for rejection the same flaw as found in those who seek popularity – 'Both have their thought fixed on mankind and do not pass beyond that sphere.' And if God alone determines who the Malāmatiyya are, if they really are His chosen people, chances are a good number of people will have imagined hearing their own names called. A.J. Arberry in his *Sufism, An Account of the Mystics of Islam* speaks disparagingly of them, describing the movement as 'this rather unsavoury development of "drunken" Sufism'. Certainly, there are stories of Malāmatiyya committing outrageous acts in public, anything from urinating to making love in the street, although probably these were not Malāmatiyya at all but Qalandarīya, such as one encounters in the *Arabian Nights*, and who certainly did go to such extremes. It is one of the more regrettable aspects of human nature to devise a loophole, a justification for doubtful practices, but Arberry appears to have either criticised the wrong people or else he described the movement as it was only after it had degenerated. There is little in the original precepts, as set down in the eleventh-century writings of Abū ʿAbd ar-Raḥmān as-Sulamī, to justify such a condemnation. According to him the Malāmatiyya are those who have achieved union with God, who were His highest grade of slaves, but who also lived according to the laws of the world.

So how did Sulaymān fit into this picture?

'When because of the oath I had taken with Ibn al-ʿArabī I re-entered the world there were thirty-five Malāmatiyya present. Beardless and turbanless, they wore modern suits and ties. They formed part of my vision but in reality they were dressed like this so that other people would not recognise them. The Malāmatiyya are the hidden and the innocent – they do not reveal themselves – you do not notice when they come and go. They are ordinary people to all appearances – educated, sociable, they marry and have complete lives – but they have total power in both ours and the other world. They are scientifically minded people who do not depend on or use miracles. If you perform miracles in their presence, they will say everything in this world is miraculous. They do not interfere in other people's lives and they do not have rules like other Sufis. Any power they have, they attribute to God. Why do they not perform miracles? They do not want fame because everything belongs to God. They save other people's lives without their noticing. The angel Gabriel knows them and so do all the prophets. St George is a Malāmatiyya with one thousand two hundred powers. One of these powers on its own is enough to destroy the world. There are thirty-five leaders of the Malāmatiyya. Ibn al-ʿArabī was one. You cannot properly read his books unless you are a Malāmatiyya. When I took the oath I became one of them.'

'Are you sure?' I asked.

'Without doubt!'

'Are the Malāmatiyya similar to holy fools?'

'No, to all appearances they are perfectly normal.'

'What is your role as one?'

'By helping other people or spreading knowledge of Ibn al-ʿArabī. The Malāmatiyya are like cashiers. A cashier does not own the money in the bank, but he is responsible for it.'

The question is, have there been any Malāmatiyya in recent times and, if so, would they so willingly reveal themselves? Malāmatiyya are about as thick on the ground as unicorns so perhaps I should consider myself fortunate in having been in the presence of one. Or was this, together with his alchemical pursuits, Sulaymān's latest folly? I wish in no way to cast aspersion over a figure of whom it can be said, as Byron did of Shelley, that beside him all other men are as beasts. I have never, not even in the most outlandish moments of our friendship, found quarrel with Sulaymān's sincerity. Later, I sought Abed's view on the matter.

'Look, we have already taken it for granted Sulaymān is a holy fool, so we mustn't judge his statements. I haven't seen him for eight months. The last time was when he had become a down-to-earth materialist. He kept saying money was important, which got on my nerves. It seems every time I see him he has a new personality.'

'I am still trying to make sense of our conversation. There is nothing in my notes that coheres, although what he was saying at the time seemed to make sense.'

'That's because he uses spiritual power. Sometimes a holy fool speaks nonsense in a way that makes you understand perfectly what he means. This is the power of Sufis in that they communicate "heart to heart" because, as the Prophet Muḥammad says, whatever you have in your heart is reflected in your face. There is another saying, "When you are in the presence of a scholar take care of what you say, but when in the presence of a Sufi take care of the heart's occurrences." A Sufi will hear what you say in your heart but, to get back to your question, when Sulaymān talks like this he tickles you.'

'So you think this Malāmatiyya business is a delusion. And, anyway, how can he know if he is one?'

'He doesn't wait to know. If this is what he wishes to be, then he behaves accordingly.'

'Surely, according to Sulaymān's own definition, the Malāmatiyya would never tell anyone—'

'But he tells! He *tells*. Why, I don't know. The conclusion of all my studies during my twenty-seven years of existence is that the human heart is unknowable. I don't know why Sulaymān is like this.'

'So when I write about him do you still think it's proper to describe him as a holy fool?'

'Yes, I do, but you should also know something Ibn al-ʿArabī said: "One can identify those equal in spiritual rank to him or who are beneath his rank but never those who are above him." Since reading this I have been spared much effort and exhaustion because I'd spent hours trying to find some explanation for Sulaymān's behaviour. We mustn't waste too much time in trying to find an interpretation for Sufi statuses or in seeking to determine whether or not somebody is a holy fool, because only top saints can recognise these things. One's attitude towards such people should be not to despise them, but to leave them as they are – do not interfere with them. Certain statuses will appear pure craziness in your eyes; some might appear to go against piety but, again, only in your eyes.'

'So in the years we have known Sulaymān, substantially your view remains the same, that he is a holy fool of some kind, although we cannot say *what* kind.'

'I am told he is a good person. Sometimes I reach the conclusion that really he is a bad person, but what I believe is different from what God knows. God always corrects. I am a weak person. So when the saints correct me, they tell me in a vision that he is good. The only clues I have, the only proofs, are metaphysical things – visions.'

'And *still* you won't speak to him?'

When I got back to the hotel that evening, I was told the Syrian poet Nizār Qabbānī had just died in London where he had been living for some years in a kind of exile. One would have to look to the Egyptian singer Om Khalsoum to obtain a measure of his popularity throughout the Arab world. This is perhaps an exaggeration, but certainly his audience extends into the hundreds of thousands as opposed to the millions the singer continues to enjoy from beyond the grave. All evening Lebanese radio played a tribute to him, which also included musical settings of his poems by the Iraqi singer Qazem al-Ẓā hir. All evening people spoke of little else and what preoccupied them most of all was the question of where he would be buried. After a strangely muted response in the Syrian media, it was announced that President Asad would send his personal jet to England to bring the body home.

The next morning I visited the house where Qabbānī was born, in the al-Ṣaghīr district, not far from the Street Called Straight, and standing near the entrance a boy of seventeen or eighteen was holding vigil there. A shy boy with intense eyes, he had come to Damascus from a distant village. When I asked him if he were a poet he said he hoped to be, which probably meant he already was. We were allowed admittance into the courtyard of the house. The rumour was that Qabbānī requested his body be brought first to his childhood home, although this was not to be. A couple of days later, which for a Muslim funeral was a couple of days late, I went to the Badr mosque in Malqī, in the new part of Damascus. Quite a few people were already there, including women in twos and threes comforting each other, artists and writers, and, of course, the *mukhābarāt* easily identifiable by their baggy jeans and mirrored sunglasses. An hour later, the funeral cortège arrived, a man at the front with a loudspeaker crying, 'Nizār, Nizār, you are our king! Our Nizār, we love you! Nizār, all of Damascus follows you!' The surge of the crowd was such that at one point, caught in a press of bodies, I was physically suspended in mid air. A public funeral is usually a passionate, somewhat dangerous affair although by and large there was little hysteria here; the tears shed were mostly quiet ones. Qabbānī's coffin with the flag of Syria draped over it was lifted to the entrance of the mosque, a sea of hands reaching out to touch it. The coffin was taken inside and only a hundred people or so were allowed in before the doors were slammed shut. There was a palpable anger in the air. I squeezed up the steps to where a furious man was pounding at the door of the mosque. After he gave up I went and knocked as I would at any door to any house. It opened a little and a policeman inside, mistaking me for a journalist, pulled me in and then immediately closed the door again. It seemed unfair that I alone should have gained admittance. As a salve to the conscience, I pretended to be what the policeman took me for. I took photographs and made notes. After prayers, the coffin was taken out the rear entrance of the mosque and from there was carried around Damascus on the shoulders of young men towards its final resting place. Qabbānī's poems blared from the loudspeakers and truly it did seem that for one day Damascus was under a different rule.

> And what is poetry if it cannot dislodge the crown
> Worn by the powerful kings of this world?
>
> ('A Very Secret Report from Fist Country')

I spoke to a journalist from Jordan, Rābiʿa Nāṣir, a deeply sensuous woman, either widowed or divorced, probably in her early forties. She spoke out of her pained solitude, although hers may well have been the voice of a million Arab women. She spoke to a complete stranger as probably she would never dare to a male acquaintance.

'A few nights ago I was in a dark mood, my whole body hard and tense. I took down Qabbānī's volume of poetry, *The History of Women*, and read his poem containing the lines, "I want you female because civilization is female" and another poem in which he asks to be allowed to hear the sound of an earring. I woke up the following morning, took a shower, brushed my hair and painted my toenails, which I hadn't done for a while. I wanted to feel soft, desirable and respectable. After I finished with my toes, I heard the news on the radio. My son had gone out to get pancakes for breakfast. When he returned I told him what had happened and he said to me, "Mother, you felt his death last night before the news came." Our culture says a poet is the salon of the people. The Arab people used to congregate in the market not just to sell but also to read their poems there. A good poem would be hung on the wall for everyone to see. We are a romantic people. Qabbānī broke all the rules of poetry whether it was in his discussion of women or politics. As women we are not supposed to talk about sex and politics. Qabbānī addressed Arab women in ways which they are unable to address themselves.'

Later, I spoke to the poet, critic and journalist, Nassreddin al-Bahra, a close friend of Nizār Qabbānī.

'I knew him personally. In fact, I boast of being from the same neighbourhood as him, in the heart of old Damascus. It is a distance of only fifty metres from his house to mine. I know most of his family. When Qabbānī was in hospital, in London, I did a half-hour radio broadcast on him and his work. Qabbānī heard this episode and was very pleased.'

'How would you assess his importance in twentieth-century Arabic poetry?'

'He specialised in two areas. Firstly, he dealt in courtship in a different way, different from any Arab poet in our history, both in the shape of the poetry and in its essence. We may find some resemblance to his poetry in the Umayyad age, in the eighth-century work of ʿUmar ibn Abī Rābiʿa which is similar to Qabbānī's in that he bravely expresses his adventures among women. Otherwise, nobody resembles him. Secondly, after the Arab defeat of 1967 he dedicated part of his poetry to politics. He criticised the Arab governments in general, but he didn't mean it personally because his aim was to awaken the crowd and to warn them of the problems in store from both the external enemies, Zionism and international imperialism, and the internal enemies, ignorance and the meaningless traditions that control people, not *all* people, but certain classes of Arab people. The most important influence that Qabbānī has had on Arabic poetry is that he destroyed taboos. Also, he gave poetry a new language and the dictionary of Arabic poetry was enlarged. Some fanatics and strict traditional poets consider this non-poetry. For example, none of these poets would ever have used the word *bustān*, which means the dress of a woman. Qabbānī writes in one of his poems, "Here are the woman's dresses which I neglected." There is a slang word *mishwār* meaning journey, which he puts into another poem. There are numerous such examples. Qabbānī was a school of poetry on his own, which was popular to the extent that I would say he was one of the very few poets in Arabic to have been able to earn a livelihood from his writing.'

'What do you say of those people,' I asked, 'who say his popularity is at the expense of psychological depth?'

'I disagree with this not because I'm a fanatical supporter of his but because if we look at his courtship poems we see he is a love poet first and foremost. Certainly, his significance as a political poet is limited but, contrary to what his critics say, Qabbānī understood women deeply.'

'The poems of Qabbānī, as opposed, say, to those of Muḥ ammad al-Māghūṭ, appear flat in English.'

'To approach the matter objectively, although I love Qabbānī I would say his poetry has a limited diction. Also, in general when poetry is translated we lose its beauty and significance.'

'And the tragedy of his wife's death, how did this change him as a poet?'

Qabbānī's wife, Balqī, was killed in a bomb explosion in Beirut during the troubles. The circumstances of her death are still hotly debated in the streets of Damascus and it was, as always, difficult to distinguish rumour from fact. A number of people said, 'Do you really suppose it was an Israeli bomb that killed her?' Whatever the circumstances, al-Bahra was not prepared to discuss them, saying only that it was commonplace for poets that when any one of them passes through a crisis he will remain tense until he expresses it in a literary work. The death of Qabbānī's wife occasioned the writing of what is probably his most loved poem, which is as political as it is elegiac in tone.

> I knew that she would be killed
> because her eyes were clear as two emerald rivers
> and her hair was long as a *mawwal* of Baghdad
> the nerves of this homeland
> cannot bear the density of green
> cannot bear the sight of a million palm trees
> gathering in Balqi's eyes
>
> ('Twelve Roses in Balqi's Hair')

I must confess that Nizār Qabbānī is a poet I have had to take on trust and even then I wonder if his reputation does not outweigh his abilities. The problems of translating Arabic poetry with its enormous tonal and verbal range into English where, for example, there is only one word for love are immense. This is not to suggest an Englishman is deficient in love, only that he might place greater emphasis on a misread train schedule. The translations of rather too many of Qabbānī's poems are perilously close to valentines. What is immediately lost is the music, of course, which I understand and accept to be Qabbānī's greatest asset. What troubles me, though, is how little the English words on the page appear to *contain*. I cannot imagine working them towards anything deeper than what is already there. There would appear to be sympathy for women, even empathy at times, but little of what I would call human depth. I wonder if the lady from Jordan was not, in her solitude, selling herself short by accepting too little. I run the risk here of coming into conflict with the Arab people, the majority of whom can recite his verses from memory, but then I have frequently heard from them similar expressions of doubt regarding a certain W.S.

Mount Qāsiyūn is a bare and rocky massif held sacred by Muslims, and because God is said to have spoken to it, it is blessed for all time. When the Day of Judgement comes and Christ, the Islamic prophet as opposed to the Christian Messiah, appears at the Ummayad mosque, at the minaret bearing his name, and from there sorts out the faithful from the infidel, the wheat from the chaff, the only thing to survive, according to legend, will be the mount overlooking Damascus. I sought in vain for a literary source. *Who* said it will survive? The oral tradition from which this may come is in jeopardy, of course, and will soon be the province of ageing scholars rather than of ordinary people. A shrug of the shoulders is often the only response to one's enquiries and at other times people will tell you what you wish to hear, but this is out of politeness rather than mischief. There is reluctance on the part of Arabs to say *no*, especially to a guest, and, for better or worse, this politeness is sewn into the very fabric of their discourse. The shame is that this should lead to misunderstanding at times, rancour even, between Arabs and Westerners. There is another story, though, about which everybody agrees. Hereabouts, the Prophet Muḥammad first came, and seeing the city of Damascus below was so overwhelmed by its beauty he declined to enter it, saying it was not for any man to enter paradise twice in one lifetime. Ironically, and here one pushes against Muslim reluctance to allow Christian ingress, what he would have seen in the distance were lovely Byzantine churches. Throughout the ages, all manner of holy men have prayed on Mount Qāsiyūn's slopes, and indeed some 70,000 of them are said to be buried there. According to Yāqūt, writing in 1225, Adam is believed to have lived at Beit Anāt and at the summit of the mountain there is a cave named after him; Eve dwelled nearby, at Beit Lihyā. There is another cave from whose entrance the prophet Abraham would view the stars, the sun and the moon, and from this experience, call it a mystical one, he drew his conclusions regarding the doctrine of the unity of God. This is described in *Sūra* vi, verses 76–8, of the Qur'ān:

> Thus did We show Abraham the kingdom of the heavens and the earth that he might be of those possessing certainty:
>
> When the night grew dark upon him he beheld a star, He said: This is my Lord. But when it set, he said: I love not things that set,
>
> And when he saw the moon rising, he exclaimed: This is my Lord. But when it set, he said: Unless my Lord guide me, I surely shall become one of the folk who are astray.
>
> And when he saw the sun uprising, he cried: This is my Lord! This is greater! And when it set he exclaimed: O my people! Lo! I am free from all ye associate (with Him).
>
> Lo! I have turned my face toward Him Who created the heavens and the earth, as one by nature upright, and I am not of the idolaters.

Abraham's birthplace is said to be at the nearby village called Berzé, but even devout Muslims say this is almost certainly untrue. It is not at all unusual for there to be several sites devoted to a single event and even a saint may inhabit more than one grave. It is fairer to say that the main purpose of such sites is often to *commemorate* rather than to *stipulate*. At the summit of the mountain is the place mentioned in the Qur'ān where Jesus Christ dwelt with his mother: 'And We made the son of Mary and his mother a portent, and We gave them refuge on a height, a place of flocks and water-springs' (*Sūra* xxiii, verse 50). Could this have been the scene of Jesus's 'missing years'? The biblical landscape is deeply suggestive.

The first time I went in search of the site where supposedly Cain slew Abel it was without benefit of map or guide. I persuaded a young Norwegian studying Arabic to join me on this crazy venture. If I had learned one thing from Sulaymān it was that folly is contagious – we would *feel* our way there. We climbed up to a road circumscribing part of Mount Qāsiyūn, little realising how close we were to the scene of the original crime. We looked down at the huge expanse of modern buildings that constitute modern Damascus. We could make out various hotels, the sports stadium, the grey bunker of the presidential palace to the right of us, but where, *where* was the Umayyad mosque? It was only after a while that I realised what at first seemed a blur in the vision was in fact a cloud of smog wholly obscuring the original site of the city with which, at a distance, the Prophet Muḥammad fell in love. Somewhere down there, hidden beneath a chemical haze, was Abū al-Ṭālib who believed the square mile containing the Umayyad mosque and his house boasted the purest air in the world.

We felt sure the place we were looking for was somewhere close, which in fact it was, and from there we sought directions. We fell upon several passers-by all of whom looked at us with bemusement in their faces. It was rather like asking after King Arthur's tomb in Milton Keynes. When the Norwegian's Arabic failed him he re-enacted the murder of Abel by running a finger across his throat. More than one person, perhaps suspecting our motives, backed away from us. A man gestured vaguely towards the western hemisphere. We began to hitch-hike and were instantly picked up by a couple of men who, appearing to understand what we wanted, drove us to the resort town of Bloudan, near the Lebanese border. We shivered in the back of an open lorry, quite unable to communicate our anxieties to the people ahead, taking us miles beyond where we wanted to be. The Norwegian told me he needed to get back home by a certain hour. Bloudan was a pleasant enough place, one that in England would have been packed with tearooms, bingo halls and fruit machines. The two men invited us for tea at their shop and, rather than display an ingratitude born of our own ineptitude, we followed them.

Our hosts raised the metal blind at the entrance to their shop.

We found ourselves inside a huge, almost empty, space in one corner of which there was a small table and four chairs, a gas burner, a kettle and some glasses, and, in the opposite corner, a ping-pong table. There was nothing else, not even an electric light, and the grand expanse of cement floor was bare.

'What do you sell here?'

'Baby food,' one of the men answered. I looked at the Norwegian and he looked at me. Was this invisible fodder for invisible babies?

'*Baby* food?'

'What did you say you were looking for?' asked the moustachioed one.

'The spot where Cain slew Abel,' we replied.

The two men held a short conference between themselves.

'Ah, Hābīl's tomb, you mean! Wadī Baradā. We passed it some way back.'

'How far?'

'Oh, close to Damascus.'

We drank our tea in silence.

'What do you do?' the other man finally asked me.

'I'm a poet.'

Yes, he said flatly, so was he. I couldn't tell at first whether he was being facetious or merely acknowledging the fact of a shared medical condition, but when he told me he had read a poem to President Asad on television only the week before, I knew then that no man would willingly fabricate such a tale. I congratulated him but he seemed not to care.

'Do you play ping-pong?' I asked him.

The panegyrist looked at me as if I were completely mad, as if that were *not* a ping-pong table in the opposite corner, as if I were blind to the stacks of baby food, as if I could not possibly be a maker of verses. I batted a couple of invisible balls, neither of which fell within reach of his comprehension. With nothing left to fill the growing silences, we bid farewell to this Theatre of the Absurd and took a slow bus home. Any faith the Norwegian might have had in me was not going to be tested a second time.

This time I was better prepared. A tour guide operator,

impressed by the fact I wished to visit the site, took me for free: Qubbat al-Arbaʿīn was, he said, one of his favourite places. The scene of the world's first murder was in fact on the northern slope of Mount Qāsiyūn, just above the area adjoining Ṣāliḥiyya. Abel's tomb, on the other hand, was where the poet and his friend said it was, at Wādī Baradā, on the way to Bloudan. The mosque of Qubbat al-Arbaʿīn is built on the site of what was an eighth-century church and is now in the middle of a military security zone. The stone with which Cain slew Abel has been replaced by weaponry of a more sophisticated nature. The stories of Cain and Abel, as related in the Qur'ān and in the Old Testament, are substantially the same, although the Qur'ānic telling of the burial of Abel is poetically an improvement on the biblical one. After murdering Abel, Cain did not know what to do with the corpse, for there had never been one before. 'Then Allāh sent a raven scratching up the ground, to show him how to hide his brother's naked corpse' (*Sūra* v, 31). Cain took note, and so buried the body of his brother, this being the first burial in the history of the human race. It is not unreasonable to suppose that the story of Cain and Abel, as with so many other legends, was built on more than just a germ of truth. It has been argued, most convincingly, that the conflict between the brothers reflects the age-old tensions between settler and nomad. After all, their story was still being enacted in the American West not so long ago.

Although the distance was not great, I was drenched with sweat by the time we climbed up to the rounded stone steps, which is all that remains of the original church. Just inside the entrance a sprightly old man offered us a slice of watermelon. Adnan Kabalan, a regular visitor to the place, explained to me how he and many other young Syrians joined up with the British when they came here in the 1940s. It may have been Second World War elsewhere, but for him it was still the period of French occupation. The reason why the Syrians loved the British more than the French, he said, was that while the latter occupied Syria for years they did nothing for the people whereas the English people were generous and helped them in their battle for freedom. 'We fought the French with stones and the British helped us. We fought them because we were hungry and because they said of us, "If they don't have bread, let them eat cake." We had neither bread nor cake.'

It seemed only proper that this old warrior, with his doubtful borrowings from Marie Antoinette, should be where his forbear cast the first stone. Adnan Kabalan said he came here often because, in this most holy of places, he felt a powerful sense of peace. What an irony, then, that we should have found ourselves in the middle of a military security zone.

Miṣbāh Ṣafī, whose first name means 'light' and his surname 'net', was the seventeen-year-old son of the keeper who was away ill at the time. One could see from his awkwardness he was still feeling his way through the role that would one day be his. The position of keeper is a family one, passed down over the generations from father to son. The keeper at Saladin's tomb, for example, is a direct descendant of the first one and the same was true at Mecca, where the keepers of the Kaʿba have been of the same family since the time of the Prophet Muḥammad, but here, on the northern slope of Mount Qāsiyu¯ n, the last keeper but one had died without issue, thereby breaking a chain extending over many centuries.

'How did they choose a new keeper?'

'It is not an official appointment nor is it exactly a religious one, although there are holy people buried here. Whoever he is, he must be a good Muslim, he must pray and hold the Qur'ān in his heart and in his mind, and he must be prepared to obey rules.'

'Will you be happy to remain here for the rest of your life?'

'Yes, of course.'

Miṣbāh took us through the mosque's various compartments that included a long room where there were forty recesses in the wall, representing the forty unknown prophets who perished or simply vanished in the Cave of Famine. An inscription at the entrance to the cave reads, 'You who enter here, wishing to be one of those forty will never be so because you do not do as they did. They underwent hunger and were very close to God. If you wish to be like them just do as they did. They spent much of their time without food, spent whole nights praying to God; they lived apart from people and spoke but little. In everything they did there was the desire to live in and with God.' One story has it that they had one scrap of bread between them, which they kept passing from one to another, none eating of it, until they all perished of hunger. Taking us into the cave, Miṣbāh pointed to a deep crevice in front of which was a screen and sniffed at the opening, inviting us to do the same.

'The holy forty disappeared through here, nobody knows where to. You can still smell their musk.'

It was the old socks smell of any cave I'd ever been to.

'This is also the Cave of Blood,' he continued, 'so called because it was here the first crime on earth took place. And because it was the first crime the mountain itself was astonished.'

Miṣbāh pointed to a second, deeper cavity in the wall.

'This is the mouth of the mountain. This, you can see, is its tongue, the gullet is there, and here at the front we have the teeth.'

Somebody had been quite liberal with the red gloss paint covering the teeth and the area forming a shelf in front of them. I didn't ask if this were the original blood. Miṣbāh touched the ceiling of the cave, saying that here one could trace the imprint of the angel Gabriel's hand, made when he pressed it there in order to prevent the roof of the cave from falling on Cain's head. It was God's will that this be the first crime and that humankind should pay the consequences therefore Cain had to be allowed to survive. It is said that if one person kills another this act belongs to Cain who carries upon his shoulders all the violence we have done to each other. And it shall remain so until the last day when God separates right from wrong. Miṣbāh said one could trace in the stone, with the tip of one's finger, the word Allāh. We were invited to do so. If God in His anger made the rock collapse why, I wondered, would one of his angels work against Him? It was an argument I chose not to voice. On the ceiling of the cave, just above the actual murder spot, were two nodules, 'two eyes', in the stone, both of which were wet and which, according to Miṣbāh, were the tears God still wept for man's crime. He invited me to taste the moisture.

'You will find it has the same taste as tears.'

'I understand people come here to be healed? Do they sleep in the cave?'

'They used to, but nowadays, because of the army station, it is not allowed.'

'Does Khiḍr come here?'

'The old keeper saw Khiḍr many times.'

'Did he describe what he was like?'

'No, except for one detail. When he shook his hand he said it was like uncooked dough. We know Khiḍr came and prayed in this cave. Jesus came here too. All the great prophets came.'

I was then invited to hold the very stone with which Cain is said to have crushed Abel's skull. I stood where the blood would have spread in a wide pool around my brown shoes, one of which I noticed had a broken lace.

'You will see', Miṣbāh observed, 'it is much heavier than any other stone.'

'Yes,' I replied, 'but unless you have another stone of precisely the same dimensions and of the same physical properties how can you be sure?'

Miṣbāh shrugged, saying the stone had always been here. As we stood there the murder weapon that was approximately ten kilos did indeed seem to grow heavier in my hands. After another five or ten minutes it might have crushed my toes. There is no mystery in this other than the interpretation we choose to place upon it, otherwise it is a small matter of gravity and muscle. There was nothing Miṣbāh showed me that could not be ascribed to natural causes and yet I could not help but marvel at the imaginative qualities which permit one to trace the name of God in stone, which enable one to discern patterns where seemingly there are none. A good Sufi might say there is nothing more miraculous than natural causes. If we can say the poetic imagination holds true and the air is full of connections only waiting to be made, why then have we become so reluctant to admit those imaginative qualities underscoring religious belief? Why do we put them down as untrue? Why have we come to mock everything sincere in this boy's face? I put the stone back on the wooden shelf, thinking to myself how easy it would be to remove the evidence. When later I asked Abed if he believed the story of the stone were true he made a fine distinction, saying he didn't think so, but that on the other hand he believed in its significance. There was for him an additional significance to this place.

'Which is?'

'It is a secret but it corresponds to a vision I had six months before I first went there, which revolves around a promise I made whose realisation would be witnessed by forty people. I did not understand then who those forty people were. I forgot the dream until six months later when I visited the place, not according to my own will, but because a friend of mine, a fool, insisted that I go. I would never have gone on my own. So you see, the dream was fulfilled. The *forty* were, of course, the saints. This is a sign that they are alive. The saints are always alive, spiritually, and they have their own functions and responsibilities. Who, exactly, these forty are I don't know. I do not like to believe in myths, but in realities. I touched this reality, it was tangible. This is what Sufism is, facts not illusions, but patience is required. At first I had wanted my vision to be realised in a single day. It was at that point in my life, by the way, I was kicked out of my father's house. Six months. It was like a preparation. It was a period of hunger for me and of living like a tramp, during which time the saints were taming my arrogance and impatience.'

A couple of days later, Abed and I hired a car to Wadī Baradā. We went through a magnificent mountainous landscape, which would have been a splendid isolation were it not for the tanks or observation posts at every second or third bend in the road, reminding us that we were in the middle of a security zone. Earlier on, a youth with a machine gun asked me to surrender my passport and camera. I was a little disappointed, therefore, to discover at this remote shrine several rows of parked buses. The building housing the tomb of Abel was nondescript, as so many Islamic shrines tend to be. We walked around the 25-foot-long tomb of Abel. 'Why such a length?' I asked one of the Druzes whose job it is to maintain the mosque. The answer was because the length represents the distance Abel's blood sprayed when he was bashed over the head with the stone. Although one's credulity is strained to the limit what strikes one with some considerable force is that the Roman village of Abila stood here. As the name suggests, even people of a different religion believed this to be the site of Abel's grave. Well over two millennia ago, Alexander the Great was said to have stationed a guard around the tomb, which was then in the open air. The Jews said this was the place; later, the Christians said so; and now the Muslims say so.

I had but a few hours to my departure and, still pondering these issues of brotherly love and hate, I met with Abed and Sulaymān at the Nofara Café. If I were to succeed in my mission of bringing them back together it would be only as a catalyst – a desire for reconciliation would already have to be there. As though in anticipation of this they almost immediately began to speak of the rupture in their friendship, never addressing each other directly but rather through me. Clearly, I was now in the position of mediator and as such would have to address them from some higher place. It was hard to resist the temptation to do so in flowery language.

'When you left Damascus last time we were exposed to many pressures,' Abed explained.

'The burden of these pressures on my body and soul was very heavy, quite beyond reason,' said Sulaymān, 'and because of this I could not communicate with other people, I could not understand other people. You must get rid of this burden before being able to communicate because when one is sad like this, although there may be support from God, the nervous system gets confused. A lot of people say to me, "Why don't you love me, Sulaymān?" I love them, of course, but I cannot love them too much because if a person is not worthy of my love then it is like handing him a pistol with which he may shoot me. So I have adopted a strategy for my dealings with people. When I hate I should hate lightly and when I love I should love lightly. But this business concerning us, Abed and I, this was different – this was a relationship of seven years. There was genuine love, so why did he go away from me? Why did he become negligent and why did he seek knowledge from other sources? And why did he forsake Ibn al-ʿArabī and so many other matters concerning himself. When I left Damascus he became confused, vengeful even, probably because in his heart he wanted to go with me.'

'But sometimes,' I suggested, 'too much dependency in a friendship can be destructive.'

'Yes, everyone must be independent in his ideas and opinions.'

'So friendship requires a certain distance. And perhaps you both destroyed this distance?'

'Yes,' said Abed, 'this is true.'

'If you know this to be true, can you not repair what has been damaged?'

'There is love and respect between us,' said Sulaymān, 'although there is disagreement too.'

'And you feel this, Abed?'

'Yes, of course.'

'If you can talk like this, why not take another kind of path? Obviously, you cannot go back on the old path.'

'What is this different path?'

'I don't know, but it may be one that will make your friendship stronger than ever.'

'Yes, of course, we both agree.'

'So why do you stand at this terrible distance?'

'Because everyone has his own orbit,' said Sulaymān.

'But all our lives are separate orbits, and it is for you to respect Abed's even if he asks questions in other places, of other people, as it is for him to respect yours. I would like to leave Damascus with your friendship if not completely repaired, then at least partially so.'

Abed got up at this point and kissed Sulaymān on the forehead. The movement from enmity to friendship was almost seamless. They began speaking directly to each other as they had always done. We went for supper at one of the restaurants on Martyrs' Square.

'I had the ticket for London,' Sulaymān said. 'I had everything, but it was not to be. Maybe London is too cold for a Bedouin.'

'So perhaps', I suggested, 'it is a place best visited in the mind. What about the desert? You call yourself a Bedouin, yet you have never seen the desert.'

'A Bedouin likes most of all his camel and his dates. This is difficult because suppose I had a camel and suppose I wanted to go to the desert – Bedouins always used to cross borders, they were free to go as they liked, but now this is impossible because they are required to have passports and visas. This would be emotionally risky, too, for then it would be hard for me to go back to the city.'

Then Sulaymān told me his dream.

'I had this dream or perhaps it was a vision. There were two Bedouins in it, both in traditional robes, holding between them a sign saying THIS WAY TO ENGLAND. They placed a turban on my head, a green one with four knots. Then there were the others, the Malāmatiyya. They were very handsome, dressed in suits and ties, and after crowning me they took me to where I signed papers to go to England. A man whom I recognised as St George said to me, "I want you in England." My uncle was also in the dream – he was for twenty years a merchant in England. This is why I have to go to England, because of this dream. When finally I get there I will not speak more than five words – "eat", "sleep", "marry", "drink" and "tea" – any more than this I am not willing to learn because if I have to go into details

I will be burdened. I would prefer my English wife to be deaf and dumb. Also, I would like a VISA card, so I can buy sneakers and clothes. And so that I will not lose my way I will measure precisely the distance from my house to wherever it is I want to go. I will measure out the whole neighbourhood. As for my life in London there will be candles and Indian incense. I will dress in Sufi clothes, but if I am not comfortable wearing them on the street I will dress this way only at home. All depends on the nature of the creatures in London. I will require a television for cosmic news, news of earthquakes, for example, and also I would like to watch nature programmes. I will make medical discoveries and in my laboratory, where I will experiment with two hundred kinds of herbs, I will discover new cures. I will see which herbs kill terminal diseases. In London, I will watch for faces that emit knowledge. One can see if knowledge is imprinted on people's faces. This is called "the science of faces" or "the knowledge of the look". Through all this I will end up with something new. I will eat lightly, for I am not going to London in order to eat. I will dress in wool against the cold. London will be an old and lovely city for me. The older the city the more knowledge you can extract from it. A Londoner might not feel this, but because I am coming from a different country I will see what a Londoner does not see. Somebody coming to Damascus will see things a Damascene does not see. This applies to religion, sects and cosmic matters. There may be more spiritual benefits in London than here. So this will be it, looking for new things. When I achieve the spiritual power I seek I might be able to help other people. A five-minute session with me might stop someone from committing suicide. A person lacking certain things will not be able to give to other people. First he must achieve security and peace. He must heal his own illness before being able to cure other people. How can one be a doctor when he is himself ill? A scientist who does not apply his science is tormented like a pagan. If you have knowledge you should teach people. Edison was kicked out of school several times, yet he made electricity. Crazy people who think too much can enter a zone from which there is no escape. The crazies love themselves. Usually great men of letters, poets, they have this craziness. People think they are arrogant but it is not true. They take their support from the zone of knowledge. A man watched the top of a casserole dish move up and down, saw there was strength in the steam, so he employed what he saw to make the first steam engine. At the time we condemned such people, whereas now we say they are great. Why? Because we have benefited from them. If not, we would say they are crazy. If we say they are great it is because of our personal interest in them. Our earth is a ball full of resources, metal, greenery – a mass flying through the universe. This is only the mass we live on. There are thousands of such masses, so why do they make these flags, these visas—'

'This is a subject that has obsessed Sulaymān for many years,' Abed interrupted. 'He greatly dislikes flags because he is a Bedouin. A flag restrains his life, his freedom to go wherever he pleases.'

'I want to visit my friend Marcie in London, so why refuse me? Would I try to create a country of my own there? After the year 2000, the problem will be solved. Open the borders! Do not be afraid! Do not be afraid of losing your resources because the earth has enough for hundreds of years to come. Just trust me. If people wish to mingle with each other, then why shouldn't they? Are you the British ambassador? No, you are greater than him because this man armed with a pen plays with people's hearts. Every time I go to the Embassy the answer is always *no*. "Why?" I ask them. "You come to us, and we love and welcome you to the extent we consider you our peers. So why can't I visit your country?" There are three hundred questions on the visa application. If you already know my life, why do you ask me? After answering all these questions you tell me, through a barrier of glass, "No!" "What will you lose if I go and learn English?" I ask them. "I have paid the fees." And still they say, "NO!" The conclusion of all this is, do you or do you not want to take me to London? If you do, then I will follow you there.'

I assured Sulaymān he would be most welcome.

'Very good. I will put your telephone number on the next application form. I am waiting for St George to order me to give you my turban and club.'

'They may prove too great a burden for me to bear.'

Later, we sat in front of the Umayyad mosque.

I was leaving Damascus soon and because there was no certainty we would ever see each other again we spoke at odd tangents, skating over issues, as though anything really important to be done was already done. We had time now to waste. Abed pulled a page from his notebook which he then tore into three strips of paper. He wrote on one of them YES and on another NO. The third he left blank. He folded the slips several times, and cupping them between his two hands shook them.

'Sulaymān, are we going to Greece?'

Sulaymān slowly unfolded the piece of paper he chose.

'Blank.'

Abed carefully refolded the slip of paper.

'Will we go to Norway?'

Abed repeated the exercise.

'Again, blank! This is getting interesting, no?'

Again Abed refolded the slip and, with something like panic building in his face, shook the three bits of paper for the longest time.

'Will we go to England, then?'

Sulaymān hesitated and just when I thought he was about to answer he went silent again.

Abed's hand began to tremble.

'Choose!'

Part Three

ELEVEN

The Shaft

One coincidence is better than a thousand appointments.

Arabic proverb

It was a standing joke between us that whenever I returned to Damascus it was always at a time of great crisis in Abed's life. I had not had a letter from him in ages. All I knew was that he had gone to Turkey, information I gleaned from a conversation I had with Sulaymān when he phoned me almost a year before. We communicated by means of the only three words of English he spoke.

'Hello, Marcie!'

'Sulaymān good?'

'Good.'

'Damascus good?'

'Good!'

'Abed good?'

'Abed, Turkya.'

'Turkya good?'

'Good.'

'Goodbye, Marcie.'

Thus I had been able to construct some kind of picture of their lives. They were friends still; Sulaymān was well, perhaps he had finally discovered the Philosopher's Stone; Abed was in Turkey, ostensibly on his way to England or perhaps he was headed for the Greek monastery and the naked woman on the beach. Alternatively, he might have been working somewhere. I had fears for Abed of a kind I might wish upon other people; the idea of him working was a troublesome one. Certainly, I could not imagine him being *gainfully* employed – Abed would never be able to carry, much less wash, crockery without catastrophe; certainly I couldn't picture him selling carpets, for he was quite insensible to their beauties; and he would never be able to rise in time to make it into a shop or office – so really it was the idea of him *being* employed that most alarmed me. I had images of him, based on nothing in his own nature, conducting punters to a seedy Istanbul dive; I had him committing random acts of violence; I even had him poking through garbage. What did one have to do in order to survive in Istanbul? And how would he begin to pay for his cigarettes? A chain-smoking philosopher from Syria, a 'non-mainstreamer', a fumbler and a drone, surely he did not stand much of a chance. At last a letter from Damascus arrived, saying only that the city welcomed me. When I got there I telephoned Abed. After several minutes of muffled phrases and awkward silences, he said he was much too unwell to be able to meet me although he hoped such an event would soon be feasible. I felt myself on a downward slide. A few hours later, however, I felt his hands on my shoulders. I was sitting outside the café we regularly went to.

'Allāh knew I would find you here!'

Abed was a bit older but he was looking none the worse. On the contrary, I thought he looked rather well, although outside, in the darkness, the light reflecting from his bright yellow sweater might have put a certain glow onto his features. Equally he might have been jaundiced.

'You must forgive me,' he said, 'but I was ill at heart. I couldn't bear to see you in this state. A couple of months ago, I suffered a bad fall in my fortunes, which is affecting me still. I want only to hide. Nevertheless, I knew I had to see you.'

I asked him about his time in Turkey. Abed had been there for three weeks and had got as far as Bodrum, or, more precisely, the nearby resort town of Kuşsadası on the southern coast. He had been enjoying his travels until one day, while lying on the beach, he was robbed. I asked him what had been so absorbing his attention.

'No,' he answered, 'it wasn't *that*. After a while, the mind wearies of naked women. They become one and the same. I had fallen asleep and that was my reward, being robbed of both money and sleep.'

Penniless, Abed took refuge on the second floor of a building under construction. One night, returning home hungry and tired, he walked down the dark corridor and turning into what he thought was his room stepped instead into an empty lift shaft. There was only a short distance between the doorless entrance to the shaft and the doorless entrance to his room. Abed fell three storeys.

'I thought you said you were on the second floor.'

'You forget the basement, so that makes three.'

A caged bird nearby made a laughing cackle.

'What were you thinking of as you fell?'

'What I discovered is that in matters of the soul there is no such thing as time. My descent seemed to take forever. Of course, I wondered if my life would end in this strange, empty place.'

'At what speed did you fall?'

'The descent was slowed down by angels and my body positioned by them in such a way, like a cat's, that I landed squarely on my back. Allāh's providence! I should have been killed otherwise.'

'Do you believe in angels?'

'I believe in God's providence and that He is free to use whatever He likes. Should it be angels, then fine.'

'What else did you think about?'

'On the way down—' Abed laughed wildly and the bird in its cage laughed too. '—on the way down it occurred to me that whatever happens to me is usually preceded by a vision or dream. When people have problems often they feel they've seen them before. I think I remembered having already had this dream.'

'You thought you were dying?'

'Let me try to remember.' Abed stared into his coffee. 'Yes, more or less, but actually I didn't think about it too much.'

'What happened when you landed?'

'At first the pain in my back was terrible. I screamed, but nobody heard me. I was completely alone. I was able to walk, however. Afterwards, there was no pain because my nerves were intact. The matter of the spine is in the nerves. I got back to Damascus, went to the hospital for an X-ray which showed a slight fracture in the spine and was told to take bed rest for a few months, which gave me an opportunity to get back to my studies. I had been fed up with everything in my life. So perhaps it was all for the best.'

It seemed to me Abed was doing in sickness what normally he did in health.

'I must agree you took a bad dive.'

'No, no! That was nothing, absolutely nothing compared to what happened later, a couple of months ago, when I fell a much greater distance. This is why I'm in such a terrible state. I fell in love with a French girl.'

'What, the same French girl as last time?'

I reminded him of the upside-down pyramid.

'No, another. This one had a much more serious effect on my emotions. This relationship deeply impoverished me, exhausted all my philosophy. What I've learned over the years is worthless in the face of this catastrophe. Abū al-Ṭālib said to me, "She gave you a rose which you embraced because it was your first rose, but she has already forgotten this rose because meanwhile she has gone and given roses to other people." Abū al-Ṭālib, you will remember, has many such analogies. He has a vivid imagination and a power in getting across what he means. Another person gave me advice contrary to his, saying I should persevere in my love for her, that I should follow her to France. I benefit from listening to contrary opinions, which is also the method of the Qur'ān where there is much use of contrast in order to make one understand better. There, every time hell is mentioned heaven is too.'

Although, for reasons of delicacy, I will not expand too much on this matter what I can say is that there was no measuring the blow to Abed's pride. She had been introduced to his family and friends, and a solemn though not official vow of marriage was made. The affair had been a disastrous one and hardly an hour passed when I did not have to persuade him yet again there was no point in pursuing a relationship that she herself had put a stop to. The differences between them, I reminded him, were greater than the similarities. She had sexual experience whereas he had none; she was free to go as she liked whereas he was rooted to one place; in short, she came from a wholly different set of circumstances. *Still* he spoke of going to see her in France despite her injunctions not to; *still* he bought cheap jewels and scarves for her; *still* he sent her absurd notes. Abed resorted to ever madder rationales. She was loyally waiting for him to make an appearance; she was pregnant and in such a parlous state she needed to know whether he would accept her; she was seeing somebody else and Abed would kill her. She was a saint, a spoiled bitch, stupid and wise. *She was, she was.* Abed had indeed come to the end of his philosophy; he had become a *majnūn*, that is, a fool for love. A step further, and he might have become a fool for hate. It got so I began to emphasise cultural differences, for he had been jealous of her every move. Why, for example, was she able to sit at another man's table? Were such things normal in Europe? Why would she not remain pure? I gave the same answers to the same questions twice a day or more.

All arguments have two or more sides, of course. I attempted to get some kind of picture of her, devised from a combination of what Abed told me and, perhaps more importantly, *what he did not tell me*. She, from her side, had been swept along by a strong tide. She fell in love with those same cultural differences, for she had even taken the veil without Abed asking her to. She followed him, not because he wanted her to, but because she was prepared to submit to her own fantasies. She was not wholly to blame nor was he. They had proceeded blindly, oblivious to social and cultural divides. They believed only in those fictions that make for the flimsiest of bridges.

The shaft down which thwarted love sends people is always

unique. The pain at the bottom is indescribable. I have lost count of the times young Arab men with glistening eyes asked me to help them write letters to real or imagined loves. Almost always, not having a clue what to say themselves, they asked me to write whatever I liked. Anything would do, and quite honestly I began to find these epistolary exercises tiresome. Abed, although he bled profusely on the outside, was inwardly more private; I had to guess at the words he himself wanted to write. And then, once found, I would have to discourage them. The job of keeping him in an upright position became an exhausting, even tedious, one. A brother's keeper must watch for his own spine. There were moments even when I was ready to let him sink in his own apathy, thinking he might then be forced to struggle on his own back to the surface. I decided upon the old military tactic of creating a diversion. When I suggested we go to the small town of Ezraʿ in the south he leapt upon the idea with relish.

'A message is waiting for me there!'

If Abed was idle, Sulaymān, by contrast, was a paragon of industry but always in matters quite outside the normal commerce of our lives. I was shown letters he wrote to multinational companies, saying that if they were interested in his metallurgical activities they could arrange for a visa to meet him. Several months passed and still he had no replies. I was glad to find him back in traditional clothes.

'I like your new turban. Do you still have the big green one?'

'No, there is no longer any need for it.'

'And the club?'

'The club is gone too.'

'What about Khiḍr, have you seen him lately?'

'He showed up briefly a couple of months ago,' said Sulaymān with a faint smile, 'but it's not up to me whether he comes. Sometimes I call for him, but he is busy elsewhere. I mustn't bother him. Allāh gives him many important jobs to do. He is reserved for great missions, universal matters, earthquakes.'

I mentioned the recent earthquake in Turkey.

Sulaymān became agitated.

'When I spoke of this four years ago nobody believed me. I told them not to make high buildings but only small wooden ones like in Britain. "Why do you want to build in the air?" I asked them. If I could afford it I wouldn't even live in this house. It's wrong! But nobody listens to me. People think I'm crazy. They only want to make money. So who, then, are the crazy ones? There was another earthquake recently, in Japan.'

'Did you know about them in advance?'

'A holy fool called Abū Nur told me. Abū Nur was short and fat, he died last year. When catastrophe is about to come to a city the holy fools are the first to know, which is why they have such terrible lives sometimes. They become, within themselves, a kind of sacrifice to the people. Also, there is a book by Caliph 'Alī, written thirteen hundred years ago, saying there would be three events – first, an eclipse of the sun, then earthquakes, these followed by the death of kings. We have had an eclipse, earthquakes, and now the deaths of the kings of Jordan and Morocco.'

'And what will happen now?'

'The Messiah will come.'

'Are you still trying to make gold?'

Sulaymān handed me a business card, embossed in gold, presenting himself as a consultant in Ibn al'Arabī studies.

'This was one of his areas of knowledge. You can't deny it is a well-established science. If you make a chemical experiment at sea level and then repeat it up in the mountains, using the same substances and measures, you will not get the same results. I read in a magazine they are planting things on the moon that will provide a cure for AIDS, which involves the use of tubes.'

'Which magazine was this?'

'I will show you. It's in English.'

'Such magazines publish only nonsense.'

'There were pictures!'

'Yes, there was also a photograph, taken from a Russian satellite, of Elvis Presley on the moon.'

'Any knowledge you think of now as unrealistic will one day be real enough. When Galileo said the earth was round nobody believed him. If he said this openly, in the souq, he would have been killed. Conservative Muslims in Egypt imprisoned Ibn al-ʿArabī for holding similar views. A holy fool will behave strangely sometimes, as though in a fit, because he sees what you can't see. He sees and reacts to cosmic explosions out in the universe and because of them he behaves in a way which we perceive to be wrong. Sometimes he sleeps for days at a time or else he eats five times the normal amount. When he reaches perfection, however, and St George supplies him with strength and secrets then he will no longer have those fits. As for my making gold, if you find compassion in your heart for me then perhaps I will demonstrate for you.'

'I will leave that to your good graces.'

The alchemists of old were often healers too. In the same way they cured metals so they cured people, by removing impurities.

'Are you still healing people?'

'Yes, of course. Only recently this man came to me. Ah, I hear problems you would not believe. Says he can't make love to his wife because he enjoys wanking more. So he is defective. What can I do? How can I cure such a man? Shake the devil all he likes, but will his wife agree? No, never! So they divorced. Sometimes, the devil won't let people sleep. You see the problems I have. Now I take only special patients, ones I can handle. If you open the door too wide, you can't live normally. They would be coming through it day and night.'

'Do they pay you?'

'Sometimes they pay cash but most of this I give to the poor. Usually they sacrifice a sheep, and this again goes to the poor. Traditionally speaking, once you slaughter a sheep certain problems are lifted. Sometimes there are cases I cannot treat at all. Some are psychologically ill – others have problems of an organic nature. A woman who is sterile comes to me. There is a physical problem here. She has no womb. How can I make a womb for her or any other kind of organ? If she already has a womb then perhaps a cure is possible because there will be enough of an incentive.'

'How do you treat a woman who is sterile?'

'Sometimes by reciting from the Qur'ān.'

'Are you allowed to touch the woman?'

'No, I must have the help of another female. She must be spiritually strong. You cannot permit any intrusion of a sexual nature, especially if the woman is beautiful. Otherwise she may destroy you. You must always be awake. If you want to marry her, that's fine. You cannot mix things up with a wife. Sometimes you treat a woman and she loves you. This makes for another problem. You must treat her in such a way that she will not love you, even if it means being a little cruel with her. And then there is my spiritual healing. As I told you before, my speciality is to do with the nerves. A woman came to me. She had been reading spiritual books. Now, not everyone is qualified to read such books. You need to be of a certain status before being able to absorb what is in them. Some spiritual authors are so dangerous that a reading of any one of them, even a short passage, can strike at the heart. This woman, she was repeating over and over a particular oath she'd read somewhere. She was entering the death zone. If you push the button of this code, that is, as in her case, if you recite a certain oath for days at a time, there may be no protection. You will enter a field where either you are killed or you escape. You will be hit, where and when nobody knows, because you will have been isolated from the world. You will be alone. Once a person has reached this rank you must hit him before he reaches the higher rank of manipulation and does harm to others. In the case of this woman I was able to cure her in time.'

'Black magic?'

'It is illegal. If one has protection nobody can harm him although he may suffer for a day or two. Still, there are people who practice black magic. I was invited to visit them once, but refused. What is their excuse for using it? A man might go to somebody, saying, "I love my wife, but she rejects me. I must have her. Whatever it costs me, I will pay you." If the man whom he is asking for help is weak enough he will accept the money and will then practise black magic on her. Sometimes, this involves the use of animals. It is very distasteful. Most people will not involve themselves in such practices whereas the weak and the greedy do. Unfortunately, black magic is a reality here.'

'Can they curse people? Can they have somebody killed?'

'If there was an order from God to kill someone that person would be destroyed in less than a second, but if there is no such order, if it comes from somebody else, how can God respond to such a request? What would His response be to someone who is practising black magic? It is the gravest sin. In Africa, they can kill you with a glance, just by focusing on you. Ibn al-ʿArabī says saints like Khiḍr will not do anything unless God orders them to. The magician, on the other hand, if you give him money he will do these things. This is the devil's way. The right way is long but beautiful. One should not seek to make money from this either. When you die you should not have money, all should be for the poor. You might be a millionaire, but you should give it all away. God curses those who bury or save their money. It should be used only for necessities. If you have money you should use it because once it is saved nobody will be benefited by it. This is our religion.'

'What about money for the children?'

'A portion is allowable, but it's not necessary for your son to be a millionaire. It would be better if he inherited your knowledge because knowledge brings money whereas money does not bring knowledge.'

'How did you learn to heal, through instinct?'

'As a beginner, I was in need of someone to heal me. I was very sick. When I first entered isolation I heard a voice saying, "Don't pray, for if you go on with this we will kill you." I prayed. There was an explosion of light and from this something began to take. I was exhausted because of the energy from this light and I would tremble uncontrollably. I went on praying during which time this same light from the other world would come, then I would meet Khiḍr spiritually, shake hands with him. I said, "You're Khiḍr, yes?" He smiled and the light that shone from his face was exactly that of the sun. From that point on, I felt comfortable. Whenever I entered isolation there was no longer any problem. I did not hear evil voices. Gradually, every time Khiḍr visited me I took strength from him by shaking his hand. The oath I took with him was my protection. Sometimes he still visits me. Saints are numerous, but he is their chief. If I want to help someone, if I don't have authorisation to do so, then I won't be able to help that person. If I want to teach someone, the saint will want him to be a good person before he is able to hear me. I can't do anything on my own. Somebody comes and I want to be of spiritual help to him, but I can't say, "All right, I'll accept you." I must pray to God for His permission. If Khiḍr says fine, I want this person, then I can give him the oath. If he is guaranteed by Khiḍr, then everything will be fine.'

'Sometimes you must meet people who have problems of a kind you have never encountered.'

'Yes, all the time.'

'How do you deal with such a person?'

'When I look at his face and eyes I know the degree and for how long he has had this problem and I will know whether he is easy to communicate with, if he will torment me or if I will have to use the stick with him. Maybe he is terrified by devils so he needs a shock to wake up. I may have to send him elsewhere. It depends on the case. I must know what his situation is. Usually, the younger he is the faster he heals. This is especially true for those from eight to thirteen years of age. Some people have major psychological problems. Professionally, I do not like to be occupied by these because when you heal someone his problem will then be inside yourself. This makes you suffer. What he has, I have. What is the solution? A patient may be in love. I enter his heart by focusing on my love for God, so gradually I feed that spiritual love into his heart and I remove from his the profane.'

At this point Abed asked Sulaymān for advice. I watched them for almost an hour, Sulaymān trying to remove the pain from Abed's eyes. I watched them both gesticulate, Abed's movements frantic like those of a drowning man's, Sulaymān's measured, always the more mellifluous of the two. This dance of the hands spoke volumes of their temperamental differences. I watched an angel and a devil at battle, a war between patience and impatience. When they finished Abed said he felt better, but both Sulaymān and I knew any cure would last for only minutes at a time.

'Will you come with us to Ezraʿ?'

'What is there?'

'An old Christian church dedicated to St George which some say contains his grave although most people would agree he was buried at Lydda. Still, I would like to investigate.'

'Impossible!' Sulaymān snapped. 'If he is Khiḍr he cannot have a tomb because, as we all know, he is immortal. It doesn't make any sense.'

Abed nodded in agreement, saying I would find no such grave there, not at Lydda or anywhere else.

'I believe this tomb is not a tomb at all but rather a monument which commemorates his having passed by there,' he continued. 'In the Umayyad mosque there is a green plaque, green because Khiḍr is green, with his name written on it. The Caliph Walīd who built the mosque said, "Who is this man I see praying over there? We have already evacuated the mosque. How did he enter?" They told him it was Khiḍr who has unlimited powers. This plaque commemorates his having passed by there.'

'So why, Abed, do *you* want to come?'

'There is a message waiting for me.'

Sulaymān politely declined the invitation.

'What do you think we will find there, Sir Marius?'

We were sitting on a bus, now entering the southern plain of Hārūn. It was an area all different shades of black and brown and jagged with sharp stones, whose bleakness was beauty of a kind, a beauty that may have something to do with these notions that from time to time we spin for ourselves, of a landscape speaking directly to the human condition, or rather, as if what is out there is a projection of ourselves, of an interior monologue rendered visible, where the word is made not flesh but stone. It could well be, of course, the earth has nothing whatsoever to say to us, not after all the abuse we have poured on it.

'Well, Abed, I didn't mention it before because I didn't want to overexcite you. We are going to meet a beautiful girl with raven hair and dark eyes. She will be waiting for us.'

'Oh my God! What is her name?'

'Cleopatra.'

Some time before, Abed had told me of an Arabic phrase, 'knocking elbows', which is what one does in order to get over a broken heart – one allows a second woman to temporarily erase the memory of the first one.

We arrived at Ezraʿ, which was the region's capital once upon a time, although there is little to indicate this was ever the case. It is now mostly flat, grey and unattractive. We stopped at a hole in the wall where we consumed a bowl of *ful*, which the cook said we could have with his compliments. Abed warned me that this was a courtesy to be disregarded, that all too often foreigners take literally words that are offered merely as a form of politeness. Afterwards, we grabbed a local bus that we were told would take us near the church of St George. We were not sure of the distance, however, so Abed made enquiries of the woman in the seat in front of us. She turned around and smiled, a beautiful young woman with raven hair and dark eyes. She was in military uniform, but somehow this vision in khaki managed to make even the dull green of her tunic shine. She offered to escort us there.

Abed stared at me in bewilderment.

'Are you St George? I think so!'

We were coming to a much older part of the town, which was the centre of what was once a flourishing city. There are still many ruins and from these a good number of houses have been made. One can find the same at Bosra where from the Roman remains people have pilfered massive stones for their houses. It may be archaeological heresy to say so, but I rather like the idea, especially when the results are so pleasing to the eye. I do not lament the building of mosques upon churches that in turn were constructed upon heathen temples nor do I always regret the cannibalising of stone. A layering of cultures is infinitely preferable to the blunt removal of all their traces. What is unforgivable, on the other hand, are the crude surrogates such as one finds at the outer wall of the Umayyad mosque in Damascus, where a couple of recently erected buttresses have been made of concrete. The idiots responsible for these drew lines on their surfaces in a vain attempt to make them resemble blocks of stone. At Ezraʿ I saw several ancient entrances to people's houses, one of which bore a primitive carving in stone of two serpents on either side of a cross. This might have been some of the earliest Christian iconography in existence. To my amateur eye these archaeological remains appeared considerably older, more primitive, than the nearby church architecture.

The church, one of the oldest Christian structures in the world, is also the earliest surviving one to be dedicated to St George. It was built in the year 410 of the Bostrian era, corresponding to AD 515, on the site of a pagan temple dating back to approximately 1400 BC. According to an inscription at the entrance, the church owes its construction to John Diomede who dedicated it to St George. The saint appeared to him, not in a dream or a vision, but in reality. This, Abed told me, with a note of triumph in his voice, was ample proof that Khiḍr is alive. I could find nothing that supported the notion I'd read somewhere that the tomb of St George was here. Actually there have been a number of tombs said to be his, but none of them are even remotely valid candidates. On the other hand both Muslims and Christians still came here to venerate the memory of Khiḍr or St George. Curiously, Christians referred to the Christian saint as Khiḍr in the same way Muslims referred to the Muslim saint as St George. And the tradition still held true, of people of both faiths spending the night in the church in order to be cured of their ailments, particularly psychological ones. The form of the church is that of an octagon described within a square and was modelled upon the church at Antioch, constructed during the reign of Constantine and which is believed to be the first octagonal church ever erected. The eight piers support a lofty dome, which was recently reconstructed by the Russians. As archaeological evidence of the origins of the cult of St George it would appear, from the dates, that there was no foreign element or inspiration at work here, as in most other churches dedicated to the saint, but a direct and local memory of his actual martyrdom. The cult was, from all accounts, still very much alive and it was this that I was most keen to investigate.

The churchwarden, a surly man in his seventies, was openly annoyed by our presence. Any questions I asked him were met with only the most perfunctory of replies. Abed told me he was illiterate and was only looking for a small livelihood, but I suspected floating hostilities. A foreigner comes and thinks he is on familiar terms with St George; a foreigner comes and cuts into his precious time – who could guess at what his anger attached itself to? She of the raven hair said the previous warden was a learned man, that he spoke English and French but was seriously ill now. This oaf was briefly filling his space. Surely though, he knew of local legends pertaining to St George. I was in a most unholy frame of mind, mentally devising instruments of torture. And, perhaps sensing my urgency, this man put up a solid resistance. As I squeezed harder, he yielded still less. I was growing irritable at the thought of a journey gone to waste and Abed annoyed me, too, saying he had found what he was looking for and was now ready to leave. Abed did not have much time for antiquities or for Christian misinterpretations of his favourite saint. The warden shook his keys, which made me all the more determined to leave only when I was ready to. When I finished taking a few, rather aimless photographs the girl asked us to follow her to her house. Abed said yes before I could say no. On the way there we met a friend of hers, another attractive woman who said that when we had finished with the first visit we would be welcome for tea at *her* house. Abed looked in seventh heaven, although just a little worried perhaps at having to socialise with Christians. Although he had no religious prejudices to speak of he did have a morbid fear of awkward situations.

A couple of days earlier, I had dragged him to a church in Damascus, also associated with St George. The priest and his family were just settling down to a meal and invited us to join them. The priest's brother was getting married in a few hours' time. Abed, fearful of making his hosts uncomfortable, asked me to say he was Christian. 'Which church?' I asked. 'Church of England,' he whispered. 'Church of England! Whatever for?' 'Because nobody here knows what it is.' I told him hardly anyone in England knew either. We sat down at the table, Abed to the left and the priest to the right of me. I refused *arak* on Abed's behalf, saying my friend had stomach troubles. The ridiculous thing was that Abed translated for me. The priest asked me if my friend attended services there. Abed replied, 'No, but I hope to soon, *inshallāh*.' All through the meal I struggled to keep a straight face. The priest gracefully pretended not to notice. As we neared the girl's house I advised Abed to remain a Muslim on this occasion. In any case, he was in a buoyant mood for the first time since my arrival in Syria. As for me, any disappointment I felt at the church was about to be swept aside.

The girl's mother greeted us. She was a widow, and seemingly very much in control of things but without the melancholy strictures this might imply, a warm, intelligent woman who regretted more than anything that she had not been able to travel in her youth and to have learned more. As she spoke of her regrets and desires, another four daughters appeared, all of them beautiful and in remarkably different ways. The five sat down in an arc, forming a respectful audience, adding comments only when they did not intrude too much upon their mother's discourse. Abed and I were in the presence of a formidable force.

The mother hoped her girls would see the world, draw from their experiences, and it was evident she wanted for them all the freedoms afforded by a healthy intelligence, which equally would be grounded within a strong Christian framework. She had worked for the General Union of Women in Ezraʿ and she was now asking me, as if I were a representative of all the places she had never been to, probing questions on social and political matters in the world at large. She accepted our compliments on the beauty and intelligence of her daughters with all the aplomb of one who knows precisely what the limits are. Abed remarked on how much easier it was to address them thus, whereas in most houses he would be under severe stricture not to. If I stress these matters it is not in order to marvel at one woman's intelligence but to present a backdrop against which she would speak of matters regarding St George. In short, hers was not a credulity born of ignorance.

'We Christians call him Mar Georgis. Although not physically alive, he would appear so in the imaginations of Christians living here. For Muslims, on the other hand, Khiḍr is still alive and will always be. There are numerous miracles associated with him. My father was in a car one night. It crashed. Then he and his companions trapped inside saw a knight on a white horse. The knight opened the door of the car and everyone was evacuated before the car went up in flames. My father said, "We should thank this knight," but he had already vanished. So my father knew then that this was Mar Georgis or Abū 'l-ʿAbbās, "the man on the horse", as many people here like to call him. You will not find a family here which has not witnessed such miracles.'

Quietly the daughters left the room one by one.

'St George appeared here many times when faith was full in people's hearts but not so much any more. Not so long ago, a plane was about to fall out of the sky and the pilot who saw St George and was rescued by him still pays homage once a year by slaughtering a sheep for the poor. We have had many miracles here. The paralysed have walked. Fifty years ago, the window in the church emitted a flame of light upon which St George came, all dressed in white. Did you notice that the cupolas were painted blue? They wanted to change the design once, but no matter how many coats they applied they were unable to paint over the blue. The government sold the ancient church of St Elias nearby to a developer who hired a bulldozer to remove its remains, but the driver was unable to knock down two pillars both of which bore a protection oath. Muslims, even more so than Christians, when their wishes are fulfilled, come to visit St George in our church. Also, they come for cures. Sick people sleep there, but whether they are healed or not depends on the strength of their faith.'

The five daughters returned with plate upon plate of food. Within minutes, we were confronting a huge banquet. So often I had witnessed the ease with which fishes and loaves are made to feed the many and almost always with people who can barely afford to.

'We live in an area where not only have there been many natural disasters, floods and earthquakes, but also the wars and revolutions that people bring upon themselves. The fact the town itself has not suffered is something we attribute to its guardian. As soon as there is a problem St George comes on his white horse, protects the town and throws sand in the eyes of his enemies. With his help we have resisted many enemies from outside. Nomads used to come and try to steal grain from our warehouses. The boss of these warehouses said there was no need to lock the doors at night because we should not be afraid of thieves. St George would force them to surrender. One bandit well known for his brutality said of his defeat, "We were slaughtered by the knight who blinded our eyes." This sentence has entered our local slang. When he was told it was not possible for a knight on a horse to ride over sharp stones he was inwardly persuaded this indeed was the immortal knight of Ezraʿ. This same man gave up his evil ways and repented in the presence of all the people.'

When we left, this woman held our hands and, speaking of

our meeting with her daughter on the bus, repeated a favourite proverb of hers, 'One coincidence is better than a thousand appointments.'

'What did the journey to Ezraʿ mean to you?'

Abed looked thoroughly pleased and this alone was enough to dispel any earlier anger I felt towards him. He seemed finally to have scaled the walls of the shaft he had fallen into.

'Our trip there was planned by St George in order that he might deliver his message to me. He warmly received us through this girl and through her we were invited by him to visit this family and to eat with them. When something is planned or preordained by a saint he will be the one in charge, he will facilitate everything. What is strange is that although we were joking on the bus we must have been expecting a feminine welcome. What this means is that sometimes jokes really are signs. In Sufism we take note of every action because every human being is a mouthpiece of God, and so by making this joke you had unwittingly become such a mouthpiece. The family we visited was a good Christian family, devout, very conservative. Every family has its own cultural background but the one we visited was surely unique. You would not normally meet such families in Ezraʿ. They are farmers mostly, uneducated people, but because this woman used to work in the General Union of Women she is cultured and educated. We heard things from her we might not have heard from other families. This is what made our visit so exceptional.'

'What was the message you received?'

'Firstly, we should know who St George is, that he is the man who is there at times of crisis, who comes when there is a great problem and in no time at all solves it.'

'Any crisis? Surely he solves only certain crises.'

'Any crisis he is ordered by God to solve, because he is a servant of God. In my case, he is backing me, showing me his strength and wants me to be confident of his support. Until now, I was backed by about four or five saints all of whom have their own specialities. Now, St George is an extra one and because he is the most powerful saint, because his speciality, which is power, is like a sword that cuts and manipulates, I feel greater confidence.'

'You needed a trip to Ezraʿ to learn this? Surely he has always been the major influence in your life.'

'No, because saints keep their own times. They have missions only at certain times.'

'And you feel it is somehow connected to your recent troubles?'

'Do you remember my telling you the story about Khiḍr and Moses? The story in which Khiḍr kills the young boy? All that at first failed to make sense was later proven to be wise. There are hidden boons and clear boons. *Boon*. This is old English, no? I can't think of a better word. When volcanoes erupt we think it is a curse, but if we read between the lines we see that unless they erupt the whole earth will explode. They are like lungs releasing the power inside. So everything in this universe is either a clear boon or a hidden one and everything in our lives likewise. Why did I fall from the second floor? Why did I fall in love? God wants me to believe that everything that happens to me is either a clear boon or a hidden boon. This, the second part of his message to me, is the essence of Islam. It is not fatalism as many people think but rather an ability to read between the lines. If I were to ask God constantly why I fail in this and why I do that I would probably commit suicide. But if I believe in God's destiny then I will be happy. So yes, it is connected to my troubles.'

'There is a painting in Krak des Chevaliers of St George on a white horse, so it is an old way of thinking in this part of the world. What interests me, however, is that the image of a knight on a white horse is European in origin.'

'I cannot speak on behalf of those people, the Crusaders,' Abed laughed, 'but what I do know is that St George is for all people, Christians, Muslims and Jews. You saw in the church those icons of St George killing the dragon. This is what Khiḍr does. St George is the representative of Good killing Evil. This is what Khiḍr is.

These details of a white horse, all these images you find here and there, are only metaphors. You remember the plane that was about to crash, which was stopped in time. If St George comes to you on a white horse, Khiḍr might come to me in a tank.'

'You may well need him to, with your problems.'

'Yes, if they are big enough he will bombard them.'

'And when this woman spoke of visions did you consider them a reality?'

'A vision is in the eye of the beholder. No one can explain it to you and give you the real feeling of that vision. And sometimes this happens to you. You dream but you cannot turn that dream into words. If you see a French woman in your dream, you can't really explain her beauty to me. This is what visions are like.'

'So a vision in that sense is a work of the imagination?'

'A vision in that sense is a work of God, but not all visions are from Him. Some, like nightmares, come from the imagination. Not every dream is a vision. Sometimes, they are hallucinations. If cats obsess me – a metaphor for women, of course – I will see them. Only yesterday I dreamed of two cats. They should have been five. If, for example, you see yourself meeting a woman with black hair and she is Spanish and you meet her three months later this was a vision from God because no one can know the future except Him. This is not from your imagination because your imagination is too weak to know the future. So regarding this visit to Ezraʿ I had this vision two months ago but I didn't know then its reality. When I visited St George just now he told me this vision had a reality, that he is backing me. I need the support of powerful figures.'

'You felt no conflict in finding this through a Christian situation?'

'What conflict? *Where* is the conflict? I can't perceive any. I was going to visit St George and for sure he was there, he passed by there. My target is Khiḍr. So where do you see conflict? We were warmly welcomed by him through those people.'

'And instead of one girl we got five.'

'Six, there was another we didn't go to see.'

'Ah yes, the one offering tea at her house. Do you think she's still waiting for us?'

'Yes, we could go back tomorrow but then we would be doomed by St George because we will have turned all this into a game.'

TWELVE

Time of the Aubergine

I was like a towering laugh in the middle of Asia.

Muḥammad al-Māghūṭ

The aubergine doesn't actually flower at this time, in late September and early October, but, metaphorically speaking, people say it does. What they mean by the phrase 'the flower of the aubergine' is that somebody is talking nonsense. A meteorologist might put this down to the changeover from summer to autumn which, when it comes to Damascus, falls like a blade, for it is then that one hears much of a foolish nature. A piffle, a bit of gibberish or a rodomontade may be dismissed with a wave of the hand, 'Oh, it's nothing to worry about, only the flower of the aubergine.' As a panacea for giddy times the belief ought perhaps to be adopted in other countries. The flower of the aubergine may be said to be at the mouth of whoever is speaking or it can be used to describe actual speech.

Robin Fedden, in what to my mind is still the best book on Syria, writes, 'The curious and the strange persist in Syria and Lebanon and the traveller will find them for himself and in the degree that he wishes.' And still those words hold true, although to speak of the curious and the strange is not to enter into exoticism but into things as they are. Should my reader be lured into thinking that most Damascenes are crazed I must emphasise here that the 'normality' surrounding Abed, Sulaymān, Abū al-Ṭālib and so many other people in this book covers acre upon acre. Much of the city is grey and nondescript and people struggle as they do anywhere else in the world and they go in pursuit of the same pleasures. There may be people with stories to tell, to be sure, but these they carry secretly within themselves. The majority of them would sooner watch television. One may step into modern Damascus for an excellent ice cream perhaps or to take a peek at what passes for progress, if progress is getting whatever the latest brand name is, but the new has little to offer that can't be found anywhere else. When one passes through the gates of old Damascus, on the other hand, one enters a zone of wondrous tales. Much persists that is both ancient and strange. I believe this to be under siege. The old is caught in a vice, as it were, is being squeezed upon from all sides, and I do not think it unreasonable to suppose the lively character of the people in the old part of Damascus is contingent upon their surroundings being preserved. Already whole areas have been threatened with demolition. Will the storytellers continue to tell their stories in fast food venues?

One of Damascus's most curious characters is buried in the relatively new Reslan mosque, just outside the old city walls, not far from the Bāb Tūmā, and in the middle of a noisy traffic circle. Abed took me there, saying I would need permission from this figure to write about him, otherwise my computer in London might crash. I should not, he warned me, underestimate the power beyond the grave. In a small cramped room, at the rear of the mosque, people devoted to the memory of this man sang prayers more beautifully than I had heard anywhere else. The man whose tomb they surrounded in a tight circle was the most popular folk figure of recent times, a true emblem of Damascene life, a joker and saint by the name of Aḥmad al-Hārūn. In him, the border between saint and holy fool begins to dissolve; in him, what may at first appear as nonsense, 'a flowering of the aubergine', fructifies into wisdom. Damascenes speak fondly of his many miracles, but to hear of them, amid peals of laughter, is almost as if those wonders were being told as jokes.

'Aḥmad al-Hārūn once booted a man in the arse.'

Born in 1900 in the Ṣāliḥiyya area, al-Hārūn was raised in a very devout house. A gifted child, he was distinguished for his memory and was able to recite whole stretches of the Qur'ān at a time. This was an important element in his upbringing. Al-Hārūn was seven when suddenly his father died. Five years later, he took up a manual trade and from then on was vital to the livelihood of his mother. He spent many years as a stone carver on Mount Qāsiyūn which probably accounted for his strong physical build and, because stone carving is painstaking work, his considerable patience. Among his Sufi peers he was certainly the best built, the most prodigious of memory and the most experienced in the ways of the world. He was also a soldier for a while and fought against the French.

Abed and I picked up a chapbook of al-Hārūn's miracles. What comprises a miracle ought to be discussed first, especially if I do not want my computer to explode, for it is a position every bit as carefully made in Islam as it is in Christianity. There is a further distinction for which unfortunately there is no word in the English language. A miracle, strictly speaking, is that which is performed by or limited to the Prophet, whereas what the saint (*walī*) does is *karāmāt*. Put simply, it is like having two grades of miracle. What they share is that they are both against natural law. So when the word miracle is employed here the reader should understand that it is in fact *karāmāt*. A great shaykh commenting on miracles wrote, 'Be a seeker of correctness; do not be a seeker of miracles because your ego is asking for them, whereas God is asking you to be correct and pious.' A saint may perform miracles but in reality they are not his but gifts from God. A miracle occurs only according to the need of the people. A person might need a miracle in order to strengthen his weak faith whereas he who has achieved religious perfection is in no need of one.

A saint will regret performing miracles much as one might regret having sins and he will ask God to prevent any reoccurrence. Also, he will ask his followers not to be fixed by the miracle, that is, not to make it their target. One should worship God and not the miracle. What often happens is when a follower of a shaykh witnesses a miracle he becomes like a baby and is distracted by it whereas he should be only with God. A miracle is therefore a double-edged weapon that ought only to be utilised and not worshipped for its own sake. At best, it is to be considered an additional proof. A miracle is not necessarily a sign of someone being a saint, although it is usually saints who perform miracles. After all, magicians might be said to perform miracles too. What is the difference, then, between a miracle performed by a saint and one that is performed by someone who is not? The former is a consequence of faith and piety whereas the latter comes of satanic influence.

'Aḥmad al-Hārūn once booted a man in the arse,' a shopkeeper roaring with laughter told me. 'This man had wanted to go on a pilgrimage to Mecca but said he couldn't afford to. Al-Hārūn, seeing him standing next to a fountain, booted him one. The man fell in and when he came out drenched he said he had just been on a pilgrimage. Afterwards, he went on a real *ḥajj*, this man who claimed he couldn't afford to. So, you see, this kick was a blessing in disguise.'

There are those miracles that have entered the oral tradition and others such as those described in the book Abed translated for me that have the sworn affidavits of reliable witnesses. The following are three such miracles.

A rich family owned a flour mill once. The town council decided that the mill should be knocked down in order to broaden the street a little. The owner of the mill sought the help of important people, politicians, businessmen, to interfere and save the mill from destruction but all in vain. One morning, the employees of the town council came with wrecking equipment to execute their mission. They gave the mill owner one day in which to remove his machines, his wheat and so forth. The mill owner was plunged into despair, such that one of his friends advised him to go to Aḥmad al-Hārūn. Although the mill owner argued against this, saying he did not know this man, he did nevertheless waver between doubt and belief that perhaps al-Hārūn would be able to help him. Was it possible, with only hours to go, that this shaykh could change the course of things? So he knocked at the shaykh's door. When al-Hārūn opened it the mill owner cried, 'Please, I beg you, help me. The town council is going to destroy my mill tomorrow.' 'But yes, of course,' al-Hārūn answered, 'and so they should because you did not grind wheat free of charge for the poor. Will you promise me you'll now do so?' The owner said he would at which point al-Hārūn lifted up part of his baggy trousers and spoke into the bunched-up cloth as though it were a telephone. 'Hello, is this the town council?' he shouted. 'Yes, good. Tell the mayor the mill is not to be destroyed. It is up to me and not up to you. Forget it! Goodbye.' The mill owner went back home and next morning opened his mill as usual and started working, all the while fearful of the arrival of the council employees. Days passed, months passed, nobody showed up. The strange thing is that the wrecking equipment, the hammers and so forth, which had been left at the mill the day before were not collected. When the mill owner thanked al-Hārūn for his help he mentioned the tools and asked what he should do with them. Al-Hārūn said, 'Go and tell them. They must be returned.' So the mill stayed in its place. And the owner fulfilled his promise by helping the poor.

One day a man who had just been fired from his job came to see al-Hārūn. Al-Hārūn took off one of his own shoes and with it made a telephone call to the manager of the company, demanding he take the man back at once. The next morning the doorbell rang at the dismissed person's house. He was surprised to find the manager himself, ordering him back to work.

There were many such miracles of a practical nature, almost all of them employing articles of clothing as telephones. There were also others of greater subtlety such as this political one.

During the French occupation al-Hārūn told an audience, 'I am going to marry an Egyptian woman who weighs three and a half tons and who has a daughter who weighs one and a half tons. This daughter snores so loudly nobody can sleep. Also, I am going to travel to Egypt with ID only, without a passport.' At that time, this was thought by many to be a joke to cheer up his audience. If there was any deeper message it was assumed to back what the Prophet himself meant when he said, 'Cheer your hearts from time to time because when bored they become blind.' Soon after, a political union was made between Egypt and Syria and for the first time people were able to travel between the two countries with ID only. Three months later al-Hārūn, together with the Egyptian narrator of this story, visited Cairo. When he entered the narrator's house in Cairo, he announced, 'I am coming to divorce her, for her folk are not good people.' At the time nobody understood what he meant by this. After a while, however, it was clear that the union between the two countries could not work for much longer. After three and a half years, 'tons', the union was finally dissolved. So who was this daughter of one and a half tons? This represents the time, eighteen months between when the union finished and the Baʿth revolution started, the beginning of a new era.

'And the snoring, Abed, what did that mean?'

'Ah yes, I almost forgot. During the union there was a famous Egyptian always on the radio, who had a spectacularly boring voice. This presenter droned on and on, making his listeners snore.'

Abed translated another miracle, but first gave some explanation as to its importance.

'A saint has secrets that he should pass on to another before he dies. Only a saint, usually a follower of the one who is about to die, may inherit them. Those secrets are frequently of an abstract nature, but ultimately their power lies in helping people. Such is their power they may be strong enough to pulverise a mountain. Obviously, one must have the reception, the ability to carry this and because he is a mould, a receptacle, once the secret is removed he will perish. Should a man give the secret away before he is meant to then for sure he will die. This secret may relate to powers, which only a chosen few have. If you were to hear an ant's footsteps this would be very strange for you. If you were to see angels this, too, would be strange. There are many things normal people cannot hear or see that a saint does.

Einstein said there are four dimensions but now, although we cannot see them, we know there are sixteen.'

Al-Hārūn met a sick saint and told him, 'Please give your secret to one of your followers. You mustn't keep it to yourself. Don't be selfish.' The sick one answered, 'No, I'd rather keep it for myself.' 'Why?' said al-Hārūn, 'You must let other people benefit from it. Pass it on. You are going to die.' This saint was obstinate. When al-Hārūn heard of the saint's death he went directly to the house where the corpse was. He told the children of the deceased to leave him alone with the corpse. What he did not know was that the deceased man's son was eavesdropping. Al-Hārūn ordered the corpse, 'For God's sake, wake up!' The son saw his father sit up in bed. Al-Hārūn took the secret from him and then the man died a second time.

'Would you describe al-Hārūn as a holy fool?'

'He was, but you must remember he was very knowledgeable. Sufism for him was the understanding of the heart and its laws. Many people used to study with him.'

There is just one last miracle that I particularly like. Already a famous figure in Damascus and one who could speak on behalf of his people, al-Hārūn spoke regularly to de Gaulle through the bunched-up collar of his *jalabīya*. Now, by some miracle when he spoke in Arabic de Gaulle heard the words in French and, vice versa, when de Gaulle spoke in French al-Hārūn heard them in Arabic. This was during the French occupation when there was a terrible famine. Al-Hārūn 'phoned' de Gaulle, demanding that he send fifty carriages of wheat for the starving people. There were many witnesses to this. The carriages arrived the following day.

Shaykh Aḥmad al-Hārūn, as famous for his jokes as for his miracles, died in 1966.

If Nizār Qabbānī was without question the most popular Arab poet of recent times Muḥammad al-Māghūṭ is the one to whom most literary people turn. This is not to say he is an intellectual poet, far from it, but as one who has set certain demons free he is considered by many the most important Arabic poet alive. A whole school of poetry has developed in his wake, although he himself abhors coteries; poets such as the self-educated Palestinian, Ṭaha Muḥammad ʿAlī, owe much to the other's absence of a polished technique. The rawness of al-Māghūṭ's work is not always to popular taste; also, it is written in free verse. We have become sufficiently inured to Modernism to be able to intermittently forget its existence, whereas in Syria there is still much regret expressed at the disappearance of classical forms. I heard several such debates, all of them in the marketplace. Nizār Qabbānī was perhaps one of the last poets to be able to exploit the classical forms and doubtless he was deeply loved, as al-Māghūṭ will never be. Indeed, al-Māghūṭ is generally better known as writer of satirical plays, many of which were written in collaboration with the comedian 'Ghawwar' and which appear regularly on state television. It is remarkable that they do, for they are brazen in their criticism of the country he loves. In one of his plays, Saladin comes back to life in this century and is stuck at the border. He is not allowed to enter the country. 'Look, I am Saladin,' he protests, 'I'm the one who did this, this and this.' And still they ignore him, saying, 'Saladin may be great, but he needs to have the right papers.' The play touches upon the nerves of ordinary Syrians, especially young people.

A mere mention of his name is enough to spark debate.

'If Qabbānī is the poet of love,' one woman remarked, 'then al-Māghūṭ is the poet of hate.'

'Nonsense!' her sister said, 'What do you know? A poet of anger maybe, but of *hate*? Never, never!'

They stared at each other in menacing silence. I was then asked to act as referee. One person I spoke to, Yasser Saghrjie, a connoisseur of poetry and nomadic textiles, was most succinct: I had asked him whether he believed al-Māghūṭ was an outsider.

'This depends upon what you mean by outsider.'

'An outsider as someone who stands outside his society, acts from outside, yet still voices the anxieties of the people.'

'In that case, I would say of al-Māghūṭ that he is a *real* insider. If you were to speak of this in biological terms there are certain kinds of viruses that build a protective layer, which enable them to survive in the body. I find this close to the character of al-Māghūṭ's work. He is the germ inside all of us, and it is as such that he feels and understands our real problems. Qabbānī is the outsider, not him. Qabbānī says things we would not normally discuss among ourselves. If you were a Syrian sitting here I would never discuss with you a woman's breasts or my sexual life. I would keep these things secret not because I am afraid or shy of them but because I feel these matters do not belong to everyone. When al-Māghūṭ speaks it is always of things that are being discussed by the people. The crisis he discusses is my neighbour's crisis. His plays are, I think, even more interesting than his poems. They address people at street level. In his plays, you might feel he is deeply bitter but you also sense that he loves his country. This is why he criticises it. You cannot be bitter about things without loving them. I would say again he is a real insider, but an insider who is not overwhelmed. I am the one who is. I am so overwhelmed by what's going on that I can't see the problems separately. I can't even begin to synthesise things.'

I spoke to a number of Damascenes, both literary and non-literary figures, all of whom said the chances of my meeting him were remote. One reason I was given is that he is unpolished in his dialogue. A man like this, a journalist told me, who comes from a simple background, does not wish to be exposed for the country bumpkin he fears he is. I was less than convinced by this, feeling that here, rather, was a man who understood that one's talent, if born of instinct as opposed to acquired skills, might perish of too much exposure. Al-Māghūṭ is a party of one. It is hardly surprising, therefore, that he does not wish to be drawn into any discussion of poetics. A poet such as al-Māghūṭ is a moving target; he will always escape the clutches of other people. All I knew for sure was that he shunned such occasions and, particularly in the years following his wife's death, was something close to a recluse. Still, I was determined to find him. I had read his poems in the lucid translations made by John Asfour and Alison Burch and I knew then I could not return to Damascus without so much as trying to make contact with him. With the help of a couple of people contact was finally made. A lady at the hotel where I stayed spoke to him on the telephone, saying I wished to meet him.

'What, a poet from England who has heard of me?' he said, 'Well, why not!'

'You mean you will meet him!' she said.

'Yes, I will come to the hotel at 10.30 tomorrow morning.'

Al-Māghūṭ arrived on the dot, the dot being almost a chimera in Syrian life. A paunchy figure in his sixties, wearing a woollen flat cap with a large dark stain on top, wide heavy-rimmed glasses, a short-sleeved shirt and red braces, a square leather satchel slung across his chest, al-Māghūṭ moved with a physical pain that suggested not weakness but rather its opposite. One would say here was a tough figure. What else? A strong, heavy face, somewhere between a farmer's and a Roman emperor's, the lid of his left eye drooped a little. Sandals, feet bare. Wooden cane. A jumbo wristwatch with three smaller faces, his one extravagance. When he sat down he leaned forward on his cane and waited in silence, with just the hint of a smile. Who was going to make the first move? I asked him if he would consent to an interview, a question that, even as I spoke, I knew to be a mistake.

'When I enter a house for the first time I feel uncomfortable.'

The voice was gentle.

When I suggested a dialogue such as one poet might have with another he replied, 'All poets are one.' I knew then I would have to appear *not* to be asking questions. We spoke for a while of domestic matters, his daughters, for example, one of whom is an artist and the other a doctor in America. Al-Māghūṭ asked me about England and expressed a desire to go there.

'England is like a paradise,' he said. 'The countryside is so beautiful it frightens me. So maybe I don't really want to go there. Anyway, I prefer hell to paradise. And besides, I don't want to go to paradise because it might be full of clergymen.'

'Where else would you like to go?'

'I gave a reading in Norway. My dream had always been to go there, although when finally I got there I found a scene of obvious spiritual battle.'

'You would like to ski?'

It must have been the memory of an earlier conversation with Abed, about his wanting to go to Norway, that got me onto that snowy slope.

'Yes, over principles!'

What is perhaps most revolutionary in al-Māghūṭ's method is the position of the poet in his own poems. Certainly, he is not a heroic figure but neither does he shrink from his fate; rather, he is something quite untameable; he is no longer a prophet although sometimes it takes a visionary imagination to see things as they are; he is not a healer but one who inflicts the wounds for which his own poetry is a burning salve.

Poetry, this immortal carcass, bores me.
Lebanon is burning – it leaps, like a wounded horse, at the
  edge of the desert
and I am looking for a fat girl
to rub myself against on the tram,
for a Bedouin-looking man to knock down somewhere.
My country is on the verge of collapse,
shivering like a naked lioness
and I am looking for two green eyes
and a quaint cafe by the sea,
looking for a desperate village girl to deceive.

('When the Words Burn')

This poem, with its curious blend of the classical and the mundane, with the figure of poet as spoiler, poet not as lover but as lecher, must have shocked his audience when it was first published in 1958. 'The lethal flower', as he mockingly describes himself, is a persona, of course, one that hides the shy and gentle man I took him to be. Certain poems are historical markers and in the development of Arabic poetry this surely was one. Satire is usually mentioned in connection with his work but I am not sure if that is quite the right word. It is too suggestive of a programme. There is something more dramatic at work here, a putting on of different clothes. When I asked if his next volume of poetry was going to include more satire he exclaimed, 'No, it will be more of *me*!' The poet as clown, sharpshooter, and rapist even – al-Māghūṭ is to my mind the wild card of Arabic poetry, the boldest and certainly the most unpredictable. Gone forever is the poet who speaks of women's eyes resembling those of gazelle's.

'The poet in my poems is a monster,' he laughed.

We like to keep at least one wild beast in the stable. The others will domesticate themselves into oblivion otherwise, which is pretty much what happened to Arabic poetry in the nineteenth, and much of the way into the twentieth, centuries. 'We must leave the others behind,' al-Māghūṭ told me, 'for they have already expired and need to be buried.' There were notable exceptions, of course, just as there were in the years preceding Eliot and Pound but something new was required in order to contain new realities, even if the vase was to be a cracked one. The time had come for change and in the 1950s Beirut was buzzing with possibilities. Beirut was where one might give voice to matters not allowable in other Arab countries. 'Wounded Beirut lay sighing on the asphalt/fondling her small breasts under clouds swollen with shame' ('The Dead Man'). When the change came, however, it was not from the pamphleteers, the bearded theorists or the aesthetes wearing berets in cafés. Al-Māghūṭ arrived with manure on his shoes. A farmer has got to be quick in his responses; there is no time for schools or fancy theories, otherwise he will lose his flock to wolves. And keeping the wolves at bay, whether they are political or literary, is something he has managed over the years to achieve. The position he occupies is probably a complex one. As he said, 'Politics, although it rules our lives, is for the minute only.' One of his most striking poems, 'The Tattoo', I will quote in full.

Now, in the third hour of the twentieth century,
when only asphalt separates the corpses
from the shoes of pedestrians,
I'll lie down in the middle of the street
like an old Bedouin, and won't get up
unless the prison bars and files on the world's suspects
  are gathered
before me to chew on, like a camel at a crossroad;
unless the sticks of policemen and demonstrators
  drop from their hands
and become again blooming branches in the forest.
I laugh, cry and write in the dark
until my pen is indistinguishable from my fingers.
Whenever I hear a knock on a door, or see a curtain move
I cover my papers with my hand
like a prostitute in a raid.

Whoever gave me this fear,
this blood apprehensive as a mountain panther's?
When I see an official paper on the threshold
or a cap through a crack in the door,
my bones and tears start to shiver
and my skittish blood jumps in every direction
as if a band of police
were chasing it like a thief from vein to vein.
Oh my love
in vain do I try to restore my courage and my misery.

The tragedy's not here alone
in the whip, the office, the warning sirens—
it's in the cradle, in the womb:
for surely I wasn't tied to the womb with an umbilical cord,
  but with a noose.

Al-Māghūṭ, it has been emphasised, has no formal education. The question of where a poet comes from ought really to be changed to the more vital question of where poetry comes from and to this, of course, there is no real answer. We do not demand of John Clare or Rimbaud their university degrees. The emphasis, really, ought to be upon the fact that when al-Māghūṭ arrived he was fully wired; his finger was on the pulse of the times. During the recent war the Arabs had been humiliated by the Israelis, a mood of despair hung in the air, but also there was a tingling in the nerves. As one who would give voice to all these things al-Māghūṭ's instincts were flawless. While he was by no means the first Arab poet to write in free verse, which had already been done in the forties, he took it to where it had never been before. Al-Māghūṭ was, after all, the first to launch an Arab into space.

Scientists and technicians,
  give me a passport to space!
  I am an envoy from my tearful country.
In the name of its widows, old men and children
send me a free ticket to space.
Instead of money in my hand
  I have tears.

('An Arab Traveller in Space')

When I first read his poetry I thought these aspects of the absurd and perhaps of Surrealism were borrowed from elsewhere, from French poetry, for example.

'Concerning the absurdity of al-Māghūṭ,' one critic told me, 'it is very much intrinsic to his personality because he was like this before ever reaching the city. He is from Salamīya, a village in western Syria, which is the centre of the Ismāʿīlī sect. One of their leaders was the Aga Khan who is buried there. We notice this particular quality in the educated people and writers from Salamīya. I lived in Beirut for three years. There I had a friend from Salamīya who worked as a builder. This man used to visit me, and we would read his poetry, which was written very much in al-Māghūṭ's style. Although he was not formally educated he had an instinctive poetry in him. It was genuine and contained this same element of absurdity. There is a specific spiritual climate in Salamīya that in turn has produced a specific culture. Among the Ismāʿīlī opposition and denial are intrinsic qualities. You should remember that as a religious branch Ismāʿīlī are criticised by Sunni people so perhaps the absurdity is a reaction to this denial by others.'

When I put this to al-Māghūṭ he laughed, saying that to speak of Ismāʿīlī influence is a nonsense, that for him the sect may be his undergarments, but that there is nothing in his work that is moved by or which derives from it, that he simply is what he is.

'So there is nothing here of Western import either?'

'Absolutely not.'

A poet is never to be wholly trusted with his denials. Any time we came close to discussing poetry I did so, from my side, as though poking my fingers into a flame, as quickly as possible. I said I'd heard him described at times, inaccurately in my view, as a poet of hate.

'As I said before, the poet in my poems is a monster, but there is no hate in my poetry. I get angry, but I do not hate. If you see my plays you might find cruelty in them and satire, but they are not mean.'

We spoke of his having extended the poetic language by the introduction of words not commonly found in Arabic verse. It is easy to forget just how far we, in the poetries of the English and European languages, have come in this direction. In Arabic, however, the process has been much slower. There is already a tendency towards floweriness in everyday discourse, and it is this that would seem to have marred much Arabic poetry if the translations are anything to go by. Whether or not we become jaded by too much beauty is a difficult line to pursue, it could well be the story of the sad decline of civilisation, but over the centuries the flowers of old classical poetry have gone to seed and when there is nothing fresh and alive for them to hold in place the forms themselves become stale. When al-Māghūṭ produces a pretty line he almost immediately weighs in with an inelegant one.

'A loser will make beautiful words into a bad poem whereas what I do is make ugly words into a good poem. Yes, I like to put words that will not normally go into poems. I like visual and tangible things; even with pain and despair I like to be able to touch them. I still feel like a burgeoning poet. I didn't even know I was one until I read about it somewhere. My daughter showed me a newspaper article that I believe was about me. When I finished reading the piece I left it in the coffee shop.'

'What do you fear most?'

I'm not sure why I asked this question, but it seemed the one he was most prepared for.

'I fear the blank page. I fear it more than I do America. The white page reminds me of a coffin.'

Al-Māghūṭ looked at his watch. It was precisely eleven o'clock. I could see he was a man of clockwork precision.

'I must go.'

I'll load my gun with tears
and confound the country with my screams
if you don't give me a wing and a storm to leave on
and a swallow's staff to return with.
Even the tall branches tremble
when I look to them and cry!

('Even the Branches Tremble')

Muḥammad al-Māghūṭ inscribed his book to me, in Arabic, 'A basis for a true friendship'.

The aubergine, a versatile plant, may also be used as a microphone.

I had been told of a famous figure who was a fierce social

critic but because he was quite mad people paid little attention to him. If, however, anyone did ask a serious question of him he would take the aubergine he always carried with him and speak into it, 'Eek, eek!' After his death, it was discovered that he had spent five years in a mental asylum. So horrendous were the conditions there that with the money he collected from people on the street he bought food which he would then take to his former inmates.

Another such figure with an aubergine, although it is not known where the money he collects goes, is the appropriately named ʿAbd al-Ḥāmid Jabber who is probably in his late fifties or early sixties. Any visitor to Damascus will encounter him soon enough. Often, he is found jabbering in front of the Nofara Café, singing into his aubergine at the entrance to the public toilets or in the square in front of the Umayyad mosque. He wears a shirt open to his waist and there are holes in the knees of his trousers. If the aubergine is an indispensable tool, his one affectation is a wooden cigarette holder. Sometimes he is seen with a walking stick, a stick worthy of a prophet, a *real* stick as opposed to a polished cane. His single English phrase, which is really one word repeated, is *goodygoodygoody* rapidly spoken like machine-gun fire. When he is not begging or spouting profanities he speaks in short parables.

'Give me money for food,' he bellowed at me, 'I'm sick and I can't work.'

'But I've already given you money for cigarettes!'

'If you weren't a good person, I wouldn't've let you photograph me.'

I gave him another fifty *lira*.

'Caliph ʿAlī says if poverty were a person he would kill him with his sword. Are you from England? *Goodygoodygoody!* Many years ago, the people wanted to move a pool. *Goodygoodygoody!* So how? Some people said with a pipe. Others said with a bucket. An Englishman came and said, "Use a teaspoon." Slowly, slowly they move the water. *Goodygoody.* This is symbolic of English patience. Give me money!'

I gave him another note.

'Somebody says to the king, "I sift all the people in a colander. Only the good remain." So he sifts all the people, the king watches and when this man is done sifting nobody at all is left in the colander. They were all bad. "Do you want to be sifted?" he asked the king. "Yes, sure," he answered, "but only if you guarantee my safety."'

At this critical juncture in the story Jabber gave a huge belch.

'*Goodygoodygoodygoodygoody!*'

A pretty girl passed by and immediately Jabber began crooning into his aubergine.

'Give me money.'

She seemed not to notice him. I got the waiter to bring him tea.

'So he sifts him and says to the king, "You have horns. You could not be sifted." What does this mean? The meaning of this is if you take somebody's blood and replace it with honey it will not sweeten him. So what do you do with all the bloodless people around you?'

Abed explained that to say in Arabic someone is bloodless is to indicate what a bad person he is.

A telephone rang inside the café.

I bunched up the lapel of my jacket.

'Hello?'

THIRTEEN

A Likeness of Angels

Whosoever adopts the likeness of angels, let him be a stranger to humans.

Aphraates, *Patrologia Syriaca*

There was one more journey I had to make, which would take me to one of the roots of holy folly, where, arguably, both Christian and pre-Islamic traditions find a meeting place. Just how far the breeze blew the seeds sown by one faith into the fertile ground of another is debatable. Muslims are not particularly receptive to suggestions of Christian or even pre-Islamic influence and Christians, such as Father Paolo, who actively seek a dialogue with Islam are rare. It is impossible to ignore the fact of a shared landscape and it is harder still to imagine the great faiths operating in complete isolation.

If anyone can be said to be the patron saint of holy fools then arguably it is Simeon Stylites. The base of the pillar upon which he stood for thirty-seven years can still be seen near the village of Deir Simʿān, an hour's drive north-west of Aleppo. The church complex, Qalʿāt Simʿān or Saint Simeon, which was later built around the pillar, is one of Syria's greatest architectural treasures.

Acanthus, the conventionalised leaf of which figures in Corinthian capitals, its adoption inspired, according to Vitruvius, by acanthus leaves growing about a basket of toys left in a cemetery, was given a fresh twist by the architects of Saint Simeon. The spiked fronds skilfully carved into stone were flattened so as to suggest the influence upon them of a strong breeze, 'the breeze itself a pilgrim to the mysteries within,' Michael Haag writes. The blown acanthus, as this new style was dubbed, spread rapidly throughout the Byzantine world. A single detail bespeaks the grace of the whole. The church of Saint Simeon, built between 476 and 491, was the greatest Byzantine structure of its time.

What Simeon, who shunned all earthly things, whose life moved through spheres beyond all concern for the beautiful, would have made of such extravagance is beyond conjecture. As it is, we can barely follow that mind. The imperial authorities at Constantinople spared no expense in the building of the church, and in this we may suspect a strong message to those pursuing alternative religious lines. The Monophysite heresy that allowed for no separation between Christ's divine and human elements had already begun to sow discord at the fringes of the Byzantine Empire. The language used by the Monophysites was not suggestive of tolerance: 'May those who divide Christ be divided with the sword, may they be hewn in pieces, may they be burnt alive.'

Simeon pulled for the orthodox side.

The church was constructed in the shape of a cross, four basilicas meeting at an octagon at whose centre we can still see the base of the pillar upon which the saint took up residence. The earthquakes of 526 and 528 which destroyed Antioch probably brought down the roof here. The pillar was still standing at the end of the sixth century when the ecclesiastical historian, Evagrius, visited the Mandra, as the local people then called it. A couple of minor details in his account lend a curiously pagan air to the scene. Rustics, and by this we may suppose he was speaking of Bedouins, performed dances around the pillar and also repeatedly led their beasts of burden around the structure. They took literally it seems the metaphorical Mandra (from the Greek *mandra*, meaning the hovels in which sheep and goats are fed).

Simeon did not leave behind any writings, so for details of his life we are largely dependent on the written testimonies of his disciples and witnesses. There are three major accounts written by contemporaries, the first and most reliable by Theodoret, Bishop of Cyrrhus, written around 444, when Simeon was still alive and had already spent twenty-two of his thirty-seven years on his pillar. Theodoret, who, according to one tradition, may have been a student of Chrysostom's, was a historian with a historian's discipline for weighing matters, even particularly irksome ones.

> For what took place surpasses human nature, and people are accustomed to measure what is said by the yardstick of what is natural. If something were to be said which lies outside the limits of what is natural, the narrative is considered a lie by those uninitiated in divine things.

The second account, by Antonius, an intimate disciple – it was he who first approached Simeon's corpse – although disjointed and lacking the former writer's Platonic style is valuable for details others might have seen fit to exclude. There is surprisingly little of the adulatory whereas the third account, by an anonymous hand, commonly known as 'the Syriac Life', begins and ends with an overpowering smell of incense. Antonius's account is the much plainer of the two, humbler in intent, unsparing in its presentation of physical realities difficult even for his contemporaries to embrace, and seeks not to place too much emphasis on miracles. The Syriac Life is almost all miracle. There is not much in it that survives the acid bath of our times. Although to ignore the miracles would be akin to cutting from the *Iliad* all the battle scenes, there is, in the more easily verifiable details of Simeon's life, a story far stranger than any attributed to miraculous causes. The three accounts present his early life as a shepherd, his early asceticism, his years in the monastery at Teleda, his removal to Telanissos and finally his years as a stylite, otherwise the narratives have little in common. Where they do meet, however – and, curiously, almost always at the seams of the probable – they command our fascination.

Simeon was born at the end of the fourth century, around

390, to a Christian family, in the village of Sisa near Nicopolis. A smallish but reportedly handsome youth, he tended his parents' flocks, work likely to be conducive to contemplation. According to the Syriac Life he would go about the fields gathering storax, a gum resin which when burned smells like frankincense. Strabo mentions its use in the worship of pagan deities. Simeon, it was said, burned the substance without understanding why he did so, and one finds elsewhere the suggestion that he unconsciously moved in the direction of the Scriptures. Such time as he had to spare was spent in the company of ascetics who advised solitude and the renunciation of bodily health and desires as vital to keeping the soul pure. After spending a couple of years as a kind of novice Simeon went, without telling his parents, to the monastery founded by Eusebonas at Teleda, not far from Antioch. There the seventeen-year-old threw himself at the feet of the abbot, Heliodorus. A good and holy man, Heliodorus entered the monastery when he was only three and, according to Theodoret, was so untouched by worldly concerns he knew neither a pig's nor a cock's shape. One suspects here a gentle joke. Theodoret who visited him frequently marvelled at the simplicity of his character and the purity of his soul.

Describing himself as low and wretched, Simeon begged Heliodorus to save a soul which although perishing desired to serve God. Heliodorus taken aback by the intensity of the youth asked him his name, where he came from and what his background was. The youth would not say who his parents were, and by this we may infer that in dissolving earthly bonds he had become *as dead* to them. There is a contemporary feel here. We find such reports in the newspapers of young people with odd religious leanings, who have severed all family ties, their parents struggling to break through a screen of silence. Antonius's account has Simeon's parents in tears, ceaselessly looking for him, whereas the Syriac Life has them already in their graves. Simeon entered the monastery where he was to spend a whole decade; at least to begin with, he was loved by his brethren, and, most vitally, he observed the rules. After a while, however, he began to move in directions that were not those of his brethren and perhaps not entirely his either. Whether divine inspiration, madness or indeed both were the spur (there is nothing in his own words to give us guidance), he began upon a course that would increasingly test the patience of the other monks. The meagre portion of bread and pulse which was his daily fare he gave away to the poor so he would go from Sunday to Sunday without sustenance, and on the seventh day consume only a few spoonfuls of soaked lentils. This did not go unnoticed by the other monks who being spiritually competitive were unable to purge themselves to such a degree. There were greater feats to come. Simeon dug a hole in the garden and stood in it up to his chest for days on end in the blistering sun. At night he would stand on a round stick so that if by chance he began to doze it would roll beneath his sagging weight, keeping him awake. The monks began to condemn more vociferously than ever those activities that put their own in the shade.

All came to a head over a length of rope.

'Behold, the new Job!' Heliodorus cried.

Maggots, this was what he had been brought to see, Simeon's bed was crawling with them. The monks gathered there agreed the boy had gone too far this time, that here perhaps was the lever by means of which he would be made to leave. Why did he go to such extremes? The stench was unbearable. Heliodorus who greatly loved Simeon was at a loss what to do. The monks had on many occasions pressed him to take measures, and because he saw in their demands something other than love his reply was always the same.

'Since he afflicts himself for God's sake, I will not be the cause of any loss to him.'

Always they spoke of the 'greater good' while never once admitting to the envy that, like scorpions at the bottom of an empty cistern, dwelled in their own breasts. This time, however, Heliodorus was deeply troubled. He had been put under severe pressure. Unless he agreed to expel Simeon the monks warned they would leave, and if that were to be the case the holy order that was entrusted to his safekeeping would collapse.

Heliodorus took Simeon by the shoulders and shook him.

'Why do you do these things? Why do you break the monastery rules? What are you, some kind of spirit come to tempt me? If you want to die, get away from this place.'

Simeon bowed to the ground in silence, tears filling his eyes. Heliodorus asked him who his parents were (if he were born of real parents that is), and from what place he came. Working himself up into a rage, he turned to the others.

'Strip him, ' he shouted, 'so we can discover what this smell is.'

When they tried to do so they were unable to peel the shirt from the boy's flesh. Cloth and flesh had become as one, an integument of decay and discharge, and for three days they soaked him in warm water mixed with olive oil. When finally the shirt was removed and with it much flesh what they saw amazed them.

The missing rope.

The monks remembered Simeon a couple of weeks earlier going out to fetch water from the well and coming back, saying that the rope for lowering the bucket was gone. They begged him to keep silent about it, fearing somebody would inform the abbot. And now here was that same object, soaked with blood and infested with larvae. What had transpired, they learned, was that Simeon had taken the rope made of palm leaves, which was extremely rough even to the touch, and going into a secluded place wound it tightly around his waist so that at first it burned and then, with every movement he made, cut ever deeper into the flesh until some days later that whole part of his body was a ghastly putrescence.

'Let me be, my masters and brethren,' Simeon cried, 'Let me die as a dog, it's what I deserve for the things I've done. I'm an ocean of sins.'

Heliodorus wept to see that wound.

'You're not yet eighteen, what sins do you have?'

'The prophet David said: "Behold, I was brought forth in iniquities, and in sin did my mother conceive me." I have been clothed the same as everyone else.'

The abbot, much struck by Simeon's answer, immediately called for two physicians to tend to him. The operation to remove the rope was such that at one point they gave him up for dead, but finally they managed to do so and for almost two months kept Simeon under their care. When Simeon recovered the abbot summoned him.

'Look, son, you are now healthy. Go where you wish, but you must leave here.'

After leaving the monastery Simeon went to a nearby well that was dry, at whose bottom dwelled numerous scorpions and snakes. The people avoided that evil place. He lowered himself into the well and hid in a cavity in the wall. A week after Simeon's departure Heliodorus had a dream in which he saw many men clad in white, holding torches, circling the monastery. They accused him, threatening to burn the place unless Simeon, the servant of God, was handed over to them.

'Why do you persecute him?' they asked. 'Do you not know what you had in your monastery? One who will be found greater than you.'

The abbot awoke, crying out to the monks to come.

'Truly I see now that Simeon is a true servant of God!' he cried, 'I beg you, brethren, find him for me, otherwise do not bother to return here.'

A search party went almost everywhere. When Heliodorus learned that they had avoided the well he ordered them to go to that place. They prayed above the well for three hours, after which five monks holding torches lowered themselves by means of ropes. The reptiles fled from the glare.

Simeon cried out to his rescuers.

'I beseech you, brothers and servants of God, grant me a little time to die. That I cannot fulfil what I set out to do is too much for me.'

The monks took him with considerable force. The way up, they said, is not as easy as the way down. They brought him as if he were a criminal to Heliodorus who fell at Simeon's feet.

'Agree to my request and become my teacher, servant of God, teach me patience and endurance.'

Simeon stayed in the monastery for another three years, but the pressure from the monks continued until finally the abbot, fearful for the future of the monastery, promised that if Simeon did not conform to their rules he would be made to leave. Another year was spent trying to persuade him to abandon his strange practices. With Lent drawing near, Heliodorus called Simeon before him.

'You know, my son, how much I love you and how I do not want you to go from here, but I cannot change the laws laid down by our fathers. Arise, go wherever the Lord is preparing for you. I will rejoice in you.'

One night, without saying a word to anyone, Simeon left and came to Telanissos where he confined himself for three years to a small hut, living only on a diet of soaked lentils and water, and, on one occasion, fasting for forty days after which he was unable to speak or move. Gradually, he was nursed back to health on a diet of chicory and wild lettuce.

The man disturbs as much as he inspires.

We are not alone in finding certain aspects of Simeon's life repulsive. It was a problem for many of his contemporaries too, even though many ascetics indulged in similar practices. Evagrius describes their activities.

> They maintain common supplications to God throughout the day and night, to such a degree distressing themselves, so galling themselves by their severe service, as to seem, in a manner, tombless corpses. . . . Indeed, their own rule enjoins them to hunger and thirst, and to clothe the body only so far as necessity requires: and their mode of life is balanced by opposite scales, so accurately poised, that they

> are unconscious of any tendency to motion, though arising from strongly antagonist forces; for opposing principles are, in their case, mingled to such a degree, by the power of divine grace combining and again severing things that are incongruous, that life and death dwell together in them, things opposed to each other in nature and in circumstances: for where passion enters, they must be dead and entombed; where prayer to God is required, they must display vigour of body and energy of spirit, though the flower of life be past. Thus with them are the two modes of life combined, so as to be constantly living with a total renunciation of the flesh, and at the same time mingling with the living.

Evagrius speaks always in the present tense, describing things familiar to his readers. There seems to be something in the very landscape which drove these 'fleshless athletes, bloodless wrestlers' to such extremes, many of them actually melding into the scorched wilderness, becoming 'grazers', permitting themselves only what the ground produced and that barely sufficient to sustain life. The desert was, after all, a spiritual home to those who rejected the comforts of an earthly home, a place where sleep and food seemed luxuries, where the devils one fought in the imagination took on an almost corporeal existence. Although the area we are speaking of does not, strictly speaking, fall into this geographical zone the desert was always close. There were reports of people who so completely transported themselves into the natural scene that neither panther nor lion harmed them.

We seek to understand the savagery of such a course.

> O Lord, Lord,
> Thou knowest I bore this better at the first,
> For I was strong and hale of body then;
> And tho' my teeth, which now are dropt away,
> Would chatter with the cold, and all my beard
> Was tagg'd with icy fringes in the moon,

> I drown'd the whoopings of the owl with sound
> Of pious hymns and psalms, and sometimes saw
> An angel stand and watch me, as I sang.

Edward Fitzgerald reports Tennyson reading aloud his poem on Simeon 'with grotesque Grimness, especially at such passages as "Coughs, Aches, Stitches, etc." laughing aloud at times'. Simeon is for Tennyson a figure swollen up with morbid pride, whose religious enthusiasm has degenerated into a fanaticism bordering on the hallucinatory, his mind set only on a crown-bearing angel who may or may not be there. 'Who may be made a saint, if I fail here?' Although he may to some degree pity this man 'whose brain the sunshine bakes', Tennyson cuts to the bone.

As does Gibbon: 'A believing age was easily persuaded that the slightest caprice of an Egyptian or a Syrian monk had been sufficient to interrupt the eternal laws of the universe.' As did a group of monks who joined Daniel on his pilgrimage, hoping they might prove Simeon false: 'Never has such a thing happened anywhere that a man should go up and live on a pillar.' As did, although rather less eloquently, a woman from Yorkshire who, standing at the base of the pillar, remarked, 'Sounds a bloody twit to me!'

A symbol must be true to the world it addresses, and among most of his contemporaries Simeon inspired not revulsion but awe. They saw in Simeon's suffering the beauty it symbolised. A maggot that fell from his leg was picked up by an Arab who when he opened his hand again found a pearl there. Simeon took into his own body the problems of the world as they really were, not abstractions or metaphors, but pain, hunger and sickness, and enacted them in the concrete. The pilgrims who came to see him spoke his spiritual language. Simeon trimmed his body according to his soul's desire. The danger of a journey such as he made is that in more impressionable beings it may lead only to a world of illusion, where sanctity is merely a cloak for pride. Although it is true he physically made, in Theodoret's words, 'the flight of the soul towards heaven' and in doing so freed himself of the distractions of the world, he remained *of* the world and spoke directly to its same distractions in other people. What his witnesses were able to vouch for, and which is the basis of all Christian perfection, was his spirit of humility. As for the scowling monks who joined Daniel, who himself later became a stylite, when they saw the saint they were moved by the love he showed towards them.

The base of the pillar is all that remained after pilgrims hungry for relics chipped away the stone piece by piece. A huge boulder that sits on the base is something of a mystery, for nobody remembers where it came from. It was not there a few decades ago. When Simeon moved to the hill above Telanissos he made for himself a circular wall of unmortared stones, and wearing an iron chain twenty cubits long remained in this fashion until a cleric, Meletius, persuaded him to remove it, saying that the fetter of reason would suffice. After approximately ten years in the enclosure Simeon became a stylite, from the Greek *stylos* meaning pillar. Whether he did so because he found the people continually poking at him quite out of place with the ascetic life or because he had already made a pact with heaven is not known. There are those who argue the case for Simeon as phallobate rather than stylite, and although there are precedents in the pagan world, such as that described in Lucian's *De Dea Syria*, where a man climbs and stays on a 'phallus' for seven days, it is unlikely that Simeon rose upon such an impulse. What he did was more in keeping with the *imitatio Christi* so prevalent among ascetics, the striking of a Christ-like posture. There were three pillars, the first four cubits high (approximately three metres); this was gradually increased to eleven metres and finally eighteen metres with a platform two metres square. Simeon wore an iron collar (presumably to prevent him from falling off), and for thirty-seven years stood exposed to severe winter winds and scorching sun.

We have a reasonably clear picture of his daily activities. According to Theodoret Simeon would prostrate himself, bringing his head close to his toes, in one instance doing so 1,244 times before Theodoret's attendant lost count. Because he ate only once a week his empty stomach allowed for freer movement, and during public festivals he would stand all night with his hands raised to heaven. Twice a day he would deliver an exhortation, and after three in the afternoon sit in judgement over the cases brought before him. From around sunset on, the whole night and next day until three o'clock he spent in prayer. Theodoret supplies a vital clue to Simeon's character, saying he did all these things with unpretentiousness (and here one thinks of Gibbon's assertion that monks were a foul-tempered breed) and was at all times very approachable, pleasant and charming. He spoke directly or through an interpreter to each person who addressed him. Simeon stood until his death on 24 July 459, when he was over seventy years old.

What is beyond dispute is the incredible presence he made in his world. 'As they come from every quarter, each road is like a river,' Theodoret writes, and by the time of Simeon's death his fame had spread from Britain to the Persian empire, and among Armenians, Ethiopians, Gauls, Spaniards, Scythian nomads, sophisticates from Rome and Constantinople, and, most strikingly, among the Arabs themselves, many of whom were converted, despite the lack of a common language, and who at Simeon's death wanted to remove his corpse for burial in their own territories. The Arabs were particularly fascinated by the strange spectacle of a man on a pillar, and if, at worst, the pillar was an attention-seeking device it certainly worked upon the nomadic imagination. The Arabs were as yet without a distinct identity and it was not until the Prophet Muḥ ammad came that they found one, but on no account should we underestimate their significant role in the development of Syriac Christianity, a matter that has been treated at length elsewhere. Christ moved among the Arab people, and it is worth noting that, according to Muslims, it will be at the minaret of Jesus at the south-east corner of the Great Mosque in Damascus that he will descend from heaven. Although Simeon may have quit human society for the company of angels, and indeed it may be that he failed in his original aim, to be alone, it was human affairs he attended to, and as such his contributions to society were concrete. Bizarre as his practices may seem to us, there was hardly anything of the fanatical in Simeon's language, if fanaticism is, as Isaac Taylor defines it, 'enthusiasm inflamed by hatred'. We are continually struck by the practicality, and, barring the miracle stories in which all kinds of ghastly retribution are made, the quick compassion of the man. He was involved in social work, spoke on behalf of slaves, in many instances securing their release, settled family disputes, sought refuge for orphans and widows, delivered the oppressed from their oppressors, had taxes remitted, unjust policies reversed and food distributed to the poor, engaged in delicate negotiations concerning ecclesiastical policy, and even took part in matters of foreign policy, mediating, for example, between the Byzantine emperor and unruly Bedouin tribes. We may ask, how did he manage to do so from such a confined space? The answer is both profound and simple: it is because people did as he told them to, such was the respect he commanded. Simeon was in possession of a quality that the Apostles had in abundance, *parresia*, a Greek word which, to give but one of its several attributes, refers to the ability to speak with the full force of one's convictions, without fear of punishment or of any human obstacle. An emperor and a beggar would be addressed in the same language. The people came hoping for a cure, divine inspiration and God's forgiveness or even in order to settle a dispute over a melon patch. Simeon was both jury and judge. As for the miracles, Theodoret writes: 'But how long shall I strive to measure the depth of the Atlantic Ocean? For just as humans cannot measure that, so what he accomplishes day after day cannot be narrated.'

Evagrius describes a posthumous miracle, or, if not exactly a miracle, then an unusual occurrence. A large and brilliant star shot along the length of the balustrade, vanishing and reappearing, whizzing back and forth several times. Apparently this, together with a bearded resemblance of Simeon's head 'flitting about here and there', occurred only at special commemorations of the saint. What are we to make of such prodigies? Evagrius was representative of an age powerfully disposed to the marvellous and in which people saw miracles even in the mundane. We may excuse that old credulity and smile, but if we mock the imagination we mock too the poetic truths to which it gives rise. Simeon would probably have winced at this blurring of religion and culture. So *what of* that heavenly sphere? Gertrude Bell who visited the site in 1905 describes 'the eye of a great star that had climbed up above the broken line of the arcade'. We may now cushion our doubts with matters of mere velocity and trajectory, and conclude that perhaps our spiritual fathers had both a weak and a strong eye. Gertrude Bell empathised with the star, finding it better to move than to remain, as Simeon did, in one place. Had she stayed longer heaven might have punished her for being a woman in a strictly male enclosure. Simeon allowed not even his own mother admittance, although when she died outside the gates of the enclosure he had her remains buried in front of the pillar so she might be always before him. It should be remembered, however, Simeon considered the small area around his pillar a monastery and not, despite the crowds that came, a place of pilgrimage. A case frequently cited of a woman who got into the enclosure being struck dead is a misreading of a miracle in which the devil comes to Simeon in various disguises, and although at times we may agree with the poet Campion that 'beauty is but a painted hell' the woman was, in this instance, a not so clever substitute. There is no evidence Simeon disliked women, quite the contrary in fact, if we consider how often he undid the injustices visited upon them. An honest doubter, Gertrude Bell washed her hands and face in a small pool of water gathered in the depression of the pillar's base, and looking up saw a star that to her greatly perceptive eye appeared to move.

A boy with a magnifying glass could have set the world ablaze. The heat was so intense that as far as one could see the land was scorched brown, almost black in places. Simeon had been suffering for a couple of days already from a high fever that gave much cause for concern among his disciples. They spoke in whispers between themselves, knowing full well any rumour would spread like wildfire. On the third day of his illness, by some fluke of nature (although others would say otherwise), a cool breeze blew about the pillar. The disciples remarked a sweet fragrance to which neither choice herbs nor Arabic scents could compare. As the maggot is to the pearl, so putrefaction to perfume. The crowds gathered there could not smell this for all their burning of incense. As the savour grew in intensity the disciples understood Simeon's time had come. Antonius climbed the ladder and addressed the motionless figure.

'You have not answered me, my lord.'

Antonius touched Simeon's white beard and seeing that he did not move kissed him on the mouth, then his eyes, his beard, and lifting the hem of his tunic kissed his feet too. And taking hold of Simeon's hand he placed it on his eyes, remaining there in silence for thirty minutes. When he came down and informed the other disciples a message was despatched to the patriarch of Antioch to come. Every effort was made to keep the assembled crowds in ignorance. There were too many people from the surrounding villages and also Arabs who had come fully armed ready to seize the corpse for burial in their own territories.

After four days troops and clergy finally came.

Ardabur, the military commander at Antioch, arrived with twenty-one prefects, many tribunes, six hundred Gothic soldiers, Martyrius, patriarch of Antioch and accompanying him six, bishops of the province. They immediately formed circles between the pillar and the crowds already assembled there. Ardabur, son of Aspar who ruled over the eastern provinces, felt a sharp pain in his wrists. It was no worse than usual, but his coming here had the effect of condensing, as it had first done, his whole being upon a single point of anguish. Only habitude had allowed his mind to occupy a wider surface. A soldier must bear his injuries, even those inflicted during peace. Ardabur had won his rank of magister militum per Orientem *after smashing the barbarians at Thrace. And not so long ago he had fought the Arabs near Damascus, forcing them to the banquet table. A man of noble character, he spent much of his time at home in Daphne or at his villa overlooking the Bay of Sosthenium near Constantinople. As of late, according to wagging tongues (yes, the scribbling Priscus too), he revelled in the company of 'mimes and magicians and all the delights of the stage'. As though sweet music should irritate the minds of the people! As though we should not with art purge our feelings of anything harsh or disagreeable! And it was said too that he indulged in 'woman-like luxuriousness'. Ha, as though a few years of peace should weaken his hinges! What does a soldier fight for but peace? The irony was that he of all men, an Alan and an Arian too, should be sent on a mission to rescue from overzealous olive growers and gatherers of dates the corpse of a man who a few years earlier he himself might have killed with pleasure. The Antiochenes had begged him to go, and, he reflected, whom one rules one serves. Simeon, darling of the skies! Ardabur had pegged him for a fake. What soul was this that fed upon its own substance? Which embraced wretchedness as though only rags, blistering sun and ice could be true? What spectacle in nature is so vile as a man who'd willingly choose physical torture? As though Christ would put himself upon the cross! Yes, glorious the man who invents for himself a fresh torture, who binds himself to a stake with the bonds of pride, who begins by worshipping God with an impure love, and because he misunderstands a single phrase compounds his error until finally he looks down from on high upon whom he despises. Ah, better the scorpion lurking in the crevice than the fiery serpent suspended in mid-air. Who but an impostor or a fool would spend year after year stuck in that posture? If man's the only fool and the only wretch among creatures it is because he alone might be virtuous, happy and wise. Ardabur watched the proceedings with a jaundiced eye. This place was the cradle of his agonies. A few years ago, wishing to demonstrate that Simeon was a fake he put an arrow to the string of his bow and aimed it at the unwashed, emaciated figure. Suddenly, a skewering pain shot through his hands and he was unable to bend the bow. Then gout attacked him. A mere coincidence, of course, but those who make a study of coincidence will call their findings miracles while all they've done really is make connections between what was already there. What simile is not a miracle? The agony in his wrists and ankles would not go, and from this Ardabur suffered ever since. And now here was his soul's adversary, a small heap of rag and bone, whom Ardabur would bear home. Simeon dead! The skinny man gone. And as death makes of all men brothers, Ardabur would conduct Simeon over the rugged terrain as carefully, as gently as he would a fragile vase.*

There was a screeching of birds in the cloudless skies.

Three bishops climbed up to where Simeon's body was and reciting three psalms kissed his robes. The corpse was then lowered from the pillar by means of pulleys. Only then did the assembled crowd know for sure that Simeon had died. The sound of weeping could be heard at a great distance. Although dead four days Simeon's face was fresh as if still alive. The patriarch of Antioch wanting a relic went to cut a hair from Simeon's beard but his hand withered at the attempt. The other bishops prayed for their leader and tearfully addressed the corpse.

'Nothing is missing from your limbs or clothes, and no one will take anything from your holy and venerable corpse.'

As they spoke the power in the patriarch's hand returned. Simeon's body was placed, to the accompaniment of psalms and hymns, in the leaden casket that had been brought from Antioch. That night there was much burning of incense. The journey to Antioch took five days during which time the body travelled in state, with people pouring in from the villages to pay their last respects.

At the outskirts of a village called Merope, about five miles from Antioch, the mules pulling the carriage which bore the leaden casket that contained Simeon's corpse stopped and despite the many proddings they received would not budge.

They were obeying some commandment audible only to themselves. The crowd stood about in awkward silence. With such a short distance to go, why this ungodly insubordination of mules? And in the middle of a heatwave too. There was a cemetery to the right of the road and suddenly from its entrance a man dressed in rags ran at full speed towards the carriage and throwing himself upon the casket cried, 'Have pity on me, holy one of God, Simeon!' All those who knew him were amazed to hear him speak.

All the people who travelled that road knew who he was, this man whose words we remember but not his name, and taking pity on him would give him food and drink as he sat on the steps of a certain tomb that he had made his home. Other times, he would pace back and forth at the entrance to the cemetery roaring aloud, his cries so terrible people were afraid to approach him. The tomb where he had stayed day and night for these past twenty years contained the remains of a woman with whom he had fallen in love. She was another man's wife. We do not know whether she warmed to his words of love, but it was certain they had not made physical love. The young woman died, her body was placed here. So maddened with sorrow 'the hater of good might gain the soul of that man' he opened up the tombstone and did to her in death what he was not permitted to in life. Almost instantly, the wretched man went into deep shock, was struck deaf and dumb, and was no longer able to recognise anyone. He remained in this state, and, who knows, perhaps by choice, or, as someone remarked later, surely he had been reserved for heaven's mercies. At Simeon's approach the demon that had consumed the man for twenty years fled, and, with his reason restored and his tongue freed from the mental shackles, he was able once more to recognise, address and understand all the people.

The mules began to move.

On this the two accounts we have of Simeon's death and his removal to Antioch roughly agree, although there are some major differences too. Antonius explains why the man was possessed in the first place, and in doing so strikes a remarkable note of compassion. The explanation he provides suggests a tolerance we would not normally associate with the times and certainly not with a rural culture. We shudder at the lunatic's fate. We can scarcely imagine the horror of that event, the coldness of the flesh, but to label as perverse what one night entered a tortured soul would be to miss completely the tragedy of what took place. Clearly, Antonius understood this. And so too did the people of the village who quite simply let him be. Such a man were he alive today, depending on where he lived might have been either stoned to death in a public place or kept fully tranquillised on drugs in a private one. The author of the Syriac Life shrinks away from the cause of madness and in his account the local people fearful of being attacked by the man keep their distance. The purpose in bringing him into the narrative at all is to add one last to the many miracles that took place while Simeon was still alive. The sceptic will find more to believe in the first, in what is, in fact, the more remarkable of the two stories.

The Antiochenes, still shaken by a recent earthquake, came out by the thousands, clad in white, carrying wax tapers and lamps, to meet the corpse. They sprinkled precious spices over the people who accompanied the saint. Simeon's body was placed in a small church called Cassianus where it remained for thirty days while its final destination was being decided. The emperor Leo wanted the body brought to Constantinople, but the Antiochenes petitioned him, saying that a city without walls, such as theirs now was, needed the relics of a saint for protection from further earthquakes. After the petition was approved Ardabur had the body moved to the great church of Constantine.

After this we hear no more of the man who lived only for a woman's corpse except that he joined the procession to Antioch and spent many days in prayer in the church of Cassianus. We know Simeon's remains were seen by Evagrius, in 588, when Philippicus, brother-in-law of the emperor Maurice, requested that relics of the saint be sent to him for the protection of the Eastern armies. Evagrius describes the body as being preserved almost entire, the hair much as it was when the saint was alive, the skin of the forehead wrinkled and the greater part of his teeth present, the others having been violently removed by the faithful. The iron collar Simeon wore lay beside his head. Many others followed Simeon's example, becoming stylites, too. Simeon Stylites the Younger took to the pillar at such an early age Evagrius says 'he even cast his teeth in that situation'. It is said when Daniel became a stylite, Simeon's garment of goat's skin was bequeathed to him. A latter-day stylite was reported in the middle of the nineteenth century. There have always been men from different cultures who ascend to heaven by stages. Of Ardabur we learn that the emperor Leo suspecting him, Ardabur's brother, Patricius, and their father, Aspar, of planning a rebellion against him invited them to his palace in Constantinople. There he had them murdered by eunuchs who then hideously mutilated their bodies. A Goth called Ostrys fled with Aspar's pretty concubine.

A single image of the great church of Constantine where Simeon lay survives in the border of the great Yakto mosaic in the museum at Antakya. There is another image too, in that same border, Ardabur's private bath, which judging by its inclusion here must have been one of the most magnificent in Daphne.

A gentle breeze blew through the ruins. An Armenian from San Francisco gave me some cucumbers, small Syrian cucumbers sweeter than those we are accustomed to. We chomped at them while he spoke to me of his ambition to go everywhere connected with the Armenian people. If he was here it was because many Armenians had gone to see Simeon. There was a church in the desert, he told me, not far from Deir ez Zor, at whose centre was an open pit containing the bones of Armenians massacred by the Turks. 'You may handle them, all those thousands of bones,' he said. A group of French tourists having a picnic grimaced over a bottle of Syrian wine. I did try that wine once. A couple of Germans shouted at a boy who charged them double for beverages. As they became increasingly abusive I regretted the boy had not charged them triple. The woman from Yorkshire continued to blare through the megaphone of her ignorance. So many people from distant places, they made this an oddly secular pilgrimage. There was, despite their numbers, a tremendous sense of peace here. We may picture the wildness of the spot as it was when Simeon was alive, darkness slowly hugging the slopes, a hyena laughing in the distance.

FOURTEEN

Fool's Gold

O student of alchemy, alchemy is in my eye.
I look with it at silver, and it turns to gold.

Yakhlaf al-Aswad

The smell of gold being made is a thin, sulphurous blue. The Umayyad prince, Khālid ibn Yazīd, is said to have had such a passion for alchemy he assembled a number of Greek philosophers and had them translate books on the subject, these apparently being the first translations into Arabic from any other language. Alexandria, with its Greek population fed on the ideas of Aristotle, had for some time been the centre for what was known as the 'Egyptian art' or *chemeia*, named after the name of the black soil of that country. A Christian hermit, Morienus, who dwelled in the mountains near Jerusalem, was Khālid's teacher. When Khālid sought from him an explanation of *this thing* called alchemy, Morienus answered, 'Why should I use many words unto you? For this thing is extracted from thee, and thou art its ore; in thee they find it, and, to speak more plainly, from thee they take it; and when thou hast experienced this, the love and delight of it will be increased in thee. And thou shalt know that this thing subsists truly and beyond all doubt.' (*De Transmutatione Metallica* in MS Sloane 3697.)

What is certain is that while Europe, if such an entity can be said to have existed at the time, slept the Arabs kept alive the flame of ancient learning. What they took from Greece, especially the writings of Aristotle and Plato, would later be returned to Europe much enriched by them. The most famous of the Arabic alchemists was Jābir ibn Ḥayyān (721–812), better known throughout the medieval world as Geber. (Dr. Johnson wrongly derives the word 'gibberish' from his name.) Far from being a crank, Jābir, arguably the greatest figure of medieval science, helped lay the foundations of modern chemistry as a branch of natural science. As well as investigating the properties of minerals, during which process he made many important discoveries, he argued for a proper scientific attitude; he counselled patience, careful observation and, most importantly, the need to support one's findings with proofs. Chemistry, whose offspring it is, is alchemy secularised; it deals only with the outward manifestations of matter, whereas alchemy activates what already exists in a latent state. If, as was widely believed, all metals were to varying degrees compounds of the same materials – sulphur, mercury and arsenic – it followed that by withdrawing one and adding another one could transmute lead or copper into silver or gold. The more precious the metal the greater was the quantity of mercury it contained. Jābir writes that he derived from the ancients the notion of the elixir or Philosopher's Stone. The alchemist was merely doing what nature herself had already performed except that by applying the elixir he was able to make it do so at an accelerated rate. The eleventh-century alchemist, Maslamah ibn Aḥmad al-Majritī, wrote, 'Alchemists must try to follow Nature, whose servants indeed they are.' After Jābir the greatest figure was Abū Bakr Muḥammad b. Zakariyya' ar-Rāzī, known in the West as Rhazes. He composed thirty-three treatises on natural science, 100 books on medicine, and various books on mathematics and astronomy, philosophy, logic and theology. He produced a systematic classification, based upon careful observation, of chemical substances and reactions. One of the main principles of alchemy, which adepts in Europe, the Arab and the Jewish worlds, China and India developed independently of each other, is the notion of the unity of matter, the belief that all things, whether mineral, animal, human or vegetable, derive from the same source. Raymond Lully sums up this view, in his *Testament*, with the formula, *Omnia in Unum*.

Why gold?

'Gold is the perfect substance, composed of mercury that is pure, homogeneous, brilliant, red; and of equally pure, stable, red sulphur that is incombustible. Gold is perfection,' writes Roger Bacon in his *Mirror of Alquimy*. Another important principle was that in the same way the human embryo grows in the womb, ores and metals in the earth develop from lower to higher grades. The object of the true alchemist – as opposed to the 'puffer' who is called so because of his use of the bellows and who merely seeks profit – is not gold but rather the 'curing' of base materials and, more vitally, the purification and perfection of his own soul. Alchemy, in its truest form, is sacred science; it is as much a process of the soul as it is of the material world. Conversely, it can be said that alchemy defies any strict definition. If alchemy is the domain of cranks, the crank usually seeks to emulate, through doubtful means, that which is true; if it is the domain of fools, then their company includes Roger Bacon, Raymond Lully, St Thomas Aquinas, Martin Luther, Sir Isaac Newton, Gottfried Wilhelm Leibniz and Robert Boyle.

Still, it should not be thought that alchemy escaped criticism in the Islamic world and any doubts I may have are perhaps best supported from that perspective. Avicenna, after showing an initial interest in the subject, wrote a refutation; the best general criticism, however, is to be found in that endlessly fascinating historical source, Ibn Khaldūn's *Muqaddimah*. 'The truth with regard to alchemy,' he writes, 'which is to be believed and which is supported by actual fact, is that alchemy is one of the ways in which the spiritual souls exercise an influence and are active in the world of nature. It may belong among the miraculous acts of divine grace, if the souls are good. Or it may be a kind of sorcery, if the souls are bad and wicked.' Of the latter he says, 'They are thieves, or worse than thieves.' Those of purer intent he finds more troublesome. After saying of Jābir's seventy treatises on alchemy that 'All of them read like puzzles', he goes on to criticise the hermetic language of adepts, saying it is simply a means by which to escape religious censure. God, in His wisdom, saw that silver and gold be made scarce, so that they should be a standard of value; if they were to be produced artificially this would not only go against His plan but gold and silver would be in such abundance they would cease to be of value. Ibn Khaldūn also points out that nature always takes the shortest path in what it does and that this makes nonsense of the alchemist's claims to accelerate its processes. 'Thus,' he continues, 'those who try to practise alchemy as a craft lose their money and labour. . . . It is comparable to walking upon water, riding in the air, [and] passing through solid substances.'

W.B. Yeats was fascinated by the subject: 'I discovered, early in my researches, that their doctrine was no mere chemical fantasy, but a philosophy they applied to the world, to the elements, and to man himself.' One might well wonder if it were not the very language of alchemy that drew him. A list of alchemical substances makes for sheer poetry – spiritus fumans, cinnabar, Dutch White, powder of Algaroth, lunar caustic, purple of Cassius, sal ammoniac, sal volatile, spirit of Hartshorn, liver of sulphur, milk of sulphur, butter of Antimony, butter of tin, aqua tofani, Philosopher's Wool, zaffre, copper glance, Thion hudor ('the bile of the serpent'), fulminating silver, horn silver, luna cornea and brimstone.

When I returned to Damascus, the enigma of St Simeon's existence still very much in my thoughts, Sulaymān announced, 'I'll show you some real madness!'

A man sold watermelons on the pavement outside the apartment building where Sulaymān's laboratory was. Sulaymān chose the biggest one. A thin man in a green turban, lugging a huge watermelon, is a sight never to be forgotten. The room was not quite the alchemist's laboratory of popular imagination with its beakers, stuffed creatures, glowing athanors and parchment texts. A patient of Sulaymān's whom he had cured of insomnia by reading him relevant Qur'ānic verses let him have the place rent-free. The melon rocked gently on a Formica-topped table. A bare mattress lay in one corner of the room. On top of a stack of three cardboard boxes was a Kelvin digital temperature controller – in short, a computerised kiln. Sulaymān plugged the kiln in, saying that he had already blown the circuit a number of times. There had been several minor explosions as well.

'Why is this oven fighting you, Sulaymān? Are you going to kill us today?'

'Truly, the last explosion shocked me. I should have used only one gram of elixir, but I put more. You should always use the right measures. If you are in a hurry and greedy, if you want to do everything in a single day, then everything will be spoiled. I was ready to quit right there and then but Khiḍr told me, "Go on, don't be afraid. Carry on."'

Sulaymān peered into the kiln, singing in his strange falsetto voice. With pincers he pulled out a short length of metal coil.

'You see this. Every time there is a break in the line it costs me 2,000 Syrian *lira*, forty dollars. Often, when the kiln reaches 900 degrees, the circuit breaks. The impure material, the refuse, cuts the line. This costs me time and money because I wouldn't let the instrument rest. I should have allowed it to sleep for twelve hours. The primitive methods are sometimes better. This machine is not good for commercial purposes, of course. I would need to buy more advanced instruments, but it is good enough for scientific research.'

'Were these explosions in line with the cosmic ones you spoke of earlier?'

'No, this is a different issue, one of technology.'

'Have you been able to produce *one hundred per cent* pure gold?'

'There can be *only* pure gold, so the question is not one of percentages. There is either success or failure. Nizār Qabbānī writes, "There is no compromise between heaven and hell." Likewise, there is none between gold and base materials.'

'Still, there are illusions – take fool's gold, for example. Could it be that when Ibn al-ʿArabī wrote of alchemy he meant it metaphorically?'

'No, no! Ibn al-ʿArabī fed half of Damascus. Where did

the food come from? You should take it for granted that he meant what he wrote. There are two kinds of gold, natural and artificial – the first one finds in the earth, the second one makes. Both require much effort to get at them.'

'What does your family think of alchemy?'

'They are not convinced. If you were to discuss these matters with physicists they would be happy to listen to you, but if you discuss them with people who come home from work, eat *ful*, dress up in their pyjamas, watch TV and then go to sleep they won't understand.'

'Can alchemy be a moving away from God?'

'Yes, because it is a double-edged weapon which you can use in either a good or a bad way. As long as one intends good then one need not be afraid. I will donate half of any profits I might make for food, charity—'

'And the other half?'

'It will go towards the bank loan.'

'You got a loan for this!'

'This kiln cost me 400 dollars, about four months' salary. Some of the money I borrowed from people, the rest I got from the bank. All this has cost me a fortune, about 2,000 dollars. Also, I made many trials, all of them failures. I met with the director of a bank in Lebanon. After I explained to him what the money would be used for he kicked me out. I have learned not to ask for such things. You must give another reason for needing the money. We will see after the year 2000. Just now, everything is in a state of chaos – all the planets are confused. They will calm down and then we'll see what can be done.'

'But it won't be 2000 according to the Arabic calendar.'

'The new era is anonymous, so it's not a matter of calendars. If I don't pay the loan back after five years the bank will confiscate my property and I will be imprisoned. Banks are not emotional. Always they say to me, "Do your experiments first and, if successful, come back to us." "But," I answer, "if I am successful why should I come to you? First give me money." But they never do. They have their printing houses, they print money, but unless you guarantee results they will not give you any support. I cannot elect a government on my own. I cannot issue my own Khiḍr bank notes bearing a picture of him. I must work according to the existing rules.'

'You will need to control the world.'

'On the contrary, one should be the weakest creature in the world. It is a matter of responsibility that whatever I do is not done out of ambition or materialistic desire, but rather because it will mean being able to help other people.'

Ibn Khaldūn, after pointing out that alchemy is an art practised mostly by those who are unable to earn their living otherwise, states, 'They have to pay for their efforts in the form of trouble, hardship and difficulties, and in the form of persecution by the authorities and loss of property through expenditures. In addition, [the alchemist] loses standing and, eventually, when his secret is discovered, faces ruin.' It was precisely this that I feared for Sulaymān, that he might drown in his own innocence.

'So all this work will give you no profit? Could it be that the making of gold is a test sent by God to see whether you will be tempted by wealth?'

'One must not be fixed by this idea of rich or poor, not when during the days of my deepest poverty I was so much happier than I am now. Concerning the spiritual zone I inhabit there is neither poverty nor riches. Those images are what other people make or observe. What difference would it make if I had so many zeros in the bank? Would this make me rich? No, nothing will change for me. Eventually, I may have enough for the price of a sandwich.'

'So why do you do it?'

'After reading about alchemy in Ibn al-ʿArabī I felt personally attracted. He says do whatever you have to in bringing the oven, the instruments and so forth. Alchemy requires technology, but remember, the ability to make gold is only a status and as such has no permanence. The true result, he says, is in the reaching of the perfection rank. Perfection of the metal will not be possible unless you reach perfection in yourself. Ibn al-ʿArabī says this knowledge has to be as natural as the materials you bring to it. Secondly, it is spiritual, a mixing of soul and matter. This is the speciality of the angel Michael and the prophet Abraham. You are on the spiritual path when your soul is supported by these two.'

'So any progression in the development of gold is equal to the progression in the soul?'

'Not only there, but also in the comfort and happiness you bring to other people. If I am righteous it is because I am of this earth.'

Sulaymān slid a collapsed cardboard box against the wall and kneeling down upon it began his prayers.

'What do you think, Abed? Is Sulaymān of this earth?'

'Yes, I have witnesses. And I know his father.'

'Do you think it's wise of him to continue with his alchemy?'

'It is not my business. If I were to attempt what he does nothing would come of it because this is his speciality. I might love the diamond-cutter, but I cannot tell him how to cut a diamond. If you were a doctor, would I give you medical advice? Sulaymān has permission to do such things from another world.'

'I've a feeling Sulaymān is going down a blind alley.'

'A *feeling*? There, you've said it yourself! The truth is in the eye of the beholder.'

Sulaymān got up from his prayers.

'Do you think alchemy leads to madness sometimes?'

'It is *all* pure madness,' he laughed. 'There is a delicate line between genius and madness and if it is removed too quickly one can be destroyed. Most great scientists, if you study them closely, led abnormal lives. On the other hand, some people achieved great results but because of the long bureaucratic processes that demand theories be proven they died mad, unable to spread their knowledge. Others – call them overly practical, secular people – lose their minds because they have reached everything in their art except the eyeing of an angel. In alchemy, for the materials to mix one requires the angel's eyeing.'

'What exactly is the elixir?'

'The elixir is the soul of the metal, that which is strongest, which is of the highest quality. Everything in the universe has its own elixir. Your sperm is your elixir. Here, we may say the womb is this kiln, the egg the copper. Everything has a soul, even objects. If the marriage between two materials which we have mixed together is successful, if there is harmony between them, then it means we have had permission from God. It would be impossible for those two materials to marry otherwise.'

The early alchemists believed there was a single prime substance in nature and that the formation from this of minerals and metals was similar to the development of the foetus in the womb. Therefore, just as there are seeds in animal and plant life so too there is a metallic seed. One of the aims of alchemy was to discover this seed which was often referred to as 'mineral sperm'. A jeweller can tell the sex of the diamond by its brilliance, and so it is with the various ores. I posed the question to which I knew I would not get an answer.

'What is in the elixir?'

Sulaymān smiled sweetly for what seemed the longest time.

'I am not trying to steal your secret but, if possible, I should like to be able to describe its circumference.'

'Alchemy is secret knowledge,' he replied, 'although I am by no means the first to have discovered the elixir. The English and the Italians knew how to make gold and, of course, the Jews – Adam, Solomon, David, Jacob, Abraham. But even if you published my findings nobody would benefit from them because the making of the elixir is something one has to do oneself.'

'So can we say it is the combination of different ingredients?'

'Yes. You have to mix the elixir for six months in the sun's rays, without fire. I put the ingredients in a container which I then hermetically seal and place in the window, in the sun's rays, just like the Egyptian Pharaoh's pyramid, and there they become one material.'

Sulaymān funnelled copper shavings into a crucible, which he then lowered into the kiln.

'This is copper, the first stage.'

We sat in silence while the lit numbers on the control panel began to increase.

'We have now arrived at the middle stage, what we call "gold in pregnancy". Those who understand gold know this stage. When you see how a baby develops in the womb, you will not be surprised by any of this.'

'Is there any gold mixed in there as well?'

'Of course not, impossible! The only ingredients are copper which is the medium and one gram of elixir which is the soul of the gold. As perfume is made of essence—'

'So "when making tea" water is merely the medium while the elixir is in the tea leaves?'

'Congratulations!'

'Are the materials non-metallic?'

'Yes, a knowledge of plants is a preliminary stage.'

'You mean essential to the finding of the elixir?'

'Yes.'

'Why do you choose some materials and not others?'

'It is written in Ibn al-ʿArabī who devotes a whole chapter to this and in other old books as well.'

'What, briefly, does he say?'

'The elixir is evidence, a key to what is going on in the universe and to how it changes. You have to be very delicate. A heavenly balance must be reflected in the employment of accurate measures. You put one gram of elixir instead of a thousand and you use only so much copper. One gram of elixir can turn one thousand grams of base material, which is the copper, into gold, metal that has reached perfection. Ibn al-ʿArabī says all metals were gold originally but they have been influenced by the name of Allāh the Hurter, one of his ninety-nine names.'

'The discovery of the elixir, did it come to you through logic or faith?'

'Both, spiritual and natural knowledge. Ibn al-ʿArabī says when you are on the path don't use your brain only – "Commit your heart to me and I will support you." There are many other factors, of course. The saints helped me. The secret was inherited. I took it from a man who passed away, a Lebanese whom I never met. I knew him only through a dream, even though I probably know more about him than his children do, for they are ignorant of his true knowledge. He married a lot of women.'

Sulaymān emphasised this, as if perhaps the man's virility were somehow at one with his alchemical abilities.

'Even though I never knew this man physically the secret was inherited from him. Spiritually first, through a vision, and the rest was practical. The actual elixir you must find on your own, however.'

'What did the old man give you, if not the elixir?'

'He told me in a dream or vision that he would encourage me. Also, he said I was of the same astrological sign as he was, which is a very important key to success. He spent ten years beside Ibn al-ʿArabī's tomb. You cannot deny the knowledge is there. The ancient Greek philosophers spoke of it, for instance. It was known in India, China—'

'Maybe the old man did not succeed?'

'Of course he did! He is famous. There are many witnesses. The Lebanese government quarrelled with him because they wanted to take advantage of his discovery. Finally, he went to Switzerland. The Swiss who respected him awarded him a medal for metaphysical sciences.'

'When you are old will you pass the secret to someone else?'

'When I die the saints will find a suitable person and will give him the secret, perhaps through Khiḍr, perhaps through a vision. We do not know who this person will be – he might not yet be born. The angels know who he is, however.'

While the figures in the temperature panel steadily rose Sulaymān took the product of the previous day's experiment and dropped it into a plastic bowl of sulphuric acid. Thin blue fumes rose and then he took the metal and dropped it into an identical plastic bowl filled with water. He scrubbed the metal vigorously with a wire brush to remove the black impurities from the surface. Meanwhile, he sipped water from a third, identical bowl. What if he put one of the bowls back in the wrong place?

'What is the connection, then, between alchemy and the cosmos?'

'If you are not connected by birth to the seventh planet – the black one, *zuḥal*, Saturn – you will not have success. The date of your birth, your astrology, this planet which is all elixir – these are all influences. As I said, the man who made gold before me was of the same astrological sign as me. I was born on the seventeenth of the first month. This planet causes me problems sometimes, produces inconsistencies in me. I flit about from place to place. Without patience I would go mad because this planet demands a lot of patience. Sometimes you are in one status and you can change to another. The seventh planet is nearly all elixir.'

'So if one is born under the right star sign, why does he need so much effort to find the solution?'

'Because this planet has its consequences. There can be a negative side – avarice, bad temper.'

This was certainly in keeping with the belief of the early astrologers who wrote that the bodily organs are connected to the actions of various media in the universe and that astrology is an essential part of the healing arts. In the Emerald Table, supposedly written by the Babylonian, Hermes Trismegistus, it is stated clearly enough, 'As above, so below.' A man born under a particular sign shares to some extent its nature and properties. In the healing arts the influence of the planets and stars was linked to the medicinal properties of certain plants. The alchemist believed the planets were connected to the maturing of metals and that they influenced the alchemist in his efforts at transmutation. The alchemist associated gold with the sun, silver was connected to the moon, quicksilver to Mercury, copper to Venus, iron to Mars and lead to Saturn.

'At 1,050 degrees the gold will be liquid.'

The kiln read 600 degrees.

'You see how they are able now to separate neutrons and protons, how they can manipulate the atoms. So what you see here is perfectly normal. We are taking only one element, the proton. The most important thing is not to be too quick in one's reactions. You require patience, wisdom, prayer, learning from other people. You should not take your decisions alone – you should consult people. This requires practice. If you fail, you will be sad. At this point you stop, look for where your mistake is. Slowly, slowly. If you get all your knowledge from the first experiment you will not cherish it. You will not learn its value. It is hard work, physically and spiritually, and expensive. And you need a guru. All that you have seen from Adam until the present day has been inherited, transferred from one person to another. In short, if you wish to have this knowledge you must be destined. You might work for forty years and not be benefited; on the other hand, you might work for only a month. There is no guarantee. If I wanted to start a car factory it would be comparatively easy but with this, no. And then there is so much greed. Jewellers offered me gold in order to tempt me. "But it is not like this," I told them. "Even if you had all the right measures you would not be able to make anything of them because unless it is in your destiny, unless you have spiritual permission, you will never convert the image of the metal." This is called "creation knowledge", the imaging knowledge. In the Qur'ān there is a verse which says God will construct you according to any image He wants you to be. It all has to do with the constructing of image. You see how the baby develops in the womb and how because of an angel he begins to move in the third month. In Europe they are playing with DNA. Cloning is evil, of course. So what's so strange about alchemy? Nothing. God says you have been given a little knowledge. If you look at the universe realistically you will see it being born all the time – labour, birth, always giving all the time. The earth is giving all the time.'

Abed announced, in a droll voice, 'I will now cut the watermelon and live normally.'

We sat around the table, devouring slice after slice.

'Would you consider the search for gold as being on the same path or line as your development as a Sufi?'

'The same, but beginners in Sufism are distracted by materials in the same way as they are by women. This is because they haven't yet reached the truth. One can say there are two kinds of Sufi – the first is practical, scientific in his approach, whereas the second kind depends on miracles that have their roots in things outside logic. The Malāmatiyya, as I told you before, are scientific people. They do not depend on or use miracles. The Prophet Muḥammad asked God, "Please, increase my knowledge." He didn't ask him to increase his spiritual status because had he done so no one would have believed him and he would have had problems in spreading Islam. Statuses come and go, they are not permanent whereas knowledge is.'

'You are simply an instrument?'

'I am nothing, a servant.'

'For how much longer will you make gold before moving on to your next stage?'

'I am almost finished, I'm getting close. I will not be fixed at this stage of making gold. I will move to another. What I am doing now is curing metal – the next knowledge will be curing people. I want to discover the origins of diseases and their cures.'

'Do you see a direct connection between alchemy and those that you would need for healing?'

'All are the same but this job requires more delicacy, more observation.'

'Do you believe nature has all the cures and all we have to do is find them?'

'Yes, but the question is, who will be the one to explore. It is a long process. Every plant cures something. I will collect them from all over the world and put them in ten thousand bottles, kept at special temperatures. And then my researches will begin. You may finish in forty years or you may not. This is knowledge. The knowledge seeker and the money seeker are both insatiable.'

The progression from alchemy to healing was once a natural enough one; many alchemists of old were physicians as well. According to one historical source, Jābir practised medicine at the court of Hārūn al-Rashīd and some years after his death the remains of his laboratory were found at Kūfā where he lived for a while. The greatest figure after Jābir, Rhazes, was chief physician at the hospital in Baghdad. He was the first to have produced treatises on smallpox and measles. According to one source, he lost his sight because of his experiments in alchemy and according to another, rather more interesting tale, he had been offered a large reward if he would apply his knowledge of alchemy, which hitherto he had applied only to medicine, to the making of gold. When he refused his tempter struck him so heavily on the head he lost the use of his eyes. As metal may be cured of its impurities, and in fact alchemy is often spoken of as the healing of sick metal, so too the human body may be cured of its illnesses.

Sulaymān handed me the piece of metal he had been scrubbing. If it did not look like gold to me it was quite unlike any other metal I have ever seen. It wasn't copper, nor was it bronze.

'But surely this is not pure gold?'

'I will put more acid and then you will see with your eyes and be compassionate in your heart. If it isn't gold, what is it then? When you heat any other metal and put it in acid it changes colour, usually it turns black, but gold, the more you wash it with acid the shinier it gets, until all the impurities are gone.'

'It still looks more like copper or bronze than gold to me.'

'It is not a matter of what it *looks* like to you. You cannot just by looking determine whether it is gold or not. If you put copper in acid you will see what happens. See, it turns green.'

Sulaymān put some copper shavings in the bowl to demonstrate.

'If the colour changes, it is for the garbage. When you drop the two metals, the gold and the copper, on the ground they have a different sound. Listen.'

I listened to the clank of one and the clink of the other.

'The gold has an inner sound, while the copper has a ringing one.'

'The sound is not affected by the shape?'

'What is your aim in life?' Sulaymān suddenly asked me, with more than a hint of exasperation in his voice. 'What do you want from this life?'

'I suppose I believe in alchemy, too, but of a different kind, one which involves language, which I hope will reflect my poetic development as the making of gold reflects your spiritual one.'

'You see, it is all art!'

'All these things are illusions. After all, when one creates a metaphor one creates in the mind of the reader an illusion and yet, with luck, it will be the expression of a greater truth.'

Sulaymān stared at me for a moment or two with what seemed to be a critical silence.

'So the pen is your happiness? Why do you write? Always there is renewal, even in your own face and in your physical movements, in your behaviour too. If you watch this continual process of renewal you will see God Himself, the true Allāh. You will discover Him because He is always manifesting Himself in a new image. That's why even in the world of spirits there will always be surprise. On Judgement Day, when they see God they'll cry, "But He is not our God!" because He will have manifested Himself to them in a way contrary to their expectations of what He would be like. And so, missing their previous image of Him, they will weep. Sometimes, when I walk in the street, I see a man cursing God, but *who* does he curse? What does he worship? Maybe it is the wall in front of him, maybe it's a car or a mansion. So really I don't know what he worships, nor do I know the name of God that is manifested in him. You can't see God in all of His names, in His wholeness, because God is not busy in one thing only. I drive a car, but I can't fly a plane. When I am sleeping I can't do other things because I am a weak creature. I am poor. Whatever rank I have reached, when I am poor and humble before Him, He will support me with His eyeing. At this stage many saints and Sufi people perish. They drift because they enter a stage of greatness in which they claim the union between themselves and God. I cannot agree with this. You have always to admit that you are a slave to God and that you are weak. You get your strength from your weakness. There is no other solution. Pharaoh and his like said, "Why are you looking for God? I am God. Worship me!" The magicians told him, "Be careful, or else Moses will come and will give you a lesson in politeness." You know the rest of the story. The stick was converted into a snake. Who is the performer? Who is the doer? It is God.'

'And in this do you find a parallel for alchemy?'

'Yes, because in all conversion God is the doer.'

I continued to turn the metal disc over and over in the palm of my hand.

'What can one do with this?'

'You could try to buy a loaf of bread with it, but I fear it may be prohibited.'

The temperature on the kiln was approaching 750 degrees. The air was full of fumes. I asked Sulaymān if they were dangerous at which point he embarked upon a lengthy mime, a performance worthy of Jean-Louis Barrault, at the end of which, after several jerks and shudders, he swooned to the floor, his eyes rolled up, his tongue jutting out just a little. Sulaymān, his turban still in place, did not rally to our applause. The newly dead follow rules.

'Sulaymān's ambition,' Abed said, 'is to get through the daily business of life by means of mime only, that is, without the burden of language. Do you not find this idea attractive?'

I told Abed that if we were to succeed in getting Sulaymān to London we would not allow him to speak English there, we would keep him exactly as he was.

'Yes,' he agreed, 'if we were sufficiently ruthless we could use him as a prop to sell carpets or perfumes.'

850 degrees.

We both stared at Sulaymān or rather his feigned corpse, mentally turning the base metal of his existence into the gold of our shared, future one. At that moment there was a dull thud from the direction of the kiln. The corpse sprang to its feet, copper shavings flying from the striped *jalabīya*. The temperature displayed in the control panel dropped steadily by tens of degrees at a time. Another 2,000 *lira* had just gone up in smoke. The alchemist Sulaymān solemnly announced that in future he would make a return to the much slower brick kilns of an earlier time.

I was leaving Damascus in a few hours, perhaps forever, and already there were tears in my eyes. Sulaymān scolded me.

'There are no goodbyes, not even in death. Such sentiments belong only to *your* language, not mine.'

Behind the anger I sensed Sulaymān's disappointment not so much in me, perhaps, as in his having failed to persuade me that gold could be made. Was I lacking in the compassion he had earlier asked of me? Why make gold, I wanted to say to him, when he had already given me the gold of his friendship, the gold Abed spoke of five years before.

'Do you remember, Sulaymān, your Bedouin dream?'

'Yes, I remember.'

'I think your real tragedy is not being unable to go to London, but that you're not a Bedouin in your tent.'

'I will find a tent when I get there.'

'There are no tents in London.'

'I'll put one inside my house. Also, I will need a camel. There is a camel in my spiritual world.'

'But there is no place for a spiritual camel in London.'

'I will find a solution.'

'The neighbours there are most intolerant of camels. You would have to build a high wall around your garden.'

'All right, then, when I arrive with the camel I will give them gifts and they will grow to like the camel. A human being is a creature of gifts, which is why for four thousand years you've loved Santa Claus because he gives gifts.'

'Two, Sulaymān, *less* than two thousand although we're almost there. I will send you a Christmas card. I do so enjoy these conversations because we enter another stratosphere.'

'Yes, we enter the depths.'

When I got up to leave I handed the piece of gold, or whatever it was, back to Sulaymān.

'No, it is a gift, Marcie.'

'What, for me?'

'Tell them in London a crazy person made this.'

Why do you write? Sulaymān asked me. I should have answered, 'So that I may pin our fleeting existences to the page. So, my friend, that I might achieve the illusion of having done so.' A whole flood of individual scenes and impressions comes rushing back at me, here, seated at my desk in London. There is one in particular, a phrase of just two words, four syllables that somehow connect to everything I have written, to all the people whom I met and loved. What will be remembered of their lives? What will be remembered of anyone's? The phrase was in a somewhat archaic Italian, deeply poetic in utterance. When I first saw those two words I knew then, although I didn't know *how* exactly, that this book would have to end with them.

At Palmyra, in the Valley of the Tombs, I entered one of the eerie monolithic towers that once housed the sarcophagi of the Palmyrene upper classes. This particular tomb tower, the inside of which was like some infernal post office, had four storeys, each of which contained three or four rows of *loculi* into which the deceased were shoved. They were mostly vacant now and beside one of these empty pigeonholes someone, perhaps an Italian archaeologist (I would like to think so), had chiselled an inscription, which from the look of it was done quite a long time ago. Also, judging from its high position, it must have been made by someone standing on a ladder, perhaps a rickety wooden one of the kind farmers around Palmyra still use to pick dates.

Chi anima?

Select Bibliography

I have tried to keep the smell of the library out of these pages as much as possible, but there are certain invaluable works which should be mentioned here and from which, in some instances, I have drawn quotations.

Bell, Gertrude. *Syria: The Desert and the Sown*, Heinemann, 1907

Binns, John. *Ascetics and Ambassadors of Christ*, Oxford, Clarendon Press, 1996

Brown, Peter. *The Cult of the Saints*, SCM, 1981

Burton, Sir Richard. *Unexplored Syria*, Tinsley Bros, 1872

Collins, Cecil. *The Vision of the Fool*, The Grey Walls Press, 1947

Dodd, Erica Cruickshank. 'The Monastery of Mar Mūsā al-Habashi near Nabek, Syria' in *Arte Medievale*, II serie, anno VI (1992), no 1

Dols, Michael W. *Majnūn: The Madman in Medieval Islamic Society*, Oxford, Clarendon Press, 1992.

Doran, Robert (tr.). *The Lives of Simeon Stylites*, Kalamazoo, Cistercian Publications, 1992

Eliade, Mircea. *The Forge and the Crucible*, Rider & Company, 1962

Evagrius. *A History of the Church, 431–594*, Samuel Bagster, 1846

Fedden, Robin. *Syria and Lebanon*, 3rd edn., John Murray, 1965

Haag, Michael. *Syria & Lebanon*, Cadogan Books, 1995

Kelly, J.N.D. *Golden Mouth, The Story of John Chrysostom, Ascetic, Preacher, Bishop*, Duckworth, 1995

Ibn Khaldūn. *The Muqaddimah: An Introduction to History*, tr. by Franz Rosenthal, Routledge & Kegan Paul, 1958
al-Māghūṭ, Muḥammad. *Joy is not My Profession*, tr. by John Asfour and Alison Burch, Montreal, Signal Editions, 1994
Matthews, J. *The Roman Empire of Ammianus*, Duckworth, 1989
Neale, F.A. *Eight Years in Syria, Palestine and Asia Minor, from 1842 to 1850*, 1851
Qabbānī, Nizār. *On Entering the Sea; The Erotic and Other Poetry*, New York, Interlink Books, 1996
Russell, Alexander. *The Natural History of Aleppo, etc.*, 2nd edn, Farnborough, Gregg International Publishers, 1974; reprinted 1969
Saward, John. *Perfect Fools: Folly for Christ's Sake in Catholic and Orthodox Spirituality,* Oxford University Press, 1980
Schimmel, Annemarie. *Mystical Dimensions of Islam*, University of North Carolina Press, 1975
Theodoret, Bishop of Cyprus. *A History of the Monks of Syria*, Kalamazoo, Cistercian Publications, 1985
Trimingham, J.S. *Christianity among the Arabs in Pre-Islamic Times*, Longman, 1979
——, *The Sufi Orders in Islam*, Oxford, Clarendon Press, 1971
Wright, Dr William. *An Account of Palmyra and Zenobia, etc.*, Thomas Nelson & Sons, 1895; reprinted Darf Publishers, 1987
Quotations from *The Qur'ān* are taken from Marmaduke Pickthall's interpretation, Everyman's Library, 1992

Acknowledgements

There were times when I almost abandoned this work and when the encouragement of certain people put me back on track. Firstly, I thank my wife, Bobbie, and my children, Alice and Johanna, for their forbearance. I must thank, too, those who read chapters and/or offered invaluable advice: Jaros≥≥aw Anders, William Blisset, Peter Caracciolo, Gabriel Levin, Christopher Long, the late Hugh Macpherson, Christopher Middleton, Eric Ormsby, Alain Richerts, Arcangelo Riffis, Norm Sibum, Adam Thorpe, Alan Wall, Gillian Webster, Catherine Willis and my wife. There are many people, too numerous to mention here, who offered other kinds of help – William and Olivia Dalrymple who first told me about Myrna and Peter Clark who gave me helpful advice on how to get up to Qubbat al-Arba'īn. I thank my agent, Peter Straus, and my editors, Christopher Feeney and Matthew Brown, for giving this book a home.

'A Full Moon over Antioch' first appeared in the special Turkish issue of *Descant* (vol. 34, no. 2, Summer 2003) and a slightly abbreviated version of 'A Likeness of Angels' in *Maisonneuve* (Spring 2004). The author thanks the editors of both publications.

My deepest appreciation goes to the Syrian people, including the staff at the al-Ḥaramain Hotel in Damascus, especially Iman, and, above all, the two 'non-mainstreamers' whose lives form the basis of this book.